Dance Lessons
for
ZOMBIES

PETER HIETT

INTEGRITY®
PUBLISHERS
Nashville

Published by Integrity Publishers, a division of Integrity Media, Inc., 5250 Virginia Way, Suite 110, Brentwood, TN 37027.

HELPING PEOPLE WORLDWIDE EXPERIENCE *the* MANIFEST PRESENCE *of* GOD.

Published in association with Alive Communications, Inc., 7680 Goddard Street, Suite 200, Colorado Springs, CO 80920.

"Teddy Bear Machine" Hidden Picture by Olivia Cole used by permission. Copyright © 2003 by Highlights for Children, Inc., Columbus, OH.

Unless otherwise indicated, Scripture quotations are taken from The Holy Bible: Revised Standard Version (RSV). Copyright © 1946, 1952, 1973 by National Council of Churches of Christ. All rights reserved.

Other Scripture quotations are taken from the following: The New Revised Standard Version® (NRSV®). Copyright © 1989, 1995 by the Division of Christian Education of the National Council of the Churches of Christ in the United States of America. Used by permission. All rights reserved. The New King James Version® (NKJV®). Copyright © 1982 by Thomas Nelson, Inc. Used by permission. All rights reserved. The Holy Bible, New International Version® (NIV®). Copyright © 1973, 1978, 1984 by International Bible Society. Used by permission of Zondervan. All rights reserved. The King James Version (KJV). Public domain. The Message (MSG) by Eugene H. Peterson. Copyright © 1993, 1994, 1995, 1996, 2000, 2001, 2002. Used by permission of NavPress Publishing Group. All rights reserved. The Holy Bible, New Living Translation® (NLT®). Copyright © 1996. Used by permission of Tyndale House Publishers, Inc., Wheaton, Illinois 60189. All rights reserved. The New American Bible (NAB). Copyright © 1970 by the Confraternity of Christian Doctrine (CCD), Washington, D.C. All rights reserved. The Holy Bible, English Standard Version. Copyright © 2001 by Crossway Bibles, a division of Good News Publishers. Used by permission. All rights reserved.

Cover Design: Charles Brock, The DesignWorks Group, Inc. www.thedesignworksgroup.com
Cover Photo: Photonica
Interior Design: Inside Out Design & Typesetting; Fort Worth, Texas

Library of Congress Cataloging-in-Publication Data

Hiett, Peter.
Dance lessons for zombies / Peter Hiett.
p. cm.
Summary: "Compelling book on how to live out our faith in a fresh new way"—Provided by publisher.

ISBN 1-59145-227-5 (trade paper)

1. Sermon on the mount—criticism, interpretation, etc. 2. Christian life. I. Title.
BT380.3H54   2005
241.5'3 dc22   2005006230

Printed in the United States of America
05 06 07 08 LBM 9 8 7 6 5 4 3 2 1

To my bride, Susan—
my editor, best friend, and favorite dance partner
(my favorite part of Christ's dancing body).

CONTENTS

CONTENTS

ACKNOWLEDGMENTS

Of course, Jesus wrote the Sermon on the Mount, and He did a "super job." What can I say? Our Lord's words are a gold mine that we'll never fully fathom. Any place that I actually understood something or expressed something truly well was the work of His Spirit. Regarding this book, His Spirit worked powerfully through His Body at Lookout Mountain Community Church. This book is the fruit of His worshipping community.

Thanks to all of those who pray for me and reach with me by receiving the Word in faith, hope, and love.

Thanks to those who share their gift of prophetic words and visions, specifically Dale, Marcia, Kate, and my wife Susan.

Thanks to those who've shared their life and let me see Jesus dancing in them. Thank you, Elaine.

Dear staff and session at LMCC, thank you for your love, encouragement, and patience when things get "different."

I am tremendously grateful for my assistant Stephanie Trahant who transcribed my sermon notes and pulled this book together with such artistry, skill, and patience.

Thank you to the wonderful people at Integrity Publishers for believing in Christ in me and in this book. Thank you, Angela.

I dedicated this book to my wife Susan, which is only appropriate . . . because she spends my money! But more than that, she really is my primary editor—she listens to all my messages before I give them, telling me to take out the booger jokes and the things that make no sense. She is my best friend. She's my safe harbor. She's full of grace toward me. And she knows Jesus in a way that continues to astound, amaze, and bless me. She is also the mother of my four wonderful children who fill me with gratitude for God's creative power: Jonathan, Elizabeth, Rebekah, and Coleman.

Finally, thank you, Mom. You have always been and still are full of love and strength for me. You sat through four Easter sermons in a row sitting right in the front! Better than that, you truly love Jesus and so live with courage.

PREFACE

On a mountain we received the law and learned that we were
dead and can't dance—
Mount Sinai.

On a mountain Jesus fully filled the law and gave us His life—
Mount Calvary.

On a mountain we will live and dance forever by grace—
Mount Zion.

On mountains God reveals Himself. At the start of His ministry,
Jesus climbed a mountain and preached a sermon, a sermon to kill us,
fill us, and set us free . . . to dance—*the Sermon on the Mount.*

What Jesus said on that mountain eventually got Him killed. It
turns out zombies lived on the mountain of law, and they didn't want
Jesus to move their mountain. I really shouldn't say "zombies lived."
Zombies are the walking dead. Zombies are dead on the inside even if
they look alive on the outside—like a whitewashed tomb.

We're all scared of zombies—they look like us yet lack whatever it is
that makes us truly human; they mimic the dance steps but can't hear
the music.

Perhaps you've seen one at the mall.

Perhaps you've sat by one in church.

Perhaps you've spied one in the mirror while you were shaving, and he looked familiar!

Aaaaah!

How would you know a zombie if you saw one? Old zombie movies can be helpful in this regard:

- Zombies are stiff. Zombies can't dance. They can mimic the dance steps, but that's not dancing.
- Zombies are hard to talk to. It's as if they're in their own world and can't hear the music. Turn up the volume, and they still won't dance.
- Zombies love crowds. They travel in groups. They're trapped in themselves yet derive strength from others. They love uniformity. Sometimes I think zombies don't really have "selves," so they feed on other "selves." That explains the next point.
- Zombies covet the body and blood of the living. It turns out that about AD 30, when Jesus preached the Sermon on the Mount, only one person was truly alive. "In him was life" (John 1:4). By AD 33 a crowd of zombies had gotten Jesus crucified. Like Adam and Eve "took" fruit from the forbidden tree, they "took" the body and blood of Jesus.

Well . . . taking the life of Jesus was the grand miracle, for the most evil day was the "goodest" day—Good Friday. They took Jesus' life, but from the foundation of the world He gave it. He *for*gave it—His body broken and blood shed. He came to make old zombies dance. He really is the Lord of the dance.

Have you ever been at a religious gathering and had a flashback to an old zombie movie? Perhaps to you, religion feels dead—one more discipline, one more law, one more dance step, one more program, one more principle to apply, one more practical application point, one more way to fake being alive even when you feel dead. That's bad religion.

In Matthew 16 Jesus warns His disciples two times, saying, "Beware of the leaven of the Pharisees" (v. 6), that is, beware of *zombification*. Jesus has just told His disciples that the "evil and adulterous generation seeks for a sign" (v. 4), and then He scolds them for thinking He's talking about physical leaven in physical bread. In Luke 12:1 Jesus tells His disciples that "the leaven of the Pharisees" is hypocrisy. *Hypocrisy* is acting, pretending, or playing a part. The leaven of the Pharisees is a focus on outward manifestations and rules, but a refusal to surrender the heart. The leaven of the Pharisees is what I call "the spirit of religion" or "bad religion."

James writes about "vain religion" and then continues: "Religion that is pure and undefiled before God and the Father is this: to visit orphans and widows in their affliction, and to keep oneself unstained from the world" (1:27). Not that our religion, our deeds, and our outward manifestation of faith don't matter; but that's what they should be—manifestations of something else. Dance steps are to manifest a dance. Religion is to manifest faith from a new heart. Signs are not the point. What they point to is the point.

Bad religion is what man does; Jesus is what God does. Jesus says, "Apart from me you can do nothing" (John 15:5). Paul writes, "It is no longer I who live, but Christ who lives in me" (Galatians 2:20). I believe Paul actually meant that. In Ephesians he writes, "For by grace you have been saved through faith; and this is not your own doing, it is the gift of God—not because of works, lest any man should boast. For we are his workmanship, created in Christ Jesus for good works, which God prepared beforehand, that we should walk in them" (2:8–10). Or should I say *dance* in them. We dance by grace, not by works. That is, we're saved by grace, and we're sanctified by grace.

Paul writes to the Galatians tempted to return to life under the law:

"You were running well; who hindered you from obeying the truth? This persuasion is not from him who calls you. A little leaven leavens the whole lump" (5:7–9). In Philippians 3 when Paul writes about his former life in "the flesh," he's not talking about vodka and MTV; he's talking about his life in the religious institutions of his day, what we'd call "his church." Paul is talking about his life as a Pharisee.

We've learned to hear the word *Pharisee* through a filter and equate it with an evil, sanctimonious hypocrite. But when folks in Jesus' day heard the term, they thought of the most popular and respected Jewish religious society. Jesus seems to have offended every religious institution of His day (priesthood, scribes, Sadducees, and zealots), yet He was probably closest theologically to the views of the Pharisees. Perhaps we ought to replace "Pharisee" with the name of any well-respected religious group of our day.

You see, it's not so much the views or deeds of a group that make a person a "Pharisee" but trusting those views or deeds more than Jesus.

A Pharisee is a legalist. As soon as we hear the term *legalist*, we tend to think of other groups of people with regulations and rules we don't like, so we judge them to be legalists according to rules we *do* like. We love to judge others as being judgmental. We can get very legalistic about not being legalists. We are often intolerant of those who are intolerant of what we tolerate.

Renouncing legalism doesn't mean renouncing law, that is, "the knowledge of good and evil." Instead, renouncing legalism means renouncing your *dependence* on law—the old fruit, the knowledge of good and evil. It means renouncing your dependence on yourself to fulfill that law.

We can debate the merits of different laws, but no law can save you, sanctify you, or redeem you. No law can give you a new heart, and if you think some law can, I think you're a legalist.

In Romans 5:20 Paul writes, "Law came in, to increase the trespass." In other words, law shows legalists that they're dead. That is, the revelation of the dance steps shows us we're not dancing. "Law came in, to increase the trespass; but where sin increased, grace abounded all the more." At the cross, Pharisees, Sadducees, priests, zealots, Romans, Jews, Presbyterians, Baptists, Catholics, Campus Crusaders . . . that is, sinners—people who trust themselves to save themselves—crucified Christ. At the cross, sin increased, but grace abounded all the more. Law came in: they crucified Jesus according to what they professed to be the law. Law came in: He bore the penalty for all our lawbreaking. Law came in: "Cursed be every one who hangs on a tree" (Galatians 3:13). Law came in, and grace abounded all the more. We dance by grace, and Christ fulfills the law in us.

I fear that much of what we call "Christian" these days is really legalism, the law appealing to our flesh—folks sitting around coming up with programs, formulas, and regulations, and then appealing to our pride (flesh) to fulfill those regulations. I suspect it's about us and what we can do instead of about Him and what He's done and is doing in us. Paul writes:

> Why do you submit to regulations, "Do not handle, Do not taste, Do not touch" (referring to things which all perish as they are used), according to human precepts and doctrines? These have indeed an appearance of wisdom in promoting rigor of devotion and self-abasement and severity to the body, but they are of no value in checking the indulgence of the flesh. (Colossians 2:20–23)

So Jesus says, "Beware of the leaven of the Pharisees." I fear that we've forgotten that the Pharisees "R" us. We worry and preach about irreligious, MTV-watching, Harry Potter-reading pagans and forget it was the religious types that crucified our Lord. Actually the tax collectors, prostitutes, and sinners got along with Jesus rather admirably. It's not that we shouldn't be concerned about the evils of prostitution, tax policies, MTV, and sorcery; it's just that perhaps we religious types ought to be most on guard against "the leaven of the Pharisees"—the lure of the zombies—bad religion.

In recent years an inordinate number of books have been written on how to do church, how to get a big church, how to have a great church. The church is the bride. She's spent a lot of time staring in the mirror as of late. That she writes about herself may be okay on some level; she should look nice for her Groom. Yet a good bride is focused on her Groom, not herself. If she gets great (big), it's because she's pregnant with His child—His fruit—by surrendering to His love and receiving Him to herself. When the bride becomes enamored with herself, it's the spirit of religion. She only gets fat with more of herself, but not with life—the fruit of her Groom. When the church is focused on the church, the church may learn some dance steps, but that's not dancing. We must surrender ourselves and follow Jesus' lead to really dance.

We in the Western church have become enamored with "how to" books and formulas. I've been told by "experts" that I should end every message with a "practical application point." Yet I've also been told to preach from Scripture. Time and again, I've come to the end of a text and realized the only practical application point is Jesus. I think the closest thing to a practical application point given by Jesus is "Pick up a cross and follow." And gosh—that's not very practical. If you want practical, if you want formulas and "how to" directions, go read Muhammad. He's got millions of them. However, Jesus acts as if we're dead, can't do a thing for ourselves, and desperately need a savior. It's true that once we're saved, He seems to expect a lot from us, yet it's all in His power, not ours. Jesus is an entirely impractical application point. He *is* the point *(logos* in Greek), and He applies us to Himself. When we surrender in faith by grace, when we worship Him, when we abide in Him, we bear fruit and we are His body—His dancing body.

He already died for you. You can't make Him love you any more than He already does. He doesn't want a robot, obedient zombie, or cowering slave. He wants a bride who will thrill at His touch and surrender to His life. God has offered us His heart nailed to a cross, and in fear we compile "to do" lists, ask for a policy manual, and busy ourselves with trivial tasks, like a nervous bride would do on her honeymoon night. That's the spirit of religion, the leaven of the Pharisees, the lure of the zombie—our love for living under law and relying on ourselves with our hearts kept safely hidden in our own private hell.

We tend to point to every other group, but the Pharisees "R" us. I am a zombie . . . a sinner, but Jesus is teaching me to dance.

Jesus said, "Beware of the leaven of the Pharisees" right after He said that an evil and adulterous generation seeks a sign (Matthew 16:4–6). The Pharisees always wanted a sign. They wanted God's stuff but not His heart. Jesus offered plenty of signs, but they happened to the "wrong people" in the "wrong places" outside the Pharisees' control. And when Jesus revealed His heart—indeed He is the heart of God— when He revealed His heart broken on a cross, they despised it. They could not control it, only reject it or surrender to it and dance. We're all tempted by control. The spirit of religion is control—the self in control—the self refusing to surrender and dance.

A couple years ago, my church moved into a wonderful new building. I figured that with all the new people we anticipated, I ought to do some "easy-listening-Jesus-loves-you" preaching. I decided to preach through the Gospel of Matthew. When I got to the Sermon on the Mount, I soon realized "Jesus loves you" isn't "easy listening," because Jesus loves *you*—a dead zombie, an addicted Pharisee. His amazing grace is an offense to our petty legalism and self-righteous religion. In the Sermon on the Mount, Jesus preaches us from a mountain of law to a mountain of grace—not so that we can do whatever we want, but that one day whatever we want, we'll do. For whatever we'll do will be what He wants. He wants us to dance, and His dance is love.

To dance is to surrender yourself to a rhythm greater than yourself, to lose yourself in the music and find yourself dancing. To dance is to forget the dance steps yet find yourself dancing the dance steps, animated by the music.

I'm talking about more than ballerinas and tutus. I'm talking about warriors in full battle gear. I'm talking about athletes straining for the prize.

I'm talking about cripples and cancer victims enduring a wilderness of pain.

I'm talking about you at your job tomorrow.

I'm talking about kids playing in a field.

I'm talking about whatever you do being done in a new way, that is, being done in rhythm and to music.

Paul writes, "The love of Christ compels us" (2 Corinthians 5:14, NKJV). We are to move in rhythm to the music of His love. God is love. God is a dance: three persons, one dance. Moving in rhythm to that music in this world can hurt. It's bearing a cross wherever you are, dying with Him and living with Him, always.

So we preached through the Sermon on the Mount. Some left, some danced, and some just ate donuts downstairs. I hope you'll hear the love of Jesus, dare to surrender, and begin to dance.

We'll begin with an introduction via John the Baptist in Matthew 3, move on to the Sermon on the Mount, and conclude with John the Baptist and some words from Jesus on dancing in Matthew 11.

INTRODUCTION:
THE WILD MAN

MATTHEW 3:1–12

MATTHEW 3:1–6: *"In those days came John the Baptist preaching in the wilderness of Judea, 'Repent, for the kingdom of heaven is at hand.' For this is he who was spoken of by the prophet Isaiah when he said, 'The voice of one crying in the wilderness: Prepare the way of the Lord, make his paths straight.' Now John wore a garment of camel's hair, and a leather girdle around his waist; and his food was locusts and wild honey. Then went out to him Jerusalem and all Judea and all the region about the Jordan, and they were baptized by him in the river Jordan, confessing their sins."*

John was a wild man different from the others. For those willing to accept it, said Jesus, he was Elijah. Remember that Elijah lived in the wilderness clothed in a leather girdle. Then there was Isaiah, who walked around for three years prophesying naked (see Isaiah 20:4). Ezekiel lay on his left side outside Jerusalem for over a year, then on his right side for forty days. And God commanded him to eat food baked over human dung (see Ezekiel 4).

These were God's wild men, the prophets of old; and John was the greatest of these . . . wild . . . uncivilized . . . uncontrolled by this world. He was free, tough, and dangerous. John ate locusts!

Israel lived in fear of the locust, the "ravager." (Joel 2:6–7: "Before them peoples are in anguish, all faces grow pale. Like warriors they charge, like soldiers they scale the wall.") Locusts would devour the sustenance of Israel.

But John devoured *them.*

In Revelation 9, demon locusts come from the pit of hell. They don't afflict the crops; they afflict the hearts of men.

John yells, "Repent, for the kingdom of God is at hand. . . . Make his paths straight." Some say that he meant by that, "Get your life in order." Perhaps he meant more, "Let go of your order."

Not "get your stuff together,"

But "forget about your stuff."

Not "get civilized,"

But "get uncivilized."

John was hardly civilized. "Let go of all your attachments; clean out your heart; get everything off the highway, because somebody's comin'! Repent, be baptized, wash this world away, get wild!"

Jerusalem, all Judea, and all the region round about the Jordan were going out to see John. Isn't that weird?

In times of sorrow, folks love wild men. I think we always love wild men.

- Like we love lions in the zoo
- Like we love gladiators and cowboys in the movies
- Like we love Rambo and James Bond (but you wouldn't want them driving your car)
- Like we love John Belushi and Dan Aykroyd (but you'd be afraid to have them over for a nice dinner party)
- Like we love John the Baptist, Elijah, Isaiah

We all love wild men because we all live such constrained, controlled, stiff lives.

In those days, the Jews were constrained and repressed, occupied by imperial Rome. They were also constrained by an extremely legalistic religious system. And of course, like all of us, they were constrained in their hearts by fear, guilt, and shame.

In his seminal work *Civilization and Its Discontents*, Sigmund Freud taught that civilization is dependent upon constrained (repressed) desires. If we acted on the deepest desires of our hearts, we'd devour each other. Therefore, our only hope for civilization, taught Freud, is repression of desire through fear, guilt, and shame: civilization and its discontents.[1]

Well, John the Baptist wasn't civilized. But he said, "Heaven is at hand," and heaven is the ultimate civilization. So we would suppose that they're all really repressed up there! That would mean the best party is in hell, Van Halen style . . . "Runnin' with the Devil" . . . and that heaven is full of unthinking, unfeeling, conformist zombies.

Perhaps your experience of church is something like that. Ironically, many religious folks would agree with Freud: civilization must be based on repression and discontent. They like law and so would label Scripture: *Heaven and Its Discontents*. They'd label the church policy manual: *Church and Its Discontent—How to Make a Zombie*.

I think deep down all guys want to be wild men. They want to be free and fully alive.

John Eldredge wrote a great book entitled *Wild at Heart*. He argues that every man wants to be a wild man . . . it's his true nature . . . born to be wild with an adventure to live, a battle to fight, and a beauty to rescue.

Men want to be wild men . . . and chicks dig 'em. It's weird, because mothers want their daughters to marry Mister Rogers types, but they themselves like wild men. I think that deep down, women want to be the beauty that is rescued. So they want a man strong enough, uninhibited enough, wild enough to storm their castle and set them free: to penetrate their defenses and impregnate them with life.

For some of you, that's terrifying, for it sounds like rape. For some of you, it's enticing, for it sounds like romance. For *all* of us, I think it's both. For if the wild man is strong enough to storm the castle and set us free and give us life, he's strong enough to storm the castle, imprison us further, and give us death.

We all live in a world that is raped. But we dream of romance. Remember, we're all feminine to God's masculine. We are the bride, and we are or were imprisoned in a castle guarded by a dragon.

Chicks dig wild men, so they marry the wild man. But they're *afraid* of the wild man, so they try to tame him. And after they do, they complain to a counselor, "The romance has gone out of my marriage."

So, bride of Christ, how's your marriage? How's your walk with Jesus? Is it boring? Is it dead?

Back to John: "Jerusalem and all Judea" were going out to him, because we like wild men, and really there are so few of them.

This world is effective at taming wild men. In Scripture, the word *world* means more than simply earth. *World* implies the systems of fallen reality, civilization as we know it. This world and its dark prince are very effective at domesticating wild men.

Many men are downright stupid and thus easy to tame. Have you ever watched beer commercials during football games? "I like football and beer and the twins! I'm *wild!*" No. This very instant you're being tamed by corporate America to the tune of hundreds of millions a year, and all they needed was a sixty-second spot during a football game.

It happens all the time, on a shallow level and a much deeper level. The world sets traps, and Satan sets traps. God warns of the trap: "Adam, don't take that fruit. It's a trap. The day you eat it you'll die." Satan sets the trap: "Eve, it will make you like God. Isn't that a good desire?"

That's how wild animals are enslaved and tamed: they fulfill their

God-given wild desire in the wrong way or the wrong place, and their desire is twisted to their shame. They eat old meat lying in a snare and they're trapped.

Men think they're wild by walking into traps and eating the bait: drugs, adultery, greed . . . "I'm wild!" No, maybe you're just entirely domesticated by Satan, firmly enslaved with shame, pride, and fear—fear that you'll be exposed and condemned, fear that you'll die. For you have heard the call of the wild, and now you're the evil one's pet, his zombie.

When people get frightened enough, they often turn to religion, because the law tells us where the traps are: "Don't steal, don't commit adultery, don't bear false witness." People come to church so I can tell them where all the traps are, so I can motivate them to be careful and cautious, so I can help them repress their desires by reminding them that if they screw up, they are jerks, and God might fry them in hell. But if they just carefully follow the rules, they can navigate their lives.

Guys don't say it, but they mean it: "Hey, honey, work stinks, the kids are messed up, and I'm getting addicted to porn. Maybe we ought to go to church. I need some repression."

Marx said, "Religion is the opiate of the people."

- That is, it is civilization's best shot at repressing the desires of the masses; civilization's best shot at maintaining order over discontent.
- That is, it is the most powerful means of enslaving men to the world, the most powerful means of turning people into unthinking, unfeeling conformists.
- That is, it is the great lion tamer.

In the Book of Revelation, the dragon calls forth the beast from the sea and then the beast from the land—the false prophet, a picture of civil religion. And that beast tempts all of us. So Satan traps us with sins, then he traps us with Sin itself, the belief that we can navigate our way through this world and make our own lives work—the idolatry of the self, the idea that the self can save the self by conforming the self to its knowledge of good and evil, the fruit of the tree from the Garden of Eden. He traps us with the belief that we can save ourselves through our obedience to the Law.

Well, religious people hate the truly wild man, because he is not repressed by them. Perhaps it's not the things repressed that are the greatest evil, but the fact that we repress them: that is, hide our hearts from the Wild Man. We hide our hearts from the One who can set us free.

John looks up and sees the scribes and Pharisees.

MATTHEW 3:7–10: *But when he saw many of the Pharisees and Sadducees coming for baptism, he said to them, "You brood of vipers! Who warned you to flee from the wrath to come? Bear fruit that befits repentance, and do not presume to say to yourselves, 'We have Abraham as our father'; for I tell you, God is able from these stones to raise up children to Abraham. Even now the axe is laid to the root of the trees; every tree therefore that does not bear good fruit is cut down and thrown into the fire."*

John did not mean "navigate the world,"
But "die to the world."
Not simply "repress your passions,"
But "*surrender* your passions."
Don't simply manage your sins,
But *confess* your sins.
"Bear fruit that befits repentance,"
Tears, mourning, lamentation.

Jesus taught in Matthew 11, "We wailed, and you did not mourn." You did not repent. You did not mourn over this fallen world.

So John was wild, but not wild enough.

MATTHEW 3:11–12: *I baptize you with water for repentance, but he who is coming after me is mightier than I, whose sandals I am not worthy to carry; he will baptize you with the Holy Spirit and with fire. His winnowing fork is in his hand, and he will clear his threshing floor and gather his wheat into the granary, but the chaff he will burn with unquenchable fire.*

"But who can endure the day of his coming, and who can stand when he appears? 'For he is like a refiner's fire'" (Malachi 3:2). When you truly see Him, you will mourn. Then your mourning will turn into wild dancing. You will die and then live.

The Wild Man's name is Jesus.

You may be thinking, *Jesus? Wild? Get out! I've seen Him on the flannel graph in Sunday school. He's meek and mild and boring.*
Dorothy Sayers writes:

The people responsible for the crucifixion of Jesus never accused him of being a bore—on the contrary: they thought him too dynamic to be safe. It has been left for later generations to muffle up that shattering personality and surround him with a yawning ho-hum atmosphere of tedium. We have efficiently trimmed the claws of the Lion of Judah, certified him "meek and mild," and recommended him as a fitting household pet for pale curates and pious old ladies.[2]

Jesus was wilder than John: Jesus gave the scribes and Pharisees the worst tongue-lashing. Jesus baptized not with water but with the Spirit that is fire.

Jesus was wilder than John. Not even death could contain Him. In fact, Jesus was the first truly wild man. Ever since Adam, humanity had been enslaved and trapped—the walking dead. Jesus is the new Adam, and none has ever been so wild.

He is the Lion of Judah!

In C. S. Lewis's *The Lion, the Witch and the Wardrobe,* Aslan the Lion represents Jesus. The children ask if he's safe, and Mr. Beaver exclaims, "Safe? 'Course he isn't safe. But he's good."[3]

The Lion of Judah is not a tame lion, but He's good. The problem is, His bride is not good, so He makes her nervous. When she's afraid, she tries to tame Him and make Him safe, controlled, and predictable.

Jesus is *more wild* than John. If John prepared the highway, Jesus rides His Harley down it, and He wants you on the back. John bore witness to the music. Jesus is the music, the rhythm, the *Logos* (Word).

Jesus not only leaves civilization, He leaves the throne of heaven, naked of all His glory. He sneaks into the dragon's castle where His bride is sleeping in bondage. He makes Himself His bride's baby, and traps her with love. And He sets a trap for the evil one himself. The Lion is a Lamb. Having all power, life, and glory in perfect freedom, He lays it all down. He takes the poison fruit of His bride, bears her dead heart, embraces the fallen world with love, "becomes sin for us," and yells to the dragon, "Do your worst!"

The Lamb is slain and descends into hell, into the belly of the dragon, bearing every sin, every wound, every sorrow, every tear of the ones He loves. Then, on the third day, He rises to baptize us with His fire—His Spirit. He is *the* Wild Man, and He makes us wild too.

You see . . .

He not only forgives us our sins, He gives us His Spirit.

He not only crucifies our old hearts, He gives us new hearts.

Christianity is not just repressing your old desires but dying to your old desires and getting new ones. Or better yet, it's baptizing your old desires with fire until they're pure like gold. It's not memorizing dance steps but surrendering yourself to the Dance. It's not dancing for Jesus but dancing *with* Jesus.

John said, "The kingdom of heaven is at hand"—the great civilization. But nobody in heaven is repressed. Nobody says, "Another day with a harp . . . *sigh* . . . I really ought to be good . . .". Everybody does exactly what they want, and what they want is exactly good.

I would imagine they get up and say something like:

"I think I'll go feast at the Great Banquet! I'll eat all I want; I'll drink all I want, for all I want is good! Then I'll go to the King's chambers and without a hint of shame, I'll surrender to the ecstasy of my Bridegroom's touch, for we are bound in an eternal covenant and His banner over me is love. Then I'll sit on my Father's lap. Knowing no fear, I'll rest in His arms. And I'll sing—sing to the praise of His extravagant and glorious grace forever, because I WANT to.

In heaven, no one is repressed. Heaven is a wild, uninhibited, free, and living dance of absolute joy. Jesus said, "I came that my joy might be in you" (John 15:11, paraphrased). Heaven is at hand, and we can begin to live there *now* by faith in Christ Jesus. "For freedom Christ has set us free," writes Paul. "Do not submit again to a yoke of slavery" (Galatians 5:1).

If you've put your faith in Christ as your Savior and Lord, He's given you a new heart and an immeasurable greatness of power. You are a dragon slayer! The Lion is in you. So Satan's only hope is to tame you with lies. The lies appeal to your old heart full of fear, so you'll stop dancing and shut down your new heart full of love. And love is God.

Our old heart says, "Be cautious; be anxious; be afraid; don't screw up! Stay in control at all times." Every move is calculated and measured.

Have you ever tried to dance like that? It's not fun and not wild. You're so occupied with yourself you can't hear the music.

Over the years, while praying with people who've had visions and received prophecies, I've been amazed at the questions Jesus won't answer. Sometimes I've been able to speak into people's visions of Jesus and ask for details or formulas and instructions, and Jesus will simply answer, "Trust Me. Follow Me." Once a friend asked, "Should I see a certain person, go on a certain trip?" And Jesus said, "Use your new heart, the one I gave you."

I always want *instructions*.
He wants me to use my new *heart*.
I want dance *steps*.
He wants me to *surrender* to the music of His love.

It's scary to surrender control to His love.
It's scary using your new heart.
It's scary being free. Who knows what will happen?

It's a frightening thing to love from the heart without constraint. For in this world it can get you crucified.

The wildest men are hanging on crosses in the Sudan. They're singing in prison cells in China. They already have one foot in the kingdom of heaven, even while the other is still locked in chains.

It's frightening to love. But love is stronger than death, and nothing is more wild. For love is God, and God is not *at all* repressed.

Let the "love of Christ compel you." Use your new heart. The Law helps you know when you're *not* using it. Are you looking at porn? Are you cheating in your business? Are you having an affair? Are you greedy? Then you're not using it.

Don't panic. Don't just repress it but confess it. Then use your new heart. Jesus didn't come to only forgive us our sins and say, "Try again. Try *harder!* Be more repressed next time." Jesus came that we might have *life* and have it abundantly.

John came to help us die to the old world; Jesus came to give birth to the new one. In Matthew 11, Jesus teaches, "John mourned, and you didn't lament. We piped, and you would not dance" (paraphrased).

When the Wild Man hangs on His wild cross, He draws all men unto Himself (see John 12:32). We mourn, and our mourning turns into dancing. We die with Him and are resurrected with Him. We're "born again to be wild." Women, don't be afraid of wild men like Jesus. They're the ones you long for, so wild they'll hang on a cross and sacrifice everything for you. And they won't settle for just your body. They want your freely given, naked heart. That's not rape; it's romance. Yes, it's scary, but it's good. Bride of Christ, stop hiding from Jesus.

Brennan Manning tells about a repressed nun in her mid-thirties who never smiled, laughed, or danced. In prayer she had a vision of a large ballroom filled with people:

> I was sitting by myself on a wooden chair, when a man approached me, took my hand, and led me onto the floor. He held me in his arms and led me in the dance. The tempo of the music increased and we whirled faster and faster. The man's eyes never left my face. His radiant smile covered me with warmth, delight, and a sense of acceptance. Everyone else on the floor stopped dancing. They were staring at us.

The beat of the music increased and we pirouetted around the room in reckless rhythm. I glanced at his hands, and then I knew. Brilliant wounds of a battle long ago, almost like a signature carved in flesh. The music tapered to a slow, lilting melody and Jesus rocked me back and forth. As the dance ended, he pulled me close to him. Do you know what he whispered? . . . "Christine, I'm wild about you."[4]

Bride of Christ, He's *wild* about you. He wants you to be *wild* about Him too.

He didn't come to earth and hang on a cross bearing the sin and shame of all humanity just to populate heaven with hordes of unthinking, unfeeling, conformist zombies. He came to earth for His bride, a bride who would respond to His advances with the most glorious, free, and uninhibited of passions—His own love.

1

When Jesus Gets Famous

Matthew 4:17, 23–25; 5:2–12

MATTHEW 4:17, 23–25: *From that time Jesus began to preach, saying, "Repent, for the kingdom of heaven is at hand." . . . And he went about all Galilee, teaching in their synagogues and preaching the gospel of the kingdom and healing every disease and every infirmity among the people. So his fame spread throughout all Syria, and they brought him all the sick, those afflicted with various diseases and pains, demoniacs, epileptics, and paralytics, and he healed them. And great crowds followed him from Galilee and the Decap'olis and Jerusalem and Judea and from beyond the Jordan.*

In Matthew 4 Jesus gets famous. He becomes big news. The gospel means "good news."

Last week driving up to our church (on a mountain west of Denver), I noticed the local news truck with the words "Real News" on the side. News trucks always seem to be parked at the overpass taking pictures of the *sky*.

It struck me that we would all go home that night and put everything else aside to watch the news, especially the weather, which would be a picture of what we drove by that day. But because society (the crowd) labels it "news," we watch with wonder. "Wow, honey! The mountain cam!"

Do you ever watch the news and think we're missing the *real* news?

1

Well, in Matthew 4 Jesus makes the news. People come from all over the province of Syria (an area larger than Israel). Jesus is preaching the gospel, the good news of the kingdom. The kingdom is at hand. And He's healing every infirmity. There are *huge crowds*. We've got some serious religion here. I think we'd call it a revival.

People sometimes ask me, "Wouldn't it be great if God sent a revival?"

In John 14:12 Jesus says, "he who believes in me will also do the works that I do; and greater works than these will he do, because I go to the Father." So according to Jesus, it seems we ought to make the news like *He* made the news.

Sometimes I wonder, *Lord, why* aren't *more people healed? Just think of the crowds. You'd be famous, and we'd be blessed. The signs of the kingdom would be evident. Why* aren't *more people healed, Jesus?* That's an involved question.

1. It certainly appears that at times God chooses not to heal. In fact, studies show that 100 percent of His disciples over 125 years of age are *dead*. So at some point their bodies were not healed.
2. It may have to do with the fact we don't *ask* for healing. So I hope we ask expectantly.
3. It may be a lack of faith. Clearly, healing is in some way related to faith.
4. It's clear some people have a special gift of faith for healing. But faith isn't something you can simply conjure up. And faith isn't simply an idea in your heart. It's a deep trusting in the depths of your heart, like a space in your heart that God fills with Himself.

With my head I know God can heal. I've encountered some remarkable medical testimonies, including my own. I believe, but I know at times I need help with my unbelief.

Several years ago I received some shocking news. One of my dearest friends had HIV. She went to a specialist who put her on meds. It appears she contracted the virus years before, when she was brutally raped by a man who abused her as a child and was sent by a coven to keep her in fear and shame. She'd been raised in that coven and abused in ways that make any movie from Hollywood seem mild.

I don't know if I would have believed her story except that on numerous occasions I've encountered the demonic spirits assigned to harass her, and better than that, I've seen the power of Jesus as He drives them out of her life. It wasn't subtle. It wasn't vague. It was extremely dramatic, a sign and a wonder. The power of our Lord at work in her was utterly astounding! Yet she still had HIV. For years she felt sick and still had to take the meds. So I agreed to come and hold her when she dies. But now I may not be able to follow through on my promise.

Recently she asked a friend of mine, a doctor, to give her another HIV test. We'd been praying, she felt better, and she had even gone off her meds for a year.

We all gathered in the back room one Sunday after our worship service. With great trepidation my friend braced herself for the news about her test from Ann, the doctor, who handed her a piece of paper and said, "Um, this is very hard for the doctors to explain, especially for someone that's been off her meds for a year. But medical science can't detect any HIV. I think you're healed."

She's been off her meds now for almost two years, and she feels great. And I believe she's healed.

But now, I don't know *when* she was healed. Was it when we cast out a certain demon? Was it when I commanded HIV to go in Jesus' name? Was it when she prayed alone calling out to Jesus in her room? I don't know. But just think: if we could heal everyone with HIV, we would be on the news! Everyone would say the kingdom of heaven is at hand.

Jesus would be famous. We'd have a revival! Just imagine the crowds!

Matthew 4:23 says Jesus healed every disease. He was famous. Verse 25 says great crowds followed Him from all over Syria. Then, at the beginning of chapter 5 (just when we expect Jesus to write a book called *Revival: How We Did It* or *Keys for a Dynamic Healing Ministry*), we see what He did:

When Jesus got famous, seeing the crowds, He "sat down." When the crowd tried to make Him king, He ran away. (Jesus is *not* a standard American evangelical pastor.) Seeing the crowds, He left and sat down.

Jesus seems rather ambivalent about crowds. Søren Kierkegaard writes, "The crowd is indeed untruth. Christ was crucified because he would have nothing to do with the crowd."[1] Kierkegaard also says we like crowds because they "abolish our conscience." Zombies travel in crowds.

Now that my church is bigger, it scares me how people will listen to my sermons. They think my sermons are true because they draw crowds.

Jesus was ambivalent about crowds, fame, and even healing. Over and over He healed people and then told them to keep it quiet. Seeing the crowd, Jesus sat down. Now I would have expected Him to tell us how He healed everyone so *we* could do it. We'd make the news, draw a huge crowd, publish a formula for success; Jesus would be famous, and we'd all be blessed.

I want the formula, because so often I pray for someone's healing, and when they don't get healed I feel . . .

- inadequate (poor in my spirit)
- sorry for the person I'm praying for (we mourn)
- humbled (meek)

I so much want to see everything put right. But . . . seeing the crowd Jesus sat down . . .

MATTHEW 5:2–12: *And he opened his mouth and taught them, saying: "Blessed are the poor in spirit, for theirs is the kingdom of heaven. Blessed are those who mourn, for they shall be comforted. Blessed are the meek, for they shall inherit the earth. Blessed are those who hunger and thirst for righteousness, for they shall be satisfied. Blessed are the merciful, for they shall obtain mercy. Blessed are the pure in heart, for they shall see God. Blessed are the peacemakers, for they shall be called sons of God. Blessed are those who are persecuted for righteousness' sake, for theirs is the kingdom of heaven.*

"Blessed are you when men revile you and persecute you and utter all kinds of evil against you falsely on my account. Rejoice and be glad, for your reward is great in heaven, for so men persecuted the prophets who were before you."

"Blessed are the poor in spirit, for theirs is the kingdom of heaven." Blessed: fortunate, deeply happy. Luke simply records, "Blessed are the poor"—the destitute. So it at least means those who have nothing to depend on in this world, not even a healthy body. I think "Blessed are the poor in spirit" also means those whose own spirits are destitute and weak, with a space in their hearts for God to fill.

"Blessed are those who mourn, for they shall be comforted." Blessed are those who weep. He keeps your tears in a bottle (Psalm 56:8). Blessed are those who mourn a fallen world and a broken heart.

"Blessed are the meek, for they shall inherit the earth." Meek doesn't mean passive or lacking in courage, but humble and surrendered. Moses was meek (Numbers 12:3). Jesus was meek (Matthew 11:29).

"Blessed are those who hunger and thirst for righteousness, for they shall be satisfied." If you think you are righteous, this doesn't describe you. Jesus says, "Those who hunger and thirst for righteousness" are blessed. If you're satisfied with your own righteousness, you've got the wrong religion.

"Blessed are the merciful, for they shall obtain mercy." The merciful, forgiving, compassionate—for "the measure you give will be the measure you get" (Matthew 7:2).

"Blessed are the pure in heart, for they shall see God." Pure in heart. Did you notice all these blessings have to do with the heart, the interior of a person? They have to do with that which never makes the news, that which is entirely personal, that which cannot be regulated with law but only romanced by grace.

You can't control the teaching you get, the preaching you hear, or the miracles you see. You can't control the crowd. But can you surrender your own heart to God's grace?

Do you want to see the kingdom? "Blessed are the pure in heart, for they shall see God." In the words of Kierkegaard, "Purity of heart is to will one thing"—God. What is God? God is love. And where can we see love? All sorts of places, even in "the last and the least."

Paul writes to Titus, "To the pure all things are pure" (Titus 1:15). The one with the pure heart can find God in every rock, every flower, even every cross. Was anything more horrifying and impure than the cross? Can you see God there? Then I bet you can see Him anywhere . . . kind of like the kingdom really *is* at hand, if only the eyes of our hearts were truly opened to see. Then the kingdom wouldn't be a matter of signs and wonders to be observed, crowds to follow, teachings to get, or sermons to hear. At any moment the kingdom is a matter of the disposition of the heart, like faith, hope, and love.

I've spent countless hours praying with my friend raised in the coven, and usually those times of prayer involve going back to horrifying pictures in her past. There we ask Jesus to help us see Him. He purifies her heart so that she's willing to see Him. He's always there, doing things like hanging on crosses; raising the dead; holding, washing, and embracing my friend. And when the eyes of her heart see

Jesus with faith, hope, and love, Satan himself doesn't stand a chance in hell. "Blessed are the pure in heart, for they shall see God."

"Blessed are the peacemakers, for they shall be called sons of God." Not the peace-*havers*. There are those who live in the suburbs and avoid all conflict, always saying nice things; they think they are peacemakers, but they are peace-*deniers*.

Shalom (biblical peace) is the presence of all good things in their place, the presence of the kingdom. Peacemakers will be called sons of God, and the Son of God is also the Prince of Peace. He said, "I have come not to bring peace, but a sword" (Matthew 10:34). Blessed are those who will use God's weapons to fight for peace.

There came a day when the Prince of Peace was no longer famous but infamous, when He performed no sign and didn't even heal Himself. It was when *the crowd* nailed the Prince of Peace to the tree, He "made peace through the blood of His cross" (Colossians 1:20 NKJV).

"Blessed are those who are persecuted for righteousness' sake, for theirs is the kingdom of heaven. Blessed are you when men revile you and persecute you and utter all kinds of evil against you falsely on my account."

When Jesus got *famous* He said to His disciples and to the *crowd* seeking the *kingdom of heaven* . . .

> Blessed are you when you're not famous and the crowd hates you, for you are the kingdom of heaven.

The literal Greek construction of this beatitude and the first is, "Blessed are the poor in spirit and the persecuted for righteousness' sake, for *autos*—" of them "—is the kingdom of heaven." Not only is the kingdom *theirs,* but the kingdom of heaven *consists* of them.

In the Revelation, John sees the New Jerusalem coming down, and his name is on the foundation. The New Jerusalem is literally built of

God's people, it's shaped like the temple, and God *lives* there.

At one point, Pharisees come to Jesus and ask Him when the kingdom of God will come, and Jesus says, "The kingdom of God does not come with observation [signs to be observed (RSV)]; nor will they say, 'See here!' or 'See there!' For indeed, the kingdom of God is within you" (Luke 17:20–21 NKJV).

So, "seeing the crowd Jesus sits down." I think He's saying:

"Guys, don't play to the crowd. Don't confuse the crowd for the kingdom."

"Guys, don't seek signs. Don't confuse signs with the kingdom."

Twice in Matthew Jesus says, "An evil and adulterous generation seeks after a sign" (Matthew 12:39; 16:4). Often when I get depressed and don't feel blessed, I run off seeking crowds, fame, and signs—bad religion. Adulterers seek the signs of love: security, gifts, and pleasure. But they don't seek Love. He is a person. Seek and you will find. When you seek the kingdom, don't seek the crowd, the signs, or the famous. Don't depend on the latest teaching or the best preaching. When you seek the kingdom, seek the *King*.

Look in your own heart and ask yourself:

- Am I destitute for Jesus?
- Am I willing to mourn?
- Am I humble?
- Am I hungry for righteousness?
- Am I merciful?
- Am I pure in my desire?
- Do I seek peace?
- Will I suffer for righteousness?

If not, confess it to Jesus. Then look at Jesus.

You see, I'm not convinced you can surrender your own heart. But Jesus can. Look! He's hanging on a cross. When you see His love for you, your arrogant heart breaks, and you become . . .

> poor in spirit,
>> mourning and meek,
>>> hungry for Him,
> merciful like Him,
>> desiring only Him,
>>> willing to suffer for Him.

Your heart is opened. A space is made, and heaven invades your heart.

So when people come to me and say, "Wouldn't it be great to see revival in our church?"

1. I want to say, "Yes!" Yes, I'd *love* it if there were more dramatic conversions, healings, and bigger crowds.
2. I want to say, "Yes!" and "I'm sorry," for I'm convinced I lack faith, which may inhibit God's work somehow.
3. I want to say, "Yes!" and "I'm sorry." But what I really want to say is, "I hope you haven't missed it. I hope you haven't missed the revival."

I'm not sure what people mean by *revival*, but I know the kingdom of heaven consists of the "poor in spirit," and the kingdom is at hand. Perhaps then "the blessing" isn't *out there* waiting to be found as much as *in here* waiting to be discovered like treasure. "For the kingdom does not come with signs to be observed. They won't say, 'Oh, it's in *this* place or *that* place,' for the kingdom is within you" (Luke 17:20–21, author's paraphrase).

I think the thing that amazes me most of all, in all the years of praying for my friend from the coven, is how utterly concerned our Lord is with her heart. Being healed of HIV just didn't seem to be a big thing to God: no visions, no words of knowledge, no shaking—it just happened.[2]

For God, healing bodies, casting out demons, and signs and wonders just seem remarkably easy. It's been obvious in my friend that God has absolute power over demons, Satan, and disease. So then many times I've asked God, "Why did we have to pray *all night*, chasing some demon?" That is:

Why the poverty of spirit?
Why the mourning?
Why the surrendering?
Why the hungering for You?
Why the areas of forgiveness?
Why did we have to go back and see You in all those places of pain?
Why did we have to witness those persecutions?

"God, in an instant you could have *fried* every demon and every disease forever in hell!"

I think He has answered me many times: "Yes, yes, I could have. But then you wouldn't have spent all those hours caring for the heart of My beloved. And you, Peter, would have missed the splendor of My kingdom and the beauty of its King." "Blessed are the poor in spirit, for of them consists the kingdom. Blessed are the persecuted for righteousness' sake, of them consists the kingdom."

Follow "the crowd" and you'll miss the kingdom. Love somebody and you've found it. You are the kingdom. That's the real miracle.

The kingdom is not the same as a religious crowd. Jesus, seeing the crowd, sat down.

I heard Clive Calver tell of a young man who played Mozart in a concert hall in Great Britain. At the end of his performance, everybody stood and cheered. But he wouldn't play an encore. The proprietor said, "They're all standing. Play an encore!" The young man said, "In the balcony in the corner an old man is sitting." The proprietor said, "Oh, he doesn't know his music. The crowd is standing!" The young man replied, "He knows his music. He is my teacher. If the whole crowd were sitting but that one man standing, then I'd play an encore."[3]

Calver pointed out the one place in Scripture where Jesus, seated, is said to stand. In Acts 7 Jesus, seated at the right hand of the Father, stands. He stands when there is no healing, when the crowd turns on a fellow named Stephen and stones him to death. He stands as Stephen forgives them, for they know not what they do.

I doubt it made the news in Rome. But it was news in the kingdom of heaven. Stephen looked just like somebody else.

Jesus is already famous in heaven forever. But when He becomes famous in your heart, that's *real news* . . . and you become famous like Him.

Don't play to the crowd; play for Him—dance for Him.

2

SALT AND LIGHT

MATTHEW 5:13–16

MATTHEW 5:13: *You are the salt of the earth.*

MATTHEW 5:14: *You are the light of the world.*

MATTHEW 5:16: *Let your light so shine.*

We are called to be *salt and light!* You are the only Bible some will ever read!

We need *spirit!* In high school we always had a spirit section at sporting events. We would chant, "Heritage! Heritage! Heritage High!" We had spirit; it psyched up the team.

Sometimes Christians walk around as if we're in mourning. We need to exhibit joy and confidence! We need to be assertive, to claim this earth for God!

We're to be a light—an example. We need to exhibit our righteousness—a moral majority of stable marriages and healthy smiles.

I'm tired of tolerance—going easy on filth, easy on crime. Personally I'm offended, and I'm not gonna take it anymore! We are salt and light!

This world is filled with so many needs. Every week my desk is flooded with information about them: abortion, drug abuse, teen suicide, poverty, starvation, corruption, and deforestation. How can we not give our hearts to all these things? We're to be the light of the world . . . the *world*.

We wage a war on all fronts, and Scripture says, "friendship with the world is enmity with God" (James 4:4). It's time to stop making peace!

I've read we are one generation away from persecution (like in Russia, Africa, and China). "Salt and light" . . . but the world looks at us and reviles us—laughs at us. We need to do something about it!

So I've developed a strategy for achieving measurable success: the 3-M Ministry—Marketing, Management, Mastery. (Professionalism is probably a better word for mastery, but it doesn't start with *M*.)

> We will *market* ourselves,
>> *manage* our world, and
>>> *master* our subject.

Marketing: We need pithy slogans. I've thought of some for my church:

- Lookout Mountain—It's the Real Thing
- Lookout Mountain—Like a Rock
- Lookout Mountain—Where Jesus Goes to Church

Management: I have learned a lot about building a successful church, thanks to a plethora of valuable resources, and found that we are woefully inadequate. So I've taken:

- "Twelve Keys to an Effective Church,"
- "Four Principles of the Disciple-Making Pastor,"
- "Six Stages of Building a Contagious Church,"

- "Five Points of the Purpose-Driven Church," and the
- "Popular Model for the Prevailing Church"

. . . and combined them all into the "Dynamic Salt and Light Strategy for Global Conquest: 27 Key Disciple-Making, Principle, Purposeful Stages of the Contagious, Prevailing Church."

Mastery: I am currently training ten key leaders who will master the twenty-seven principles. They in turn use the workbook and multi-media resources to train ten more people. They in turn train ten more. Through this Dynamic Exponential Discipling Strategy (do the math: 10 x 10 = 100, 100 x 10 = 1,000, 1,000 x 10 = 10,000), in *ten years* we make 10 billion disciples! That's the *world!* Then Jesus comes back, and we get His stuff.

Marketing
    Management
        Mastery (Professionalism)

Some say, "I don't like this . . ." Well, la de freakin' da! If you don't want to be salt and light, you can just be *Jack Squat* singing "Kum Ba Ya" in a van down by the river! (I hope you know I'm kidding.)

MATTHEW 5:13–16: *You are the salt of the earth; but if salt has lost its taste, how shall its saltness be restored? It is no longer good for anything except to be thrown out and trodden under foot by men.*

You are the light of the world. A city set on a hill cannot be hid. Nor do men light a lamp and put it under a bushel, but on a stand, and it gives light to all in the house. Let your light so shine before men, that they may see your good works and give glory to your Father who is in heaven.

He didn't say you *could* be salt or what *if* you were light, He said, "You *are* the salt of the earth . . . you *are* the light of the world." Who is the "you" He's talking to? Surprisingly, verse 13 follows verses 1–12.

MATTHEW 5:3–13: *Blessed are the poor in spirit . . . Blessed are those who mourn . . . Blessed are the meek . . . Blessed are those who hunger and thirst for righteousness . . . Blessed are the merciful . . . Blessed are the pure in heart . . . Blessed are the peacemakers . . . Blessed are those who are persecuted for righteousness' sake, for theirs is the kingdom of heaven. Blessed are you when men revile you and persecute you . . . for your reward is great in heaven, for so men persecuted the prophets who were before you. You are the salt of the earth.*

Years ago at Penn State, a young Jewish student converted to Christianity. One of his professors encouraged him to go to a well-known evangelical church. When the professor, Dr. Tony Campolo, met him some weeks later and asked how it was going, the man said, "You know, if you put together a committee and asked them to take the Beatitudes and create a religion that contradicted every one of them, you would come pretty close to what I'm hearing down there at that church."[1]

Jesus says to His disciples: *"Blessed* [which can be translated *happy*] *are the poor in spirit."* Blessed are those who sense their own deep, spiritual need—insufficiency.

Paul defends his ministry in Corinth by writing, "Who is sufficient for these things? For we are not, like so many, peddlers of God's word" (2 Corinthians 2:16–17).

"Blessed [happy] *are those who mourn."* We live in a broken, fallen world. Blessed are those who don't live in denial of that fact. Joy and sorrow are not opposites of each other but they are *both* opposite of

denial and deadness. They are both opposite of bland, plastic people—
the walking dead, zombies.

"Blessed are the meek"—those who don't demand their rights, those
who are not easily offended.

Before Pilate, Jesus was meek and stronger than steel. His meekness
terrorized Pilate.

"Blessed are those who hunger for righteousness"—not those who think
they *are* righteous, but those who ache to walk in righteousness.

I've felt guilty a trillion times, but three or four times I think I
sincerely ached to be righteous.

"Blessed are the merciful, for they will receive mercy"—they need it. I
suppose they are merciful because deep in their spirit they know they
need mercy.

"Blessed are the pure in heart." In a world of a million demands,
purity of heart is to will one thing according to Kierkegaard: as Jesus
said, "Love the Lord your God."

"Blessed are the peacemakers, for they shall be called sons of God."

*"Blessed are the persecuted, reviled, slandered for righteousness' sake and
for me,"* says Jesus. *"Yours is the kingdom of heaven, and great is your
reward there."*

"You are the salt of the earth." Poor, mourning, meek, hungry,
merciful, pure in heart.

"You are the salt"—who live in this world with integrity and
authenticity . . . not playing a game or acting a part. *"You* are the light
of the world."

A. W. Tozer writes:

Christians have fallen into the habit of accepting the noisiest and most
notorious among them as the best and the greatest. They too have

learned to equate popularity with excellence, and in open defiance of the Sermon on the Mount they have given their approval, not to the meek, but to the self-assertive; not to the mourner, but to the self-assured; not to the pure in heart who see God, but to the publicity hunter who seeks headlines.[2]

In Jesus' day, the Romans, scribes, priests, and Pharisees made the news. "But God chose what is weak in the world to shame the strong," writes Paul (1 Corinthians 1:27).

In Jesus' day, the Romans exercised power through military strength. The scribes and Pharisees exercised power through religious strength. People obeyed out of fear of those strengths, obeyed them but secretly despised them.

In our day, in our society, we exercise power through capitalism—economic strength. America no longer invades with armies to take people's territory (at least I hope not). We invade with *marketing, management,* and *mastery* (professionalism). It's definitely better than bombs, but people still resent our power. So they eat at McDonald's in Cairo, Egypt, but their hearts are far from us.

As the early church was tempted with the power structures of its day, so our churches are tempted with the power structures of *our* day. We think if it works for selling cola, it should work for spreading the gospel! *Marketing.*

The modern advertising industry began about one hundred years ago in order to sell people things they didn't need. Now thirteen years of an average American life are spent watching TV. Three full years of that are commercials.[3] We're used to being lied to—hearing promises that can't be kept.

Our marketing society has led to what sociologists call "a depletion of meaning."

"Coke is the real thing."

"Volvo can save your soul."

"Chevy is like a rock."

When the church depends on marketing, we are in danger of the depletion of meaning. People don't really believe our meaning, and the true Meaning leaves our conversation.

Jesus is the Meaning, Logos, Word, Truth, Real Thing

How did Jesus market His church? "Do you want to be my disciple? Pick up your cross and come follow."

How did Paul market himself and his church friends? "We have become, and are now, as the refuse of the world, the offscouring of all things [the scum of the earth (NIV)]" (1 Corinthians 4:13).

My friend Mike pastors a church named Scum of the Earth. When I first heard that name, I was so . . . *jealous.* Why? Why would you want to market yourself as scum of the earth? Because scum of the earth need a savior. Wretches need grace.

Who would know a savior best? Those who need to be saved; those who know their own poverty, hunger, need for mercy; the meek, the persecuted, the reviled. They *are* the salt of the earth . . . and they make us thirsty for living water.

A preacher once said, "You can lead a horse to water, but you can't make him drink." After the service a rancher said, "That's not true. You can feed him salt."

Live your life with integrity and authenticity—be honest about your struggles and doubts, honest about your faith—and you will make people thirsty for Jesus. But market yourself, and you'll be bland like everyone else.

The church is not to market herself as if she were a product to be consumed. The bride who markets herself is called a whore. If we market anything, it's Jesus. But He's not a product to be consumed; He's a person to be known.

We live in a market society with a management economy—hundreds of companies with the same product. The one that markets and manages best *wins.*

This is Jesus' management scheme:

- He chose twelve guys to be with Him—twelve guys the world and religion considered losers. (As far as we know, not *one* of them chose twelve more guys, duplicating the scheme!)
- At one point the crowd tried to make Jesus king, and He ran away. How's that for management?
- In the New Testament, Jesus healed people, raised the dead, and then commanded people not to tell. If *we* think there's a miracle, we market it and manage it.

A few years ago, a national survey ranked seventy-one professions regarding their perceived honesty and integrity. TV evangelist was sixty-eighth, right after prostitute and right before organized crime boss.[4]

It seems the more we market ourselves and manage our churches like big business, the less people believe, the less we must look like Jesus, and the less it must seem that we're relying on Jesus. Maybe that's why the church in the United States is *not* growing.

However, the church in Russia, Africa, and China is growing like crazy . . . where marketing, management, and professionalism are often *illegal!*

I'm absolutely inundated with literature and conferences on "How to Build a Successful Church" and "How to Manage a Successful Discipleship Program." Discipleship is not a *program*; it's a life that rubs off on another life, seasoning, flavoring, and permeating that life like salt.

You Are the Salt of the Earth

In Mark 9:49 Jesus says, "For every one will be salted with fire." It's in trials, persecutions, and struggles that the world tastes salt on you—faith in Jesus. You can't program those trials; you don't know when they're coming.

Marketing, Management, and Mastery/Professionalism

We *pay* professionals to tell us how to raise our kids, marry our spouse, and serve our God. We *like* it that way because it avoids the confusing, hard work of love. We don't have to sweat blood in a garden in prayer, just read the manual. We don't have to surrender to the great lover of our souls, just follow a formula. We don't have to dance, just do some dance steps.

I have a Master of Divinity degree. However, I didn't master divinity; divinity mastered me. Christians don't *master* a subject; they bear witness to a mystery. We're not spreading a curriculum; we're introducing people to a living mystery—the person of Jesus Christ, who has invaded our self-centered, bland, little world and is now seasoning our lives with His gospel of grace.

When we market our "wonderful selves," manage our entire world, and act as if we've mastered our subject, we've lost our saltiness. We've stopped trusting our Savior, because we trust ourselves. We've stopped loving Jesus.

Love is not *marketing* yourself but *losing* yourself.

Love is not *managing* your world but *surrendering* your world.

Love is not *mastering* your subject but being mastered *by* your subject. It's following His lead.

But now, please understand: corporate communication is important, and you could call it marketing. Administration is critical, and it's a kind of management. Hiring professionals is key to organizing and equipping large groups for the work of the ministry. Marketing, management, and professionals build big saltshakers and construct large lighthouses! But saltshakers without salt and lighthouses without light are worthless.

All these "how to" books on building churches are great as long as by *church* we mean a saltshaker or lighthouse. But never forget: "You are the salt of the earth," and "you are the light of the world."

And Jesus said, "I will build my church" (Matthew 16:18). The true church isn't a building, program, human organization, or institution. The true church is people redeemed by the blood of Christ.

This is a personal message for me. Years ago I was on staff at two large and influential churches on the West Coast that were pastored by two high-profile leaders.

It turns out both men led extensive, secret lives of corruption and deception. Yet they both presided over glorious saltshakers (wonders of marketing, management, and professionalism).

When I learned of their hidden lives, I was so devastated I think I would have left the ministry had I not been salted—I had met Jesus in my dad. Not because he was a pastor but because some nights at 2:00 or 3:00 a.m. I would bump into him downstairs while I was getting a drink. I'd say, "What are you doing?" He'd say, "Oh, I couldn't sleep, and I was just praying."

> I was poor in spirit, and He let me see.
> He let me see that he needed a Savior.

I also met Jesus in my youth pastor Gary, not because he was great at marketing, management, and professionalism, but I had talked to him about stuff like doubt and masturbation, and he was honest, authentic, and meek . . . like Jesus.

I have seen Jesus in the people who have told me of their failures; who shared their sorrows and hungers, pains, and struggles. None of them consider me "their disciple," yet I *am*, for they hunger for righteousness, and in them I see Jesus (the righteousness of God). I taste salt, and I see light.

You are the salt of the earth, and you are the light of the world. Get out of the shaker and let your light shine. Your light is your sincere and authentic faith in Jesus in the midst of your own inadequacies.

It's true that you are the only Bible some people will ever read. But have you ever *read* the Bible? The Bible is full of losers. Only one succeeds; only one is good; only one is a hero. All the "heroes of faith" are heroes of a faith that's not in themselves. They are poor in spirit.

Abraham the pimp

Moses the timid

David the murdering adulterer

Rahab the harlot

Paul, chief of sinners

They confess, even advertise, their failures, so their lives are testimony to God's grace.

Jesus says, "Let your light so shine before men, that they may see your good works and give glory to your Father [not to *you*] who is in heaven" (Matthew 5:16). God gets the glory. You are an earthen vessel, "poor in spirit" that you may be filled with His Spirit.

Paul writes, "I will all the more gladly boast of my weaknesses that the power of Christ may rest upon me" (2 Corinthians 12:9).

Will Willimon led an evangelism program in his old church. Helen and Gladys got the map telling them where they would be witnessing door-to-door. Helen and Gladys were both church ladies in their eighties, couldn't follow the map, and evangelized the wrong neighborhood. They only got one prospect.

Verleen lived in the projects with her two children and had never been to church. But the following Thursday Verleen came to the women's Bible study, proudly clutching a brand-new Bible. Will led the study and then said, "Have any of you ever faced temptation and with Jesus' help resisted?"

One of the church ladies shared a story about paying the correct amount for groceries. Will said, "Good." Then Verleen spoke:

A couple of years ago I was into cocaine really big. You know what that's like. You know how that stuff makes you crazy. Well, anyway, my boyfriend, not the one I've got now, the one who was the daddy of my first child, that one, well, we knocked over a gas station one night—got two hundred dollars out of it. It was as simple as taking candy from a baby. Well, my boyfriend, he says to me, "Let's knock off that 7–11 store down on the corner." And something in me, it says, "No, I've held up that gas station with you, but I ain't going to hold up no convenience store." He beat the hell out of me, but I still said no. It felt great to say no, 'cause that's the only time in my life I ever said no to anything. Made me feel like I was somebody.

Through the stunned silence Pastor Willimon muttered, "OK. Let's pray." Outside afterward, as the pastor helped Helen into her Plymouth, she turned and told him, "You know, I can't wait to get home and get on the phone and invite people to come next Thursday! Your Bible studies used to be dull. I think I can get a good crowd for this!"[5] *Salty.*

24

Obviously Jesus doesn't want us to sin. We've already sinned plenty. He wants us to be honest about sin so we can be honest about grace, honest about Him.

Marketing, management, and professionalism help us get our act together as large institutions, but please don't get some act together as a person. (That's called *hypocrisy.*) Your honest life and faith is salt and light. "You are salt and light."

Sometimes I worry that all our American marketing, management, and professionalism, all our fancy seminars on *how to be* salt and light

- might just intimidate the poor in spirit so that they hide under a bushel;
- might make those who mourn keep silent;
- might make those who hunger for righteousness feel so guilty they won't share;
- might make those who are persecuted, slandered, and reviled for Jesus feel as if they're doing something wrong when, in fact, they're doing everything right. In fact, they already are salt and light.

In the midst of our gorgeous new saltshaker, we have an old rugged cross that looks as if someone was recently crucified upon it. That cross in the midst of our church building is there for a reason: we are to preach "Jesus Christ and Him crucified." Picture the cross:

- How's this for poor in spirit? He cried, "My God, my God, why have you forsaken me?" (Matthew 27:46 NIV).
- How's this for mourning? "The LORD has laid on him the iniquity of us all" (Isaiah 53:6).
- How's this for meek, hungering for righteousness, and merciful? He prayed, "Father, forgive them" (Luke 23:34).

- How's this for purity of heart? He said, "Nevertheless not my will, but thine, be done" (Luke 22:42).
- How's this for peacemaker? He is the peacemaker called "Son of God."
- How's this for persecuted, reviled, and slandered for righteousness sake? A cross.
- How's this for *marketing*? To be His disciple you must pick up His cross and follow Him (Matthew 16:24).
- How's this for *management*? At the cross his disciples abandoned Him.
- How's this for *mastery*? The cross is where slaves die.
- How's this for *romance*? . . .

I Corinthians 11:23–25: *On the night when he was betrayed [Jesus] took bread, and when he had given thanks, he broke it and said, "This is my body which is for you. Do this in remembrance of me." In the same way also the cup, after supper, saying, "This cup is the new covenant in my blood. Do this, as often as you drink it, in remembrance of me."*

Jesus is the salt. If He's in you, you'll be salty . . . a living sacrifice. In Israel, every sacrifice was to be salted, seasoned for God.

Jesus is salt on you to the glory of God. He is light through you to a dark world.

Speaking of His crucifixion, Jesus said, "And I, when I am lifted up from the earth, will draw [romance] all men to myself" (John 12:32).

3

TROUBLE WITH ZOMBIES

MATTHEW 5:17–20

A news bulletin flashes across the screen of a 1950s black-and-white TV set. The newscaster intones:

> I think we have some late word that's just arriving. And we interrupt to bring this to you. This is the latest disclosure, a report from National Civil Defense headquarters in Washington.
>
> It has been established that persons who have recently died have been returning to life and committing acts of murder. Widespread investigational reports from funeral homes, morgues, and hospitals have concluded that the unburied dead are coming back to life and seeking human victims. It's hard for us here to believe what we're reporting to you, but it does seem to be a fact.

That newscast comes from the cult classic movie *Night of the Living Dead.* The poor people trapped in farmhouses and old cars are having trouble with zombies—the walking dead. Zombies look like us on the outside but are dead on the inside, empty of that elusive, indefinable property we call "life." They look like us, so how do you know one when you see one?

1. They're stiff, because they really *are* stiffs.

2. They usually travel in groups (a crowd), because they don't think or feel for themselves.
3. Zombies feed on the living. Being dead, they *hunger* for life— the body and blood of the living.

According to professor David Chalmers at the University of Arizona, there are three kinds of zombies:[1]

1. *The classic Hollywood zombie.* They have usually been animated by space aliens or radiation.
2. *The voodoo zombie.* A soulless body that has been revived from the dead and made to work as a slave. In Haiti, zombie is the snake deity that inhabits the dead.
3. *The philosophical zombie.* According to the *Dictionary of Philosophy of Mind,* a zombie is "a being that behaves like us and may share our functional organization and even, perhaps, our neurophysiological makeup without conscious experiences." These zombies are a hot topic in philosophical circles, for their conceivability is an argument against materialism, a way to discuss human consciousness, or the soul, and what it is to be human and why we are not *all* zombies . . . or maybe we are. For if the materialists are right, we're all just empty matter consuming each other.

While philosophers argue over the feasibility of zombies, society worries that they could be real. Frankenstein, Dracula, cyborgs, the Terminator, the evil Santa in *Santa Clause 2*, the Hebrew legend of the Golem—all express our anxiety over zombies.

We conjecture about zombies, but my wife and kids believe they're real, because Dad turns into one every now and then, usually after the church service on Sunday morning. Sometimes while driving home I'll gradually become aware of my daughter's voice: "Dad! Dad! Hello?

Where are you?" I'll realize I've been operating on autopilot and maybe even missed my exit. I've been totally disengaged.

Worried, afraid, ashamed, insecure, we all tend to turn into zombies. We hit autopilot and go through the motions, disengaged and self-absorbed. Maybe we're so afraid of zombies because we're terrified we might *turn into one!*

Perhaps the most frightening zombie movies you've ever seen were on religious TV. Maybe you've run from church because you felt surrounded by a group of empty-headed, non-thinking, stiff people who wanted to suck the life out of you. Or maybe you have a strong suspicion that what God *really* wants is zombies—robots—unthinking, unfeeling slaves to do His unthinking, dispassionate will.

In so many of those old Jesus movies, Jesus looks like a zombie. And you wonder, *Why are folks following Him? Has He turned them into zombies too?*

Well, reading through the Gospel of Matthew we find that in reality Jesus is anything but a zombie. Jesus is the wild man who in chapter 4 battles the evil snake deity in the wilderness. Jesus will not be tamed or zombified by the devil.

In Matthew 4:18–19 Jesus calls us to be who we truly are, as He called Peter and Andrew to be fishers of men. He nurtures and baptizes our little desires and dreams all the way into the kingdom. Then in verse 23 Jesus delivers and heals. He *exudes life*. Then He *exudes grace* in the beatitudes as He delivers His "Sermon on the Mount."

By now we can see that Jesus is so full of power, life, joy, and freedom that He fills us with hope that God is not a zombie! Maybe He doesn't want to turn us into zombies either. So we can blow off all those painful commandments and endless laws, right?

Catch Jesus' answer:

MATTHEW 5:17–20: *Think not that I have come to abolish the law and the prophets; I have come not to abolish them but to fulfil them. For truly, I say to you, till heaven and earth pass away, not an iota, not a dot, will pass from the law until all is accomplished. Whoever then relaxes one of the least of these commandments and teaches men so, shall be called least in the kingdom of heaven; but he who does them and teaches them shall be called great in the kingdom of heaven. For I tell you, unless your righteousness exceeds that of the scribes and Pharisees, you will never enter the kingdom of heaven.*

Sometimes Paul preached
    and people said,
        "Shall we sin that grace may abound?"
Sometimes Jesus preached
    and people thought,
        "He's come to abolish the law and prophets."
Sometimes I will preach
    and people will use it to justify sin.
That drives me *crazy* and I want to scream, "Don't think I'm preaching to abolish the law! 'Till heaven and earth pass away, not an iota, not a dot, will pass from the law until all is accomplished.'"

In our ignorance and blind consumption of culture, we tend to think that sin makes us wild and free. But Scripture is clear: sin turns us into zombies. Breaking God's law makes us slaves, but walking in God's law is life and freedom.

Jesus said, "Love God with all your heart, soul, and mind, and your neighbor as yourself. On this depends all the law and the prophets." God's law then is a description of what love looks like. When we violate the law, we violate love: we harden our hearts, numb our minds, disengage our souls, and enslave ourselves to the Serpent. To sin is to *zombify* yourself: dead to others and dead to the God who made you and suffers for you.

A Christian confesses that Jesus suffers the penalty of his every sin upon His cross. How can we say we love Him and at the same time continue to pound nails in His hands and feet?

People will say, "I know it's a sin to divorce my husband, but God will forgive me. I'm a Christian." I try to be all pastoral and stuff, but I want to *grab* them and scream, "*Liar!* You're being deceived! You're being zombified! 'No one who lives in Him keeps on sinning. No one who continues to sin has seen Him or known Him' [see 1 John 3:6]. *Wake up!*"

People have the absurd idea that Jesus came to say the law of God is *no big deal.* Just the opposite! He came to *fulfill* it.

It's tempting, then, as a pastor to just preach the law—

> to define the law,
>
>> amplify the law,
>>
>>> so we can live by the law,
>>>
>>>> so I can be *safe* . . .

because I don't want to be least in the kingdom.

In Jesus' day, the religious leaders took the law so seriously that they defined it, refined it, and simplified it, just to be safe. So the law says, "Keep the Sabbath," and the Sabbath is rest, not work. Well then, what is work? Lifting a burden is work. So, what's a burden? The scribes and Pharisees figured it out:

A burden is: food equal in weight to a dried fig; milk enough for one swallow. Less is okay; more is sin.

A burden is: ink enough for writing two letters of the alphabet.[2]

They went on like that ad infinitum. It was the scribal law, which would become the Mishnah. Those dedicated to carrying it out were called Pharisees. They were *serious* about doing the law.

MATTHEW 5:19–20: *Whoever then relaxes one of the least of these commandments and teaches men so, shall be called least in the kingdom of heaven; but he who does them and teaches them shall be called great in the kingdom of heaven. For I tell you, unless your righteousness exceeds that of the scribes and Pharisees, you will never enter the kingdom of heaven.*

Yikes!

We've been inoculated by a million Sunday school lessons that taught us the Pharisees were the bad guys. But you could make a strong argument that the Pharisees, of all the groups in the Bible, bear the most striking resemblance to American evangelical believers. They *were* the Moral Majority, the Promise Keepers, the Bible study leaders.

So this is utterly *shocking!* Even *they* are not serious enough about the law. Even *they* don't enter the kingdom of heaven.

It's tempting to preach law, law, law just to be safe. And people say, "You can't be too careful; you don't want to make anyone stumble, for those who relax the law are least in the kingdom of heaven." Okay, but the scribes and the Pharisees *don't even get in!*

In Matthew 23, the week before Jesus is crucified, He cuts loose on the scribes and Pharisees. He delivers His most stinging condemnation— seven woes, perfect woes:

MATTHEW 23:23–28: *Woe to you, scribes and Pharisees, hypocrites! for you tithe mint and dill and cummin, and have neglected the weightier matters of the law, justice and mercy and faith; these you ought to have done, without neglecting the others. You blind guides, straining out a gnat and swallowing a camel!*

Woe to you, scribes and Pharisees, hypocrites! for you cleanse the outside of the cup and of the plate, but inside they are full of extortion and rapacity. You blind Pharisee! first cleanse the inside of the cup and of the plate, that the outside also may be clean.

Woe to you, scribes and Pharisees, hypocrites! for you are like white-washed tombs, which outwardly appear beautiful, but within they are full of dead men's bones and all uncleanness. So you also outwardly appear righteous to men, but within you are full of hypocrisy and iniquity.

Do you hear what He's saying? "You're *zombies*—the undead, the walking dead. You're beautiful on the outside but dead on the inside."

MATTHEW 23:15 (NRSV): *Woe to you, scribes and Pharisees, hypocrites! For you cross sea and land to make a single convert, and you make the new convert twice as much a child of hell as yourselves.*

Let me rephrase: "You take secular zombies and turn them into religious zombies, and the religious ones are worse than the secular ones."

We church folks can get good at identifying the secular zombies in the world. But the ones we really ought to be concerned with are the religious ones in the church. Steve Brown commented in *Christianity Today:* "It's worth noting that Jesus didn't condemn bad people. He condemned 'stiff' people. We condemn the bad ones and affirm the stiff ones."[3]

Jesus taught, "We piped to you, and you did not dance" (Matthew 11:17). Zombies are stiff. Their hearts don't dance to the music of the kingdom. By itself the law makes us stiff in our hearts and our heads. The law even entices us to sin—to *harbor* sin.

A few years ago we invited Philip and Janet Yancey over for dinner. Philip is a best-selling Christian author and probably my *favorite* author in the world today. Janet is more imposing than Philip. Back then we didn't know Philip and Janet very well, and having them over for dinner was a really big deal. But we have four kids. So Susan and I sat our kids down and said, "Okay, guys, we need to make some rules. There will be no booger stories, there will be no burping stories, and there will be no *passing gas* stories. The following words are forbidden: *butt, booger, and a few others*."

We laid down the *law:* not *God's* law but Mom and Dad's law for impressing guests. We figured surely Philip and Janet wouldn't be interested in an unbroken stream of second-grade booger stories but in Dad's deep biblical wisdom and the casual, fun-loving, freely wholesome nature of his wonderful family.

Well, the Yanceys came over. We had dinner. The kids were good, but entirely stiff, like little zombies. Usually kids are zombies around unknown adults, but mine were *twice* as zombied as usual. I knew why. In their minds they were reviewing the list of unspeakable words and untellable stories.

Not only did it make them stiff, it made them constantly occupied with what they were not supposed to say (which only made them more stiff). That is, they were living by *my* law and dying by *my* law. The law may have been good, but it was killing them.

Finally Becky cracked. I think Janet said something, and Becky laughed and said, "That's like the time Coleman—" Then all at once she put her hand over her mouth, her eyes got big, and she said, "Sorry. I'm not supposed to say that."

Janet said, "What do you mean you're not supposed to say that?" Becky looked nervously at Susan and me and said, "Well, um, I'm not . . ." Janet said, "Becky, is there a list of things you're not supposed to say in front of us?" Becky knew the law of God was more binding than the law of Mom and Dad, and she couldn't lie. So she said, "Uh huh."

Janet said, "Oh, wow! Well, Becky, tell me everything on the list."

Becky looked at me, and I nodded (what was I supposed to do?), and we spent the rest of the evening talking and laughing about boogers, burps, gas, and the unspeakable words. We had a pretty good evening.

Basically, we all confessed our broken humanity. And our little zombies came to life.

Well, that was the law of Mom and Dad, and violating it is no big deal. But violating the law of God is an insanely big deal, for it kills us and turns us into zombies.

Yet if we *live* by the law (like the Pharisees, like my kids at dinner), we become twice the zombies we were before—even stiffer, even more preoccupied with the things that kill us.

About fifteen years ago I was riding in the back of a minivan with my friend Scott and his family, on the way to the National Youth Workers Convention. Scott's preschool-aged son was playing the rhyming game when he began to rhyme words with truck: "Truck, duck, muck, f . . ." and he said it, the mother of all unspeakable words.

In a fury Scott said, "Colin, don't you *ever* say that word!" And Colin said, "What word? Truck?" "No!" "Duck?" "No!" "Muck?" "No!" "F . . . ?" "*Colin,* I told you never to say that word!"

Colin asked:

"But, Daddy, why can't I say F . . . ?"

"*Colin!* I said don't say that word!"

"But Daddy, why can't I say F . . . ?"

"Colin, don't *say* that word!"

By the time it was over, Scott was furious and red in the face. Colin was crying in fear and shame, undoubtedly totally preoccupied with one question: "What does that word mean? And why can't I say it?"

Colin didn't realize how profound his question was. In our country, religious people sometimes make a big deal out of that word but not that deed—whatever that word and deed may be. That way they can judge others, feel good about themselves, and still indulge in various actions in practice and in heart that they wouldn't dare speak of.

Jesus said, "Woe to you, scribes and Pharisees. You strain at gnats and swallow camels."

Sometimes in sermons I'll say certain "potty" words or refer to the biblical concept of God damning something. I understand why folks get nervous at that point. They don't want me to violate the law of God, and that's good.

Some people think I play loosely with the law of God, and so they think *they* can too. Listen closely. I *never* want to play loosely with the law of God, for that is an evil trap set by the snake to turn us into zombies.

Yet I will make it a point to offend the man-made laws of the Pharisees, for living by that law can make us twice the children of hell, turn us into the worst kind of zombies, and shut others out of the kingdom.

Though the law of God is good, Paul was clear: "All who rely on works of the law are under a curse" (Galatians 3:10). The law may be good, but the law can't make me live. It can't make me dance. At best it only describes the dance steps.

I love the church. I believe in the church. She is God's creation. But I also grew up in a church. I make my living doing church. I know how to play church, so maybe I should be more scared of religious zombies than secular zombies, for I'm more likely to turn into one of *them.* Maybe in many ways I already am.

I'm constantly amazed at how worried we American Christians are about "the world" out there (sex, drugs, and rock 'n' roll), while we are blind to "the world" in here, blind to scribes and Pharisees in the church. Have we forgotten that the religious people crucified Jesus? Do we think that spirit is no longer our enemy?

The Pharisees were stiff. They traveled in religious groups, not thinking or feeling for themselves. They feasted on the living—biting and devouring, judging and condemning others to justify themselves and steal life. Outside they looked good, but inside they were empty of life, which is love. They could tell you love was the aim of the law. "Love with all your heart" wasn't a new law. It was Deuteronomy 6. They knew it in their heads; they just couldn't do it from the heart.

That only makes sense. Hold a gun to a person's head and say, "This is the law: love me with all your heart, mind, soul, and strength, or you'll die!" That person would have a hard time doing it. Yet that's been our human situation since . . .

- we stole the fruit from the tree of the knowledge of good and evil (the law, that is);
- we chose a description of what love looks like (the law) over Love Himself (God is love);
- we learned the Law is Love, so now we can no longer love.

To obey is to live, and so we've learned we are dead. To obey is to live, and Jesus obeyed perfectly. He is the love of God poured out. His life was the Pharisees' condemnation and also what they craved. So they tried to take His life.

Never forget: a group of religious zombies crucified Jesus on a tree in strict compliance with their law, in violation of God's law, all in order to consume Jesus' life.

So what am I saying?

If you *break* God's law, you die, zombified, the walking dead.

If you try to *live* by the law by relying on your ability to *do* the law, you're double dead.

You say, "Gosh, I'm a zombie if I do, and I'm double zombified if I don't!"

Well, God did say, "The day you eat of the fruit of the tree you die" (see Genesis 3:3). You say, "Well, yeah, but see? I'm still walking around." Exactly! The walking dead. Apart from Christ, we're all zombies.

Maybe the problem is we won't confess that we're dead. In Scripture, death is not really a lack of self-consciousness but a lack of anything *but* self-consciousness. It's being cut off from God and cut off from others, trapped in our self, utterly alone, unable to love, unable to join The Dance. To join a dance, you must hear music that comes from beyond yourself.

Maybe we're afraid of zombies the way we're sometimes afraid of mirrors: afraid to see ourselves. And the law of God is a mirror. We look in the mirror and see that we're dead. And if we try to clean ourselves up by using the mirror, we're still dead, even *doubly* dead.

I must be *so serious* about the law that I admit I'm dead. "Did that which is good, then, bring death to me?" asked Paul in Romans 7. "By no means! It was sin, working death in me through what is good, in order that sin might be shown to be sin, and through the commandment might become sinful beyond measure" (v. 13). The law is a mirror, and it tells me, "You're dead! You're dead! You're dead!" A mirror can't raise the dead; only God can raise the dead.

So Jesus sat on the hillside and said, "I haven't come to abolish the law and the prophets but to fulfill them" (the Greek means fill them to the full). You fill something that's empty. So apart from Christ, the law is empty of love and life and meaning. The meaning of the law is love, which is life, and Jesus is the Meaning (the Logos), the love and life of God for us.

- He fulfills the law: He gives it meaning.
- He fulfills the prophets: He is all that's hoped for.
- He fulfills the moral law: He's the only one who ever obeyed it.

- He fulfills the ceremonial law: He's the perfect and complete sacrifice for sin.
- He's the music that turns dance steps into dance.

When Jesus died on the cross, He satisfied justice for us all. He took our death and gave us His life as a gift.

The zombies crucify Him, but the night before, He takes bread and breaks it saying, "This is my body given for you—forgiven to you." He takes the cup and says, "This is my blood poured out for you." He told us, "Unless you eat my flesh and drink my blood you have no life in you" (see John 6:53).

ZOMBIES

He is the life that we all crave.
He not only fulfills the law; he fulfills the law in you.

God sent Jesus "in order that the just requirement of the law might be fulfilled in us, who walk not according to the flesh [the old, zombie way] but according to the Spirit [Christ's Spirit in us]" (Romans 8:4).

Through Jesus, God forgives all our sins, and then "we love, because he first loved us" (1 John 4:19). He even loves *through* us. Jesus not only fulfills the law, He fulfills the law in you. Even more, He fully fills you with Himself.

Paul writes, "[May you] know the love of Christ which surpasses knowledge [including knowledge of good and evil—the law], that you may be filled with all the fullness of God" (Ephesians 3:19).

God so loves zombies! God so loves you! When you were dead in your trespasses and sins, God made you alive together with Christ (see Ephesians 2:5).

It's God who raises the dead. If you take Christ's body and blood in faith, God raises you. He raises Christ Jesus *in* you, and begins to fill you with all the fullness of Himself.

Jesus doesn't want zombies; He wants a bride.

The Father doesn't want zombies; He wants children.

So Jesus sits on the mount and begins to expound the law (Matthew 5:21–48). If we aren't "poor in spirit, mourning, meek, and hungering for righteousness," we soon will be. He expounds the dance steps so we'll admit we can't dance. He'll make us "poor in spirit" that He might fill us with His Spirit.

ROMANS 5:20–21: *Law came in, to increase the trespass; but where sin increased, grace abounded all the more, so that, as sin reigned in death, grace also might reign through righteousness to eternal life through Jesus Christ our Lord.*

So Jesus sits on the mount and begins to expound the law that He might . . .

kill us,

fill us,

and make us dance.

4

Church Chat (and Hell)

Matthew 5:21–26

Thou shall not murder"—the sixth commandment (Exodus 20:13 NKJV). Murder is at least killing out of personal passions for private reasons. It is forbidden, for human life is sacred.

Since 1973 an estimated forty million abortions were performed in the USA, after the U.S. Supreme Court established a new right to privacy and ruled that preborn babies were only potentially human, "not persons in the whole sense."

Modern people tend to define personhood as "that which can reason or make moral decisions," which usually means, "that which is reasonable and good to *us*." But before a government can sanction the death of forty million lives, it must redefine personhood with new words, like all of us do.

A "baby" is a mystery of personhood.

An unwanted baby is a "fetus," just tissue, no mystery.

In Scripture personhood is a mystery defined by God, like breath or spirit from God. Ecclesiastes 11:5 states: "You do not know how the spirit comes to the bones in the womb of a woman with child."

Perhaps personhood happens when the seed is implanted in the egg; that's what science would point to. Clearly unborn babies, like Jesus and John, are considered persons in Scripture. Yet there is a *mystery*—God's mystery—to be left to Him. *Sacred.*

But out of fear and anger we attack great mysteries with words, and we justify murder. We look back on Nazi Germany and ask, "How could law-abiding Germans murder six million Jews?" They redefined them—"not persons in the whole sense."

I wonder what future generations will say about the forty million aborted babies and us?

This in itself is horrible enough, but according to Jesus, there may be an even greater holocaust occurring now in our midst.

MATTHEW 5:21–22: *You have heard that it was said to the men of old, "You shall not kill; and whoever kills shall be liable to judgment." But I say to you that every one who is angry with his brother shall be liable to judgment; whoever insults his brother shall be liable to the council, and whoever says, "You fool!" shall be liable to the hell of fire.*

"Every one who is angry with his brother shall be liable to judgment." Judgment for *what?* Murder. So I may not move a muscle; I may not speak a word; I may simply think a thought and harbor a private feeling and be guilty of *murder!* God judges the heart.

Thumos is Greek for anger that flares up like a flame and then dies down. *Orge* is anger that is nurtured. Jesus uses *orge* here as a present passive participle: "He who is giving in to angering"—an "orgy" of anger. Have you ever been angry like that?

Perhaps you're feeling ashamed and alone because you've been party to an abortion. One morning at church I said to the congregation, "If you've ever had an abortion *or* ever been angry in an "unrighteous manner," would you raise your hand?"

I saw a lot of hands go up. It seems we're all in the same boat.

If you've ever been angry, perhaps your orgy of anger reached such a fevered pitch that you *said* something. In verse 22, Jesus says, "But I tell you that anyone who is angry with his brother will be subject to judgment. Again, anyone who says to his brother, 'Raca,' is answerable to the Sanhedrin. But anyone who says, 'You fool!' will be in danger of the fire of hell" (NIV).

Raca meant something like *blockhead* or *butthead,* someone without much ability to reason. *Moré* is translated "fool." From *moré* we get our words *moral* and *moron.* A *moré* was a moral fool incapable of good, moral decisions. The psalmist writes, "The fool says in his heart, 'There is no God'" (Psalm 53:1). To call someone a *moré* was to judge their heart by saying, "You don't really believe in God, and you're morally deficient."

Raca moré: stupid moron. With such words we demystify persons into tissue; we desecrate what's sacred; we murder in our hearts; we kill other hearts, murdering even in effect.

We could all tell stories of words heard in childhood that have kept us in bondage. Words that kill hearts, stunt growth, and snuff out potential life. "Raca," fool, moron, retarded, stupid, and others that make us wince . . . Such words are used for cursing.

Words carry power. *Kakologeo*: malicious words, curses. A curse murders not only psychologically but *spiritually.* Demons ride on curses. Witchcraft isn't a joke, for curses are empowered by demons.

"Whoever says, 'You fool!' shall be liable to hell," said Jesus. I remember when I first read that as a young boy. It really stressed me out, because I have a little sister named Rachel. I remember thinking, *Yikes! Be careful. Mental note: never call Rachel a fool; stick to* stupid *or* butthead."

Obviously cursing is not simply a matter of vocabulary. We get all worked up over "cuss words" and "unspeakable words." Meanwhile, we curse each other up and down the street, right into the sanctuary!

Jesus spoke the word *raca.* However, Jesus went to hell and back to break a curse.

My grandpa Ralph used the phrase "God d*** it" more than anyone I've ever met. It's a curse. In fact, I have a theory that hell is absolutely overrun with broken irrigation equipment from central Nebraska, sent there by my grandpa. But maybe not . . . I don't think there was much power in those curses, for he didn't *mean* what he said.

As far as using God's name for their own vain purposes ("taking God's name in vain"), I think a lot of church folks do that more than my grandpa. Yet because he said those words, as a good church boy I judged him: "Grandpa doesn't know God" (*more*). I always kept my grandpa Ralph at a distance . . . and he loved me. So who was most guilty of murder? Many times I've wished he was still alive. I'd say, "Ah, Grandpa, I love you too."

I've prayed against some powerful curses and satanic incantations to which demons were attached. In all that weird, demonic world some curses seemed to carry the most power. Do you want to hear them?

- "I hate myself."
- "I wish I were dead."
- "I'll never tell."
- "I'll never be free."
- "I'm a fool."
- "God can't forgive me."

They're curses, agreeing with the curses of the evil one. *Evil judgments.* I suspect we curse others and ourselves all the time, and although we mean what we say, we don't even *know* it's a curse!

Have you ever said to a person, "You'll never change"? You just denied the gospel and may have somehow aborted new life in Christ. Have you ever said to a person, "You don't have God's Spirit" or "You don't know God" or "You're a fool"? You don't even have to *say* it; you only have to *think* it in anger, and you're liable to the hell of fire.

Yikes!

Matthew 23:15–17: "Woe to you scribes and Pharisees. . . . Woe to you, blind guides. . . . You blind fools [*moroi*]!" Jesus said that.

Wow! Did Jesus sin? No! Was Jesus lying? No! They *were* blind fools, and some *didn't* know God. Did Jesus know this about them? Yes! He is the judge. Would *you* have known this about them? Probably not. But even so, the apostles said stuff like this. Paul looked at Elymas the magician, and "filled with the spirit" (Acts 13:9) he said, "You son of the devil!" (v. 10). Paul is the *same guy* who wrote, "Bless and do not curse"!

Well, I'm not sure I understand all that. But when Jesus rebuked the Pharisees, it was *good.* And what made it good? Well, He said He came to fully fill the law. He fills it with Himself. Who is He? He is the love of God poured out. So what made it good? His love. He rebukes the Pharisees and then dies for them at their hands.

If you really love someone, you will tell them when you think they are being foolish or neurotic, or when they need God. But you will tell them in the pain of sacrificial love. You'll feel nails in your hands and feet.

I don't believe Jesus *cursed* the Pharisees but *blessed* the Pharisees. Words spoken in the sacrificial, furious love of Christ are blessings. But words spoken from the sinful passion of our own flesh are curses, no matter what language we use. But if it's the language of the church, I think the curses are doubly evil. The *world* knows that. It's a tragic joke on *Saturday Night Live.*

Sadly, one of the funniest skits on NBC's *Saturday Night Live* was the Church Lady, played by Dana Carvey. The Church Lady hosts a show called *Church Chat,* full of gossip.

On the show, she accuses guests of all sorts of sins, and gossips about their failings. She has a signature line that always gets a laugh.

Here's an example:

"And who could have been in the back of that cab, Jimmy? Who? Who was behind the wheel of our Lincoln Town Car when we drove into the hotel? Who could it be? *Who could it be? I just can't imagine who. Could it be . . . Satan?*"

Well yes, actually, it could be. But, you see, this is the tragic joke that the world laughs at: who's behind our "church chat," our church gossip, slander, and hatred? Could it be . . . Satan? Of course! Or are we "ignorant of his designs" (2 Corinthians 2:11)?

I've been told that satanists are assigned to go to churches and curse them. I don't doubt it. But *big whoop!* They have no power unless we give it to them! I'm not worried about *that*; I'm far more concerned about *church chat*—the church cursing herself.

> MATTHEW 5:23–24: *So if you are offering your gift at the altar, and there remember that your brother has something against you, leave your gift there before the altar and go; first be reconciled to your brother, and then come and offer your gift.*

I don't think that means go to everyone who is offended with you before you worship. Thousands were offended with Jesus, yet they had nothing of substance against Him. But if you curse your brother, he has something against you. You need to go to him and provide atonement for reconciliation.

The picture here is of a worshiper handing a sacrifice to the priest. A Jew would put his hand on the animal and confess his sins. Then the animal would be slain in his place—an atonement to work reconciliation with God.

Jesus says, "Leave it at the altar and go be reconciled to your brother." Where is God anyway? Jesus, the Judge on the throne, says,

"Whatever you did for one of the least of these brothers of mine, you did for me" (Matthew 25:40 NIV). It's as if they actually *are* His temple, and by cursing them, you curse Him. Your religion cannot be private, for you worship a God who makes His dwelling in temples of flesh. Go to them. Confess and be reconciled. Reconciled for what? Murder. And what's the payment for murder? Death. How can we make atonement for that and not be killed thousands of times over?

I'm a boss, a pastor, and a Christian. I'm charged with speaking the truth to the staff, but never in unrighteous anger and always in love. Anything less is murder. I'm convinced I've murdered everyone on my staff. And Jesus is in them. Whatever I do to the least of these, I do to Him. How do I make atonement for that? There will be an accounting.

MATTHEW 5:25–26: *Make friends quickly with your accuser, while you are going with him to court, lest your accuser hand you over to the judge, and the judge to the guard, and you be put in prison; truly, I say to you, you will never get out till you have paid the last penny.*

Clearly Jesus is talking about more than just a human court. The Father is the Judge, and perhaps Jesus is our adversary here, because we have cursed Him and made ourselves the enemy of God. Perhaps the adversary is Satan, and he's taking us to court with a watertight case: we've cursed Jesus, and Jesus is the *Judge*! We not only cursed Him; we really did murder Him.

Yet no matter what:

- There is a way to settle our accounts before we get to court.
- There is a way through which the accuser will have nothing on us.
- There is a way out here on the road, on the way to court.

This is the gospel—God's Word—good Word—*eulogeo*—the "eulogy." The Father has made Jesus Judge, and to the horror of the adversary (Satan), the Judge has made Himself an atonement for our sins. He died the thousand deaths in our place to reconcile us to Himself, us to each other, and all things to God the Father.

Jesus made Himself the gift, His cross the altar, and us the temple. Jesus absorbed all those curses. Jesus absorbed *the* curse. "Christ redeemed us from the curse of the law, having become a curse for us—for it is written, 'Cursed be every one who hangs on a tree'" (Galatians 3:13). Jesus took the curse of death so we could be born of His Spirit into life (the children of God). And this was all according to the Father's plan. Jesus is the Father's Word of blessing, and He fully fills the law in us.

1. I can reconcile with my brothers because the blood of Christ is my atonement, giving me the courage and strength to confess and forgive. I must carry the blood in myself as a weapon against evil. I must come to the table of the Lord and claim the blood over us all. For at the table *every curse* is defeated!

2. Believing the Father's blessing, I'm *uncurseable* and entirely *bless-able*. I can receive your words as blessings. You could even say, "Peter, you're acting foolish," and I could say, "Thanks for the valuable input. I may have been acting foolish, but I am not a fool; I'm a child of God." If you don't believe the Father's blessing, you won't be able to receive criticism, and you'll be stunted in your growth, for every kindhearted rebuke you'll receive as a curse.

3. Believing the Father's blessing, you'll *become* a blessing. The blessing (Jesus Himself) fulfills the law in us. But apart from Jesus, trying to fulfill the law ourselves, we're cursed. In fact, we're dead:

- raca – stupid
- moré – morally insane
- not fully human
- truly unborn and yet sacred

For everyone is God's mystery. That is, you don't know which zombies may be destined to dance.

As Solomon said, "As you do not know how the spirit comes to the bones in the womb of a woman with child, so you do not know the work of God who makes everything" (Ecclesiastes 11:5).

Apart from Christ, one is truly unborn yet sacred, for everyone is God's mystery. *Be careful* not to curse His mysteries. "Bless and do not curse" (Romans 12:14). Bless, and sometimes (although we can't comprehend it) His Spirit—Christ's Spirit—like a seed comes to the unborn through us. And we give *The* Blessing.

Paul writes, "God . . . through Jesus Christ . . . has given us the ministry of reconciliation, that is, that God was in Christ reconciling the world to Himself, not imputing their trespasses to them, and has committed to us the word of reconciliation" (2 Corinthians 5:18–19 NKJV). Jesus is the Word, and the Word is a seed, and we can speak the seed into another and give birth to eternal life.

The real church lady—Mother Church (Revelation 12)—*that* church lady is now the one called to give birth to our Lord in others, by speaking words of blessing: the Good Word, *eulogos,* Jesus Himself.

Years ago Fred Craddock, professor of preaching at the Chandler School of Theology in Atlanta, was on vacation with his wife in the Smoky Mountains in Tennessee. It was the last day of vacation, and they'd stopped at a favorite little café called the Blackberry Inn. They didn't want to be bothered.

Well, this old country fellow walked in . . . just talking to everybody (you know the type). Fred thought, *Curses,* as he hid behind the menu. Sure enough, the old guy came to Fred's table:

"You folks on vacation?"

"Yes."

"Having a good time?"

I was, thought Fred.

"Gonna be here long?"

"No, not at all."

"What do you do?"

That was the question Fred had been waiting for, because he could shut people down with his answer: "Well, I'm a professor of homiletics and theology." The old man lit up and said, "You're a preacher man! Well, I got a preacher story for you!" He pulled up a chair and sat down.

"Yeah, I was born back in these mountains. My momma wasn't married. We lived in a shack outside of town. The other women in town used to spend their time guessing who my daddy was. And I didn't know who my daddy was. That was a real problem back then.

"My momma worked a lot. Other kids weren't allowed to play with a boy like me. I would hide in the weeds at recess, and I ate my lunch alone. They said I wasn't any good and I'd never amount to anything.

"Kids used to call me Ben the Bastard Boy . . . Ben the Bastard Boy . . . I thought Bastard Boy was my last name."

The old man was weeping now, but he collected himself.

"Well anyway, there was a church in Laurel Springs. It had this preacher. His voice was big like God. I knew church wasn't a place for boys like me."

(We know at church they wouldn't call him Bastard Boy; they'd find other ways to say the same thing.)

"Sometimes I'd sneak in and sit toward the back so I could sneak out before the service ended. But this one day I just got lost in what the preacher was saying. Before I knew it, church was over. The aisles got all jammed up. Folks were looking at me. I was making for the back door quick as I could when all at once I felt this big hand on my shoulder.

"This big voice boomed, 'Boy!' It was the preacher man himself! He said, 'Boy!' I froze. He talked so loud everybody heard as he said, 'Boy, who's your daddy? Boy, I *know* who your daddy is.' That was a knife in my gut, and I wondered did he know who my daddy was. He said, 'Boy, now let's see . . . why, you're a child of . . .' He paused and everyone listened. 'Boy, why you're a child of *God,* and I see a strikin' resemblance!' Then he swatted me on the bottom and said, 'Now you run along and go claim your inheritance.'"

Fred looked at the old guy. He seemed familiar, so Fred asked, "Sir, what's your name?" The old guy said, "Ben Hooper." Fred replied, "Ben Hooper . . . Ben Hooper . . . Oh yes! I remember my daddy telling me about you, the illegitimate boy elected twice the governor of Tennessee."

Old Governor Hooper looked up at Fred and with tears in his eyes said, "I was born that day."[1]

Receive the Father's blessing—*Jesus.*

Give the Father's blessing—*Jesus.*

5

ADULTERY (IN THE WORST PLACES)

MATTHEW 5:27-32

A visitor to an insane asylum found one of the inmates rocking back and forth muttering, "Lulu, Lulu . . ."

"What's this man's problem?" he asked the doctor.

"Lulu . . . she was the woman who jilted him," was the doctor's reply.

As they proceeded on the tour, they came to a padded cell whose occupant was banging his head repeatedly against the wall and moaning, "Lulu, Lulu . . ."

"Is Lulu this man's problem too?" asked the visitor.

"Yes," said the doctor, "He is the one Lulu finally married."[1]

We will now discuss sex, lust, marriage, and divorce. And I know that makes people uneasy, because it taps into the deepest desire of our hearts. And deep in our hearts lies a wound.

- Some are single, and they feel the wound in their singleness. They think, *If only I were married . . .*
- Some are married, and they feel the wound in their marriage. They think, *If only I were single . . .*
- Some deny the wound, but we all are wounded in the place of our deepest desire.

"So God created man in his own image, in the image of God he created him; male and female he created them" (Genesis 1:27).

The first thing we learn about the substance of the image of God is sexual. And God's first commandment—first law—is, "Be fruitful and multiply, and fill the earth and subdue it" (Genesis 1:28).

A church friend said to me, "We don't want to hear any more sermons about infatuation with sex." That's also what the world says: "Church, do your religion thing, but don't be talking about sex. That's private." But God seems to be infatuated with sex. It's central to His image, and all through the Old Testament He strictly guards the sexuality of His people. Through the Old Testament prophets, He yearns for His bride.

In Ephesians 5, Paul tells us we are the bride and Jesus is the Groom and earthly marriage is a reference to that:

- Marriage is a covenant; our faith is a covenant (the new covenant).
- Sex is a sacrament in the sanctuary of the covenant of marriage; communion is a sacrament in the sanctuary of the new covenant of grace.
- Fruit is born of the sacrament of the covenant of marriage through seed; fruit is born of the sacrament of the new covenant through seed—the Word of the Father.
- Adultery is the enemy of the marriage covenant, for it desecrates the sanctuary and limits life.

In our faith, adultery is called idolatry.

Sexuality in marriage is a parable of worship.

Jesus got the Samaritan woman to tell Him about her sexual sins, and then He spoke about worship and the deep desires of her heart. Israel weeps because they don't sense God's blessing in worship, and Malachi speaks about their sex lives. Then he prophesies, "The Lord whom you seek will suddenly come to his temple; the messenger of the covenant in whom you delight. . . . But who can endure the day of his coming, and who can stand when he appears?" (Malachi 3:1–2).

Then, the Angel of Yahweh—the Messenger of the covenant—the Glory of God sits on a hillside in Matthew 5, speaking to His future sanctuary, temple, and bride—about sex:

> MATTHEW 5:27–32 NKJV: *You have heard that it was said to those of old, "You shall not commit adultery." But I say to you that whoever looks at a woman to lust for her has already committed adultery with her in his heart. If your right eye causes you to sin, pluck it out and cast it from you; for it is more profitable for you that one of your members perish, than for your whole body to be cast into hell. And if your right hand causes you to sin, cut it off and cast it from you; for it is more profitable for you that one of your members perish, than for your whole body to be cast into hell. Furthermore it has been said, "Whoever divorces his wife, let him give her a certificate of divorce." But I say to you that whoever divorces his wife for any reason except sexual immorality causes her to commit adultery; and whoever marries a woman who is divorced commits adultery.*

Unfortunately, Jesus has just said, "Whoever relaxes one of the least of these commandments and teaches men so, shall be called least in the kingdom of heaven." So I don't want to relax it! Actually, the Gospel of Matthew is about as relaxed as it gets.

In Malachi God declares, "I hate divorce" (2:16). Divorce is always at least a wretched consequence of sin. Mark and Luke record similar statements but without an exception. "Every one who divorces his wife and marries another commits adultery, and he who marries a woman divorced from her husband commits adultery"—*period* (Luke 16:18).

For Jesus, divorce is not the only issue. God hates divorce, yet it's with remarriage that divorce seems to equal adultery, as if people are divorced, yet may still have a commitment to their old partner.

Did you know God was divorced? But He never committed adultery. In Jeremiah 3:8, God tells the prophet He has sent Israel away with a decree of divorce. But six verses later God calls to Israel saying, "Return . . . for I am married to you" (NKJV) or "I am your husband" (NIV) or "I am your master" (RSV). Whatever the case, God divorced Israel but remained faithful.

When I marry people I say, "I've read these vows, and there's *no escape clause!*" So even if you get a divorce, perhaps God still expects you to fulfill your promise.

Well, the Gospel of Matthew does contain an exception. It's most explicit in chapter 19: "Whoever divorces his wife, except for unchastity [sexual immorality], and marries another, commits adultery" (Matthew 19:9). The Pharisees had said that Moses had commanded them to give a "certificate of divorce." Actually, Moses never commanded that. In Deuteronomy 24 he simply says that if a man does divorce his wife, and she then marries another, he can't take her back, because she's polluted and defiled. It's a regulation against remarrying a divorced and remarried wife, because she's become polluted.

That's relevant to all of us (the "Israel of God"), because Isaiah 28 tells us that Israel had a "covenant with death, and with Sheol" (v. 15). That is, she left God—divorced God—and bound herself to others. She was "defiled" and "polluted." So how could God take her back? He would have to, like . . . cleanse her, kill her, and remake her.

Well, anyway, there is some kind of exception for sexual immorality in Matthew.

Paul also mentions an exception for divorce in 1 Corinthians 7. He suggests that if a spouse is an unbeliever and wants to divorce, a believer should let his spouse go, and he is not bound.

In Ezra 10, it appears the Israelites are told to divorce their unrepentant, pagan wives.

You'll notice there's no divorce for mistakes or incompatibility. I think you're *supposed* to be incompatible. There's no divorce for "no longer loving the person," or even for abuse. (That doesn't mean you shouldn't call the police and have your husband arrested, but that's not divorce.)

Perhaps you're thinking, *Yikes! This is harsh. Maybe I'm an adulterer.* Perhaps you feel condemned and alone. One morning at church I said to the congregation:

If you've been divorced and remarried,
   or if you married a divorced person and you're not sure the divorce was entirely biblical and therefore you're an adulterer,
   or if you've just committed adultery,
   or if you've ever looked on a woman or man to lust after her or him,
   or if you've ever fantasized about being married to someone else,
   would you raise your hand?

I saw a lot of hands go up.

Jesus said, "Whoever looks at a woman to lust for her has already committed adultery with her in his heart." We get worked up over divorce—and we really should—but *just lust* makes you an adulterer in your heart! I can't think of any worse place to be an adulterer than in your heart. God sees the heart, and everything flows from the heart.

The word *lust* is also translated "covet." When a man lusts after a woman, he takes the mystery of personhood and reduces her to a consumer item, coveting her as a thing. Unwilling or unable to make a covenant to the *person,* he just covets her beauty and glory (that is, glamour). Men don't normally lust after an elderly woman, for her glamour is gone. Yet she is still there.

When a woman lusts after a man, she usually covets riches and power (the man's glory). Women *do* covet elderly men, but only if they're rich and powerful.

When we lust and covet, we consume and desecrate. "Whoever looks at a woman to lust for her has already committed adultery with her in his heart." And Jesus just says "a woman." My *wife* is a woman. Maybe there's a way in which I can look even on my covenant partner and lust and covet in the spirit of adultery. That is, I may consume her beauty and glamour, and not commune with her heart.

Guys, when you make love to your wife and picture another woman, it's adultery. Maybe even when you make love to your wife but only care for her glamour, it's adultery. And you really haven't made love to *her* but to her attributes. She might say, "Depart from me; I never knew you"—that is, "You never knew me, only my attributes."

Now, don't get me wrong; desire for beauty and glamour isn't a sin. But such things always come attached to a heart. In fact, God uses those desires to lure us into making covenants to hearts. And if it weren't for sexual desire, there would be very few children. And how could Adam "be fruitful and multiply" in obedience to God's command?

But Jesus teaches . . .

"Don't lust."

"If your right eye causes you to sin, gouge it out and throw it away."

"If your right hand causes you to sin, cut it off."

The early church father Origen had himself castrated because of this text. Yet according to Jesus, it probably wasn't Origen's eye, hand, or genitals that caused him to sin. In Matthew 15:19, Jesus says, "For out of the heart come evil thoughts, murder, adultery, fornication . . . ."

Origen needed to rip out his own heart. Yet that's death, suicide, and even *more* sin.

Now some of you are saying, "Okay, Peter, I get what you're saying:

1. "We're all adulterers in some way, and we all deserve to die. In fact, we're all dead zombies apart from grace." *That's right.*
2. "Jesus died for our sins, and if we only repent and confess, He forgives us all that sin." *That's right.*
3. "He not only forgives us but gives us new hearts." *That's right.*

Yet you rightfully say:

I understand. But I still need to know: what is sin? I'm divorced, and I have this girlfriend. Am I free to marry her? Does that match the exceptions in Scripture?

or perhaps,

I'm married and my husband's an absolute jerk. Am I free to divorce him for someone else? *Surely* God doesn't want me to be abused and belittled and dehumanized! He's a God of love. How could *that* be love? His law is love. Explain the law and its exceptions.

Perhaps I should use a case study. I've been talking to a young man named Josh. For years now he's been absolutely consumed with his wife. He rescued her from a poor, abusive family. She was absolutely enamored with his wealth and good looks, but also very intimidated and reserved. She had a hard time opening up.

Her heart began to wander. For a long time she kept up a facade, but it turns out she was sneaking out at night and having sex with other men. She denounced her faith. She even became a prostitute.

Josh would walk the streets to find her and buy her back from pimps. She gave herself to vile men, but she was frigid to Josh. The counselor said she was caught in a cycle of shame. She was dying inside for intimacy but wouldn't surrender to her husband's advances.

At one point, Josh gave her the divorce papers. He hoped she'd turn back to him, but she didn't. Still Josh wouldn't look at another woman. He thought of her; he dreamed of her; he followed her and tried to rescue her. She'd pay the pimps and johns to beat him. She even married a pimp, such that she was polluted, as in Deuteronomy 24. She was an adulterer, a whore, and an unbeliever who wanted a divorce. And early one morning she tried to kill Josh.

If anyone ever had a valid reason for divorce, his name was Josh.

"Joshua" is Hebrew. In the Greek, His name is "Jesus." And we are His whoring bride. We did kill Him. But through that cross, Joshua—Jesus—romances His bride to Himself. And there He washes her and shapes her in His image.

Do you want to be made in His image?

Do you want to know Him, commune with Him, be like Him? Do you? Because all of our questions seem to be going the wrong direction:

- How can I get out of my covenant when it hurts?
- How can I get away from this cross?
- How can I look as little as possible like Jesus?

People say, "My marriage isn't working. I want a divorce." Well, if marriage is to shape you into the image of Jesus, your marriage is *most working* when your bride is ugly, cheats, lies, and spurns your love, and is now nailing you to a cross. And you hang there saying, "Father, forgive her, for she doesn't know what she's doing."

Bride, your marriage is most working when your Groom is naked, beaten, and emptied of His power, glory, riches, and knowledge, covered in spit and shame. Yet you adore Him and see Him as He is in weakness.

Your marriage is most working when you still worship the Bridegroom from prison cells, gutters, and alleys at the expense of your own life.

Guys, are you willing to die for your bride—not her attributes but her? The world says, "You only go around once, so get all the gusto you can get!" That is: riches, power, glory, and pleasure. Well, *it's true*: you only go around once. But for all eternity you will have all the riches, power, glory, and pleasure you're capable of wanting. Yet there will be some things you can no longer get:

- There will be no mourning, crying, or pain.
- There will be no opportunity to experience Christ's sufferings for His covenant bride.

So . . . "Go for the gusto," pick up your cross, and die for the sake of a love like His. "You only go around once."

I'm not preaching what *I* would do but what Jesus does and did do. I have an easy marriage. But those I suspect I'll see at the Lord's right hand *do not*.

You may be married to an earthly bride, or you may be married to the people He died for—the church. Either one can crucify you. But as they do, you are made in His image. And He gives you His heart. He is removing your old heart and giving you His new heart. He's killing the old you and birthing the new you.

Marriage is God's sneaky way to get a person crucified.

You marry a young bride for her beauty and glamour. God gets you to enter a covenant with *no escape clause*! That's insane! And before you know it, you're hanging on a cross for the sake of love, looking a lot like . . . *Jesus.*

And by the time you die, probably all the beauty and glamour will be gone. The groom's strength, power, and vigor will be gone, and you will begin to love him, or love her, in spirit and truth—body broken and blood shed.

Robertson McQuilkin resigned as the president of Columbia Bible College to care for his bride who had Alzheimer's disease. She no longer had her old glamour, beauty, and wit. He writes:

> Love is said to evaporate if the relationship is not mutual, if it's not physical, if the other person doesn't communicate, or if one party doesn't carry his or her share of the load. . . . I count off what my beloved can no longer contribute, and then I contemplate how truly mysterious love is. What some people find so hard to understand is that loving Muriel isn't hard. . . . I think my life is happier than the lives of 95 percent of the people on planet Earth.[2]

Jesus hides in people like Muriel and calls us deeper. He hides in our spouse and calls us to love deeper. "Love deeper, past the glamour, past the flesh, past the knowledge, and into the spirit."

Perhaps you married Jesus when He was glamorous and beautiful, when He made sense of your world and showed you His power. But now He seems ugly, you can't see the glory, and the world doesn't make sense. God is *so weak* . . . it's like He's hanging on a cross.

Will you divorce Him?

Will you fantasize about another lover because it feels as if He's no longer giving you what you want?

Perhaps He's giving you His heart—His greatest gift—and turning you from a consumer into a creator. Perhaps it's more blessed to give than to receive (Acts 20:35). Or maybe in the kingdom, giving *is* receiving; that is, loving is its own reward. Giving is receiving, and receiving is giving: like a great dance in which you lose yourself and find yourself.

Perhaps worship isn't *taking* but *giving,* and the giving is the greatest taking: a communion where you drink God and He drinks you, a communion where two become one flesh just as in the sacrament of marriage. The greatest sexual ecstasy is the pleasure of giving pleasure. Two become one. Then you're no longer a consumer but a creator of life. It's there that life is made in the form of babies . . . and new hearts.

Larry Crabb says that most marriages are like "two ticks and no dog"—two bugs trying to suck the life out of each other. And they die. But Jesus gives us His life. He gives the old zombies His blood. And we love because He first loved us (1 John 4:19). He fulfills the law in us. He fills the empty wound with Himself and fulfills the first command *through* us. *He* "is fruitful and multiplies and fills the earth." (He "fills all in all" [Ephesians 1:23].)

Some of you have very difficult marriages and divorces. And you may live with a great longing all your years on this earth. Well, I believe Jesus didn't fully consummate His marriage on this earth. We are going to our wedding banquet, you know. So endure.

And some of you are single, and you think I'm not talking about you. But I am. Jesus was single, yet He was married. And so are you.

Jesus is the King, and He's speaking to His bride.

Søren Kierkegaard used to tell of a king who fell in love with a peasant. He wanted her for his bride, but he knew if he disclosed his identity—his riches, power, glory, and beauty—she wouldn't love *him* the *person* but only his things. Yet if he *didn't* disclose his identity, he couldn't give her himself, for his life would be an act, and she wouldn't know him.

His only hope was to empty Himself of riches, power, glory, and beauty and come to her in weakness. I think the king's name was something like *Josh*. And that's the story of Christmas. That's the story of the body broken and the blood shed.

". . . [W]ho, though he was in the form of God, did not count equality with God a thing to be grasped, but emptied himself, taking the form of a servant, being born in the likeness of men. . . . [He] humbled himself and became obedient unto death, even death on a cross" (Philippians 2:6–8). He did it to win His bride to Himself.

Now He sits on the hillside speaking to His bride, and His words are deeply personal and passionate, for He knows that she will not see Him, will divorce Him, and will crucify Him. He knows, because she's already committing adultery in her heart.

Both in Matthew 12 and 16, the religious people come to Jesus saying, "Show us a sign," and He says, "An evil and adulterous generation seeks a sign." As if to say:

> You talk of the days of old, of the pillar of fire by day and the pillar of cloud by night; you talk of the power and the wisdom and the glory of God . . . and that is who *I AM!*
>
> I'm standing right in front of you, and you don't know Me. You may even do "mighty works in My name," but you don't know Me. And so I am your judgment.
>
> You don't know Me, and that means you were using Me all along.

You married Me for My things and not My person, your image of Me and not Me. An evil and adulterous generation seeks a sign.

I think the religious leaders wanted signs of love but not His love, signs of His presence but not His presence. They wanted His things and not His heart; manifestations of His Spirit but not His Spirit.

Here's the irony: there *were* signs that Jesus performed in the power of the Spirit—*great signs*. But the scribes and Pharisees refused to see. And if they saw, they refused to believe, for the signs happened:

- in those they judged unclean;
- in places they were unwilling to go;
- in places outside their control;
- away from the crowd;
- in the last and least of all kinds of these, the Lord's brethren, lepers, Romans, Gerasenes, unforgivable paralytics, hemorrhaging women, demonized prostitutes;
- on the Sabbath, at inconvenient times, in the midst of storms.

And when they would happen, Jesus would tell people not to make a show. But when a group of religious people got together and demanded a show, Jesus said, "No sign shall be given . . . except the sign of the prophet Jonah. For as Jonah was three days and three nights in the belly of the whale, so will the Son of man be three days and three nights in the heart of the earth" (Matthew 12:39–40).

So Jesus . . .

the Word, the Presence, the Glory,

the Power, the Beauty, the Wisdom,

the Word of God

. . . stood in their presence.

But because they committed adultery in their hearts, because they coveted and lusted after His attributes and not His person, because they served their own idol, they killed Him. And the world received far more than just a sign.

Jesus said in Matthew 24:24, "False Christs and false prophets will arise and show great signs and wonders," but they won't love like Jesus; they won't give you their body broken and their blood poured out.

Worship is an act of loving our Lord. The most ecstatic lovemaking happens when you give yourself, not to consume but to create joy in another; when you give yourself to the other as they are—not as you *wish* them to be; as they are in naked weakness, like broken body and blood.

You know, there are people like me who actually leave the worship service and say, "I wasn't fed. But they ate Jesus' body and drank His blood."

There are people like me who leave saying, "The glory wasn't there. The Spirit just wasn't there. The sermon was confusing. The songs were flat. There must be more. I want more. That wasn't enough. Nobody got healed. Nobody fell down. There were no signs."

Well, it may be that all there was, was the broken body and the shed blood of Jesus: the life, the Word, the seed to be implanted in the womb of His humble bride.

Perhaps you missed Him . . .

Perhaps you were lusting after an idol . . .

Perhaps you were coveting His riches, power, glory, and pleasures as He handed you His heart.

Perhaps you didn't discern the body and the blood, in which case you drank judgment on yourself.

I suspect that in America we wound the heart of our Lord terribly, for we come to His banquet table—we come receiving His body broken and blood shed, all the while demanding "signs and wonders," "healings and revivals," "power and glory," as we belittle His heart. All those attributes and gifts are wonderful and good, but please don't commit adultery in your heart at the table of the Lord.

You thought this message was about your marriage—and it *is:* your marriage to Jesus. We have committed adultery against Him. I suspect we do every day in our hearts when we don't receive His grace with gratitude, and we demand more "signs" of His love.

Well, the gospel is that He came to forgive you all your adulteries. He cleanses you with His blood, and He fills you with Himself—His body broken. Receive Him now in prayer. Go to church and receive Him at communion. You are His bride. Receive Him, and He will bear life through you. Reject Him, and you reject life.

In John 12, speaking of His crucifixion, Jesus said, "Now is the judgment of this world" (v. 31). His body broken and His blood shed is judgment.

The weekend that I preached in church on this passage from Matthew, a young man came forward after the service weeping. He has become a friend now and often sees visions during the sermon, but this was his first. Dale is an engineer used to being in control, but what he saw had him rattled. He said: "Peter, I looked up and saw two angels on either side of you. They had wings outspread and held broad swords in front of them with points resting on the ground. Then I saw oil poured from above. It flowed over you and turned to blood. The blood spilled off the stage and all across the sanctuary floor. Some people dove off their chairs and rolled in the blood. They let it wash them and flow through them."

Then through tears Dale said, "But some lifted their feet." They didn't want to get wet or messy with the blood of Jesus, the love of God poured out. They didn't want the blood, but they were sitting in church.

That's bad religion.

I suppose they wanted God's stuff, but not His heart.

I suppose they wanted to maintain control rather than surrender control.

I suppose they wanted to be their own saviors and not depend on the Savior.

I suppose they were committing adultery in their hearts at the table of the Lord.

May the blood of the Great Bridegroom be precious to you. May you receive Him. And one day you will receive all things with Him.

6

THE OATH
(IS "JESUS" A SWEAR WORD?)

MATTHEW 5:33–37

In biblical Greek, the word for "oath" is *horkos*. Traditionally an oath calls upon a deity as a witness to a statement. It implies a self-imposed curse if the oath is broken, and possibly a blessing if it is fulfilled.

There are assertive oaths, asserting what's true now, and promissory oaths, asserting what will be true in the future. It's hard to define what exactly constitutes an oath, but an oath is *at least* a statement to which we try to add some weight or veracity . . . as when we say, "I promise."

• When I was a Boy Scout, I took the scout oath:

On my honor, I will do my best to do my duty to God and my country and to obey the Scout Law; to help other people at all times; to keep myself physically strong, mentally awake, and morally straight.

• If you testify in a court of law, you're supposed to take an oath, usually with your hand on the Bible.

I hereby swear to tell the truth, the whole truth, and nothing but the truth, so help me God.

- When I was ordained I took vows.
- We're supposed to ask our church elders to take vows.
- At my wedding, I made promises and I took vows.
- Many churches require vows and oaths before a person can come to the communion table.

MATTHEW 5:33–37 (NKJV): *Again you have heard that it was said to those of old, "You shall not swear falsely, but shall perform your oaths to the Lord." But I say to you, do not swear at all: neither by heaven, for it is God's throne; nor by the earth, for it is His footstool; nor by Jerusalem, for it is the city of the great King. Nor shall you swear by your head, because you cannot make one hair white or black. But let your "Yes" be "Yes," and your "No," "No." For whatever is more than these is from the evil one.*

Jesus says, "Do not swear at all."

Recently, young Andy Mott was riding in a car with some friends when they happened to drive by our church. Being a good little evangelist, Andy asked his young friend, "How come you guys never come to church?" The little boy replied, "I don't know if we should go *there* . . . they use *swear* words there!"

Well, Andy pressed him and asked, "What do you mean 'swear words?'" The boy said, "They say *God* and *Jesus* all the time there."

Well, if God and Jesus are swear words, should we repeat them?

I hope you realize cursing and swearing are not a matter of specific words on a vocabulary list. The demons in hell must get a kick out of us American evangelicals. We curse and swear all over the place but pride ourselves on our clean vocabulary.

Still, I think my scout leader would say that being moral and a good citizen is at least not cussing or swearing. So when I took my scout oath, I swore not to swear. And I swore to be a good citizen, which includes testifying under oath and pledging allegiance. So I *swore* not to *swear* while I *swore* to *swear*.

Do you realize that if you take an oath to live by God's Word, you're swearing not to swear? Because to swear (*omnyo*) is to make an oath (*horkos*). So should I renounce the scout oath? Refuse to testify under oath? Rewrite my marriage vows? I don't know.

Most commentators basically say, "Well, surely Jesus is only prohibiting casual swearing where you don't really mean it." But that sounds like saying, "Casual adultery is wrong, but if it's formal adultery in a court of law, and you *really mean it*, it's okay."

This is all very confusing for several reasons:

1. At places in the Old Testament, people are commanded to swear oaths.
2. It's hard to define when something becomes an oath. Paul said, "As God is my witness . . ." That sounds like an oath, yet isn't God always our witness?
3. Is a promise an oath? Are ordination vows and wedding vows oaths? Is the scout oath really even an oath or only a promise?
4. Is responding to an oath the same as making an oath? In Matthew 26, Jesus appears to respond under oath in court.
5. Is worrying about scout oaths and the nuances of ordination vows a bit like "straining at gnats and swallowing a camel"? Where's the camel? Well, if there's a camel, I suppose it has something to do with this sixth complication . . .
6. God seems to swear all over the place. In fact, in a real sense the entire Bible is an oath. It's the Old Testament and the New Testament. A testament is a covenant; a covenant includes an oath.

In Luke 1, Zechariah prophesies that God has remembered "his holy covenant, the oath which he swore to our father Abraham" (vv. 72–73).

So people say, "If God swears, then surely I should do it." Well, maybe there are certain things God does that I *shouldn't* do . . . like curse and swear: that is, judge the world. And maybe there are certain things God does I can't do or wouldn't *want* to do . . . like save the world or myself. And if I thought I could, it would be like swallowing a camel.

Well, I can't strain all the gnats and explain every detail, but I can help you ask some questions and ask *the* question: do I believe?

On the surface in Matthew 5:33, Jesus is at least making some rather obvious points:

1. First of all, when we "swear to tell the truth, the whole truth, and nothing but the truth," aren't we confessing that most of the time we don't? Or at least that you can't count on most people to do so?

If you go around feeling the need to always make promises, it probably means you're not too trustworthy. Have you ever hung around an alcoholic or a drug addict? Talk about promises, vows, and oaths! And the more they promise, the more you're convinced they're lying and hiding from truth.

Well, we're all "sin-aholics."

"I'll do better, I promise."

"I'll try harder."

"Look at my New Year's resolutions!"

2. Second, when I "swear to tell the truth, the whole truth, and nothing but the truth, so help me God," I'm under oath. And that assumes there are places I'm *not* under oath; places where God witnesses and places where He doesn't.

The Pharisees were rightfully concerned about casual swearing, that is, taking God's name in vain. So they used *kinnuyim*—surrogate objects—by which to swear. The Pharisees had all sorts of rules about various oaths and how binding they were. To swear by heaven or earth or Jerusalem or their head certainly wasn't as binding as swearing by God Himself.

> *Jesus points out:*
> *"Look, it's God's heaven, earth, and city. It's all holy."*

Folks get so concerned about what we say in the church sanctuary (which really isn't the true sanctuary). They worry about vocabulary we use, movie clips we watch, jokes we tell. Yet I know they wouldn't be concerned at all if we were at the park. But the park is *God's park!* And we are His sanctuary in the park or at the movies.

"To the pure all things are pure," Paul said (Titus 1:15). John Ortburg says, "God is not concerned with your spiritual life. He's concerned with your life."[1] There is no place that God is not a witness. We're always under oath, and not just us but the *entire world.*

God said, "The soul that sins shall die" (Ezekiel 18:20). Every lie merits death. Adam and Eve hid themselves where they hoped God would not see. They became a lie. Maybe we died long ago . . . a dead lie. Zombies.

3. So here's another problem with our oaths: how can they be true? "I swear to tell the truth, the whole truth, and nothing but the truth." Let's be honest. That's got to be a lie! Does anybody know the *whole truth?* Maybe some facts, but truth?

Who's guilty?

Who's innocent?

What's good?

What's evil?

What's really going on?

Jesus said to some Jews, "You are of your father the devil. . . . He . . . has nothing to do with the truth, because there is no truth in him" (John 8:44). The devil can be accurate with facts, yet he doesn't speak a bit of truth. What *is* truth? If you define it, how do you know your definition is true? Modernists say truth is what can be verified scientifically. How do they know that statement is true? It can't be verified scientifically.

Truth is something you have faith in or don't have faith in.

Truth is not like fruit hanging on a tree that *you* can pick. It's not facts you can master.

Truth is a man hanging on a tree crucified, who picks you and verifies you . . . masters you.

Truth tells *you* before *you* tell *truth*.

You can't define truth; truth defines you. Truth reveals Himself to you. Jesus said, "I AM . . . the truth." John tells us He is the Word of God—God's true Word—the Word that is truth. Paul writes, "In [Christ] all things hold together" (Colossians 1:17). Jesus, the truth, is like the fabric of reality. So when we tell a lie, it's like cutting ourselves off from reality and life, and choosing death, insanity, and hell . . . utterly alone.

Someone said, "The chief punishment of the liar is not so much that he is no longer believed but that he can no longer believe." Truth can only be known by belief, that is, faith. When we lie, we deny truth—Jesus. When we say, "I don't know Him," when we deny Jesus and imprison ourselves in death and hell.

C. S. Lewis taught that the door to hell is locked from the inside. But praise God that the truth Himself died and descended into hell for the love of you!

"Speak the truth, the whole truth, and nothing but the truth." I think the closest you could ever get to doing that would be to whisper a name: "Jesus . . . Jesus . . ."

Is that a swear word?

Well, there are assertive oaths and promissory oaths. Assertive oaths assert what is true; promissory oaths assert what *will be* true. Scouting is great, but I must confess: I broke the scout oath the moment I took it, because I swore not to swear. And honestly, has there ever been a day when I did my best to do my duty to God, and helped other people at *all times*?

Have you fulfilled the scout oath? If you answer yes, I bet you're lying and just broke the oath again.

We can argue about whether our promises and vows are oaths, but they are at least lies. "I vow to be your loving and faithful husband as long as we both shall live." And Jesus just said, "Everyone who looks at a woman lustfully has already committed adultery with her in his heart" (Matthew 5:28 paraphrase). *Yikes*! I broke that marriage vow pretty quickly.

I suspect that when we just say yes or no to things still in the future, we're saying we *intend* these things to be true. When we promise and vow, we're saying, "It will be true, and I will make it true."

How, then, could we promise anything? Our promises must be lies, for we don't know the future. We can't make one hair black or white. And why would we make a promise to God? He's eternal. He already knows the future and every sin you'll ever commit.

"God, I vow never to touch alcohol again!"

Why are you telling *Him*?

Are you trying to con Him? Convince Him?

That's insanity!

I used to sing: "I have decided to follow Jesus, I have decided to follow Jesus. . . . Though none go with me, still I will follow; though none go with me, still I will follow." And I love this song: "Jesus, lover of my soul, Jesus, I will never let you go." Often now I don't sing that last line, because every time I sin, every time I doubt, every time I get anxious, I let Him go, and I stop following.

> *So will I make it better by lying in worship?*
> *I can't promise anything;*
> *I can't predict the future.*

James writes, "Come on now, don't say, 'I'm gonna do such and such tomorrow.' You don't know. You ought to say, 'If the Lord wills'" (4:13–15, author's paraphrase). Then later, quoting Jesus in Matthew, he writes, "Above all . . . do not swear, either by heaven or by earth or with any other oath, but let your yes be yes and your no be no." Why? "That you may not fall under condemnation" (5:12). Now I think we're getting closer to the camel.

You know, when we make promises and swear oaths, we write law for ourselves. "Why do you submit to regulations, 'Do not handle, Do not taste, Do not touch' . . . according to human precepts and doctrines? These have indeed an appearance of wisdom in promoting rigor of devotion and self-abasement and severity to the body, but they are of no value in checking the indulgence of the flesh" (Colossians 2:20–23).

When we vow, we try to live by that law in our own energy—the flesh. We make vows, they fail, and we feel condemned. So we make bigger vows and fail and feel more condemned. Then, perhaps, we fail more in despair and make bigger vows, which are bigger lies.

You see, we're becoming addicted—enslaved—
to sin, flesh, lies, hell, and demons.

Did you know the word "exorcist" comes from the Greek *exhorkistes*—meaning out of oaths? Satan is the accuser, and he enslaves us through oaths, laws, and broken laws.

Some say Alcoholics Anonymous is basically the only successful program in treating alcoholics. It's not really a *program* but a *philosophy*, and the philosophy comes from Jesus. When it truly works, addicts surrender to Jesus.

In AA you don't make vows and oaths and promises for the future. You make *confessions . . . now.*

You don't vow, "I'll never touch alcohol again": a law that brings condemnation.

You confess, "I'm a powerless alcoholic *now*, and I need help."

You confess, "I'm poor in spirit, I mourn, I'm meek, I hunger for righteousness."

You realize, don't you, that the beatitudes are all about a person's heart *now.* Jesus meets us *now.* Eternity touches time *now. Now* is the day of salvation. We confess our *now,* and *Jesus* makes a promise for the future:

> *Yours is the kingdom of heaven.*
> *You will be comforted.*
> *You will inherit the earth.*

Jesus is our promise for the future.

I couldn't think of any places in all the New Testament where anyone (other than Jesus) took oaths or made promises in any real, positive way. But they made them all over the Old Testament (even though they continually broke them). Then I read through Matthew again:

- In chapter 8, these guys vow, "Jesus, we will follow You wherever You go." Jesus says, "Foxes have holes, birds have nests, but the Son of man has nowhere to lay His head," and we never hear from those guys again.

- In chapter 14, Herod makes an oath, and it traps him into killing John the Baptist.
- In chapter 17, on the Mount of Transfiguration, Peter says he'll build shelters for Moses, Elijah, and Jesus. And God basically tells him, "Shut up! Listen!"
- In chapter 26, Jesus breaks bread saying, "This is My body." He takes the cup saying, "This is the new covenant in My blood." And just after that He says, "This night you will all fall away." Peter declared (like an oath): "Though they all fall away . . . , I will never fall away!" "I have decided to follow Jesus. Though none go with me, still I will follow." And then they all pledged the same thing.

It's fascinating that churches get so nervous about guarding the Lord's table that they have people take oaths and make pledges before they come. (Paul didn't guard the *table*; he guarded *people from* the table [1 Corinthians 11:29].) The only pledges the disciples made near the Lord's table that first night were all *lies,* and Jesus knew it! But He still said, "Take and eat. Take and drink."

Later that night Satan "sifted Peter like wheat" (Luke 22:31–34). Peter denied Jesus three times. The second time he denied Him with an oath; the third time he began to invoke a curse and to swear, "I don't know the man." Immediately the cock crowed, and Peter remembered Jesus' words and went out and wept bitterly (that much more bitterly for all the oaths).

Maybe we shouldn't make promises and vows and oaths at the Lord's table before the broken body and the shed blood of the Eternal Covenant.

Now, if you're paying attention, you ought to be saying, "Hey, wait a minute. If you form a covenant, don't you swear an oath?" Yeah. In the old covenant of law, God promised to bless, and the people promised to obey. It was a covenant between God and humanity. Both swore.

But there is an older and deeper covenant, an eternal covenant. In Genesis 15, God promises to bless Abraham and his seed. Abraham watches as smoke and fire pass through the broken bodies of slaughtered animals. But Abraham says nothing. God is making a covenant with Himself. He recites an oath to bless the seed of Abraham.

In ancient days, two men would form a covenant by walking between the broken halves of slaughtered animals, reciting an oath and a curse: "May it be done unto me as it was done to this animal, if I break this covenant."[2] In Genesis 15, the smoke and fire walk the covenant, and only God swears the oath. Abraham only watches, for he has only to believe.

At the Lord's table, Jesus, the seed of Abraham, makes the new covenant—the eternal covenant. On His cross, Jesus redeems us from the curse of the law (the old covenant). He pays for every broken oath and suffers our hell. His body is broken for us. And on the cross, Jesus ratifies the new covenant—eternal covenant. His body is broken, and a way is made.

God made a covenant, and He's keeping both sides. Jesus is our priest forever, uniting us to God.

"The Lord has sworn and will not change his mind, 'Thou art a priest for ever'. This makes Jesus the surety of a better covenant" (Hebrews 7:21–22).

- Jesus is the smoke and fire that walks the covenant.
- Jesus is the Lamb that was slain to ransom us from the old covenant.
- Jesus is also the Lamb that is slain from the foundation of the world to ratify the eternal covenant—the surety of that covenant.
- Jesus is the oath of God, promising to bless the children of Abraham. "All the promises of God find their Yes in [Jesus]" (2 Corinthians 1:20).

- Jesus is the Word of God, and God swears . . . God swears with His Word.

Is "Jesus" a swear word?
Yes!
Jesus is God's Swear Word.

Behold! God is swearing, "I love you, I love you, I love you . . . every where, every when, every how."

This is the question: Will you believe God's oath? Or will you make your own? All your promises—all your oaths—are lies, for all your promises assume that *you* are the answer—the savior. And you are the problem. But believe the truth—Jesus—and live.

We are saved by grace, and we are changed by grace.

Jesus said, "Unless you eat my flesh and drink my blood, you have no life in you." He said, "I am the way, and the truth, and the life. . . . Abide in me, and I in you . . . apart from me you can do nothing" (John 14:6; 15:4–5).

It's not your oaths; it's not your promises and vows; it's the oath of God in you. Ingest Him, believe Him . . . every where, every when, every how.

Awhile back, Randy shared his testimony in a conference at our church. Randy lived a homosexual lifestyle for years and then came to Christ. Yet even after he confessed Christ, homosexuality seemed to be lord of his life. He believed a lie about his own sexuality, and he lived a lie. I'm sure he made promises and pledges, but time and time again he failed. He desperately needed help in order to change. He needed the Truth.

He shared that one day in his apartment he prayed, "Jesus, what does it mean that You are Lord?" Immediately he had a vision of the truth—what was really going on. He saw himself and Ron, his first homosexual partner. They were in bed together, and Jesus was standing beside the bed weeping. Randy said he felt such grief that if he had felt any more, he would have died.

The Lord spoke:

This is just a taste of the love I have for you and Ron. And you were so blind you didn't even know. I have seen every single sexual act you have done with every person, and I loved you so much. I loved you so much that I wanted you to know Me. It hurt Me [the heart of God] to know that you couldn't hear Me.

It was then that Randy saw Jesus, saw the truth. God loved him every *where*, every *when*, every *how*. The love of God descended into his hell. He was set free; he was changed. That was ten years ago.

The cock crowed, and all of Peter's vows were broken. All other oaths dissolve in the presence of the One Oath. All other covenants are undone by the Eternal Covenant. Nothing is more powerful than the blood of the Lamb slain from the foundation of the world.

The cock crowed, Peter realized that all of his vows were broken, and he wept bitterly. Just a few days later as he saw the Sacrifice, the Oath of God risen from the dead, he realized all of his vows were broken, and he was "exorcised"—delivered from his oath and from the curse. And his mourning turned into dancing.

The resurrected Jesus with nail prints in His hands and feet appeared to Peter at breakfast on the shore of Galilee and asked three times, "Do you love me?" He didn't say, "Peter, will you do better? Will you try harder? Promise you won't do that again." He asked, "Do you love me? *Now?*" Then Jesus said, "Feed my sheep" (see John 21:15–17).

As far as we know, Peter made no more oaths, but he went on to be the rock. On "this rock" Jesus built His church. Peter followed Jesus and wouldn't let Him go. Though none went with him, still he followed. He followed Jesus all the way to a cross outside Rome where he was crucified upside down.

> *Stop making new covenants.*
> *Believe the new covenant.*
> *Stop making oaths.*
> *Believe God's oath—Jesus.*

Take a moment to come before Him in prayer. Don't say a thing, don't intend a thing, don't promise a thing; above all, don't make any oaths. See Him, body broken, blood shed. He loves you *right now* as you are, even in hell. You cannot make Him love you more.

If you feel like making oaths, turn your oaths into prayers. Not "Jesus, I'll be good," but "Jesus, please be good in me."

> His oath, His covenant, His blood,
> Support me in the whelming flood.
> When all around my soul gives way,
> He then is all my hope and stay.
> On Christ the solid rock I stand,
> All other ground is sinking sand.[3]

Bad religion is constantly making new covenants, for it doesn't believe the new covenant: God's eternal covenant that is forever new for you.

Bad religion binds you up with oaths: pledge this, pledge that, promise this, promise that. The gospel is the declaration of God's oath—Jesus.

7

STUPID PHILANTHROPISTS

MATTHEW 5:38-48

Several years ago near the seminary in Pasadena, I stopped to get some lunch at a chicken stand. I was waiting in line when an underprivileged-looking youth approached me and said, "Man, I'm so hungry. Could you spare just a few bucks so I could get a piece of chicken?"

I looked at him and my heart began to swell with Christian love. I smiled and said, "Sure," as I handed him some cash. As soon as I had handed him the money, his expression changed. He spun around, waving the bills in the air as he yelled to his friends, "Hey guys! I got the money!"

He and his buddies ran off laughing, as everybody at the chicken stand gave me the *look*, which meant, "You are the most gullible, bleeding-heart liberal, stupid philanthropist I've ever seen. And what does your charity accomplish? Now these boys are rewarded with booze and drugs while they learn the value of lies and irresponsibility and that crime pays. What kind of society do you want to produce? What's *wrong* with you?"

I felt stupid . . . and I was.

If we are to be God's servants accomplishing His will on earth, shouldn't we think through the results of our actions? Every school kid learns "the strong survive." And life itself is the result of the "will to power," not giving but taking, and certainly not stupid philanthropy.

Indiscriminate giving is suicide.

President George W. Bush recently said, "The free people must rule the world. In order to do that, we need a strong military." In Scripture, Israel had a strong military without, and enforced justice and responsibility within, all in order to protect life and produce the great society.

In Leviticus 24:20–22, God says, "Fracture for fracture, eye for eye, tooth for tooth. As he has injured the other, so he is to be be injured. . . . Whoever kills a man must be put to death. You are to have the same law for the alien and the native-born. I am the LORD your God."

Jesus says:

MATTHEW 5:38–42: *You have heard that it was said, "An eye for an eye and a tooth for a tooth." [And yes, check it out: God did say it.] But I say to you, Do not resist one who is evil. But if any one strikes you on the right cheek, turn to him the other also; and if any one would sue you and take your coat, let him have your cloak as well; and if any one forces you to go one mile, go with him two miles. Give to him who begs from you, and do not refuse him who would borrow from you.*

Well, Jesus presents us with several crises. First, either Jesus is God, or the Sermon on the Mount is one of the most arrogant, deluded, evil pieces of literature in all history. Jesus quotes God and then says, "But I say to you . . ." Who does He think He is?

Secondly, doesn't He care for God's people Israel? Israel was an occupied country, and it was Roman law that a Roman soldier could make a Jew carry his burden one mile. Jesus is saying, "Carry it two. Don't resist."

Remember that the Jews tried to *make* Jesus king, but Jesus refused to be involved in a military revolt for the country of Israel. Who is Israel?

I often get stuff in the mail from churches begging us to support the military conquest and settlement of old Israel by Jews. How bizarre is that? "Do what Jesus didn't do, and instead of turning a cheek, turn a tank."

Jesus presents crisis on top of crisis: Jesus seems to redefine the Old Testament.

- An "eye for an eye" is no longer our law, it seems.
- We find ourselves having to ask, "Who *is* Israel? Who is truly a Jew? Who is a child of Abraham? What is this New Jerusalem coming down?"
- Jesus *is* King of the Jews, but His kingdom is not of this world.

If you're a Christian, you must read the Old Testament in the light of Christ, or you're reading it as one under the law and therefore judged under the law. Yet that doesn't mean you can blow off the law! Jesus just said He came to fulfill the law and the prophets. So how does He fulfill "an eye for an eye and a tooth for a tooth"? How does He fulfill the promises to Israel?

You see, Jesus is a crisis. It's no wonder He got crucified. *And* He's a crisis for us.

To be slapped on the cheek was the height of insult. Jesus says, "Let them insult you some more."

In that day, a normal peasant only owned one tunic and one cloak. The cloak was the only possession under Old Testament law to which every Jew had a right. Jesus is saying, "Give up all your rights." If someone sued for your tunic, and then you handed them your cloak, you'd be standing buck naked in a court of law before all those witnesses!

"If the Roman oppressor makes you walk a mile, go two," says Jesus. "If anyone begs from you, give. If anyone wants to borrow, don't turn away." Doesn't Jesus realize that if you really believed this, that after one trip to Tijuana, Mexico, or downtown Denver, you could basically lose everything and end up looking like . . . Mother Teresa or St. Francis of Assisi? That's entirely impractical for wealthy Americans like us!

The Roman Catholic Church dealt with this problem by dividing Jesus' commands between "precepts" and "counsels." Verses like these were only meant for "special orders": monks, nuns, St. Francis- and Mother Teresa-types seeking perfection.

Many dispensationalists say the Sermon on the Mount really isn't even *for* us but for Messianic Israel. Israel didn't go for it, so then Jesus went with the whole dying on the cross thing. So many say these verses don't really apply to us, and then they quote a lot of Old Testament verses about blessing Israel. So they bless Israel with guns and tanks and blow off the Sermon on the Mount.

Augustine, Luther, Calvin, and most Protestant denominations said and say, "These verses certainly do apply to us as individuals, but not as officers in a government." They point to Romans 12 and 13 where Paul talks about our individual duty to never avenge ourselves, but then talks about the fact that government has been given a sword as a minister of God to execute wrath on the wrongdoer. So the reformers argued that a soldier or police officer doesn't turn the other cheek, for it's not their cheek to turn. They're acting on another's behalf. It is interesting that Jesus didn't say, "If someone slaps your daughter on the cheek, let him slap her on the other cheek." Policemen and soldiers use force to save our cheeks. It even appears Jesus used force on behalf of another. He made a whip and chased moneychangers from the temple, for they were insulting His Father and all nations.

Anabaptists, Mennonites, Amish, and other pacifists say these verses should not be limited *at all.* Serious pacifists would argue that if a madman is threatening your daughter with a gun, you shouldn't shoot him, but you should trust the results of your pacifism to God. Real biblical pacifists are not cowards but are supremely courageous, hoping to glorify Christ by dying well.

Perhaps the most famous commentary on the Sermon on the Mount is *The Cost of Discipleship* by Dietrich Bonhoeffer, published in 1937 in Germany. Bonhoeffer was a pacifist. He stated that the distinction between person and office is alien to Jesus' teaching. He argued that you can't separate your person from your office. You always have some kind of office (father, pastor, and so on), and you're always a person responsible to Jesus no matter what the government says.

There are great arguments in all directions. And no matter how hard I try to fully explain these commands of Jesus, no matter how much I want to relax them for me and for you, no matter how hard I try to make them reasonable, practical, and understandably applicable to every situation in your life . . . I don't think I *can* or *should.*

You say, "Oh *great.* I go to church, and for *what?*

To be more confused?

To feel more inadequate?

To be more . . . poor in spirit?

How am I to make the kingdom come and produce the great society?"

One really does wonder why Jesus wasn't more clear about certain things. Didn't Jesus think through the results of these statements before He said them? Does Jesus not care about the consequences of these actions? Is He a "stupid philanthropist"? What does He hope we'll accomplish?

MATTHEW 5:43–48: *You have heard that it was said, "You shall love your neighbor and hate your enemy." But I say to you, Love your enemies and pray for those who persecute you, so that [in order that, for this reason] you may be sons of your Father who is in heaven; for he makes his sun rise on the evil and on the good, and sends rain on the just and on the unjust. For if you love those who love you, what reward have you? Do not even the tax collectors do the same? And if you salute only your brethren, what more are you doing than others? Do not even the Gentiles do the same? You, therefore, must be perfect, as your heavenly Father is perfect.*

Henri Nouwen used to tell a story of an old holy man who saw a scorpion floating helplessly in the water of the River Ganges. The old man leaned out over the water, hanging to some roots, and tried to rescue the scorpion. As soon as he touched it, the scorpion stung him. Instinctively he withdrew his hand. A few seconds later, having regained his balance, he stretched himself out again. This time the scorpion stung him so badly that his hand became swollen and bloody. The old man's face contorted with pain.

Just then a passerby saw the old man stretched out over the roots struggling with the scorpion. He yelled, "Hey, stupid, old man! What's wrong with you? Only a fool would risk his life for the sake of an ugly, evil creature! Don't you know you could kill yourself trying to save that ungrateful scorpion?" The old man turned to the stranger and said calmly, "My friend, just because it is the scorpion's nature to sting, that does not change my nature to save."[1]

God is three persons and one substance—love. It is His nature, no matter how much it hurts.

In the beginning, God said, "Let us make man in our image, after our likeness" (Genesis 1:26). Jesus teaches to *always love*. Why? To make a great society? To evangelize the world? To protect the innocent?

To make a radical sociological statement? Because of the effect it will have on the youth of Los Angeles? No! To be sons of your Father—like your Father. He is your Father, and you are being made in His image.

"He makes his sun to rise on the evil and the good." He also makes His *Son* to rise on the evil and the good. Jesus is the "light that enlightens all men," and He is risen. All will see Him. But that doesn't mean all men respond to the same light the same way.

Speaking of His crucifixion Jesus says, "Now is the judgment of this world" (John 12:31). The painful, sacrificial love of God in Christ is the judgment (*krisis* in Greek) of the world. Jesus is the *crisis* of the world. To those who refuse Him, He tastes like consuming fire. To those who receive Him, He tastes like the finest wine. But He is one substance, the love of God poured out.

"Father sends His rain on the just and the unjust," said Jesus. Perhaps one field produces fruit and one field produces thorns. But His rain, His fire, and His love are the same. God is one. Jesus commands us, "Love like your Father." But please see, you don't control the just and the unjust, the good and the evil, the fruit and the thorns. You don't control the harvest, the results, the future, or the great society.

Jesus does not command you to be successful. He commands you to love now, that you may be sons of your Father, "in His image."

Jesus is the Son of your Father. He is the perfect image of the invisible God. He commands you to turn the other cheek, give your tunic and cloak, and carry your enemy's burdens.

- Matthew 26: Angry Jews in the court of the High Priest strike Jesus on the cheek with the palms of their hands and mock Him.
- Matthew 27: Having beaten Him, Romans strip Jesus of cloak and tunic. They sue (cast lots) for His tunic, and He gives us His cloak, His robe. He is crucified naked before heaven and hell.

- The Roman soldiers made Him carry the cross, but He carried the burden more than a mile; He bore it to hell.

Jesus fulfilled the law, "An eye for an eye, a tooth for a tooth," for "He has borne our griefs and carried our sorrows. . . . And the Lord has laid on Him the iniquity of us all" (see Isaiah 53:4–6). He satisfies His own justice for us evil beggars—His enemies. We sued for His tunic, and He gave us His cloak—His rightful robe—His righteousness.

You are to love like Him. You must trust Him to love like Him. When you're "poor in spirit," He blesses you, puts His righteousness on you, and begins to live His love through you.

If you say, "I don't look a thing like Jesus," maybe you don't trust His love. Maybe you're not "poor in spirit." Maybe He's making you "poor in spirit" right now no matter who you are and what you do.

Tax collectors and soldiers came to Jesus and said, "What shall we do?" He didn't tell them to quit, but to do what they did differently. It's as if all the stuff we worry about isn't the *real issue.* At all times in all places, love is the issue. Sacrificial, painful love is what makes us different. Abide in Him . . . tax collectors, soldiers, even pastors.

He says, "Be perfect as your heavenly Father is perfect": a perfect image. And Jesus is the perfect image, perfect man. *Perfect* in the Greek means "flawless" and also "finished," "completed." We have been completed in God's image, not when we answer all the questions and understand all things, but when we love like Jesus. From His cross He cried, "It is finished"—perfected. Then He died.

Dietrich Bonhoeffer was arguably the most brilliant young theologian of the twentieth century. But his theology was in direct opposition to the policies of the Third Reich. As the Nazi threat grew, scholars in America arranged for his exile to the States and a teaching post in New

York. No sooner had the boat docked in July 1939 than Bonhoeffer knew he must return to Germany and suffer with his fellow believers.

Back in Germany and seeking to love like Christ, he was unable to maintain his pacifist convictions and became involved in a plot to assassinate Hitler. In April 1943 he was arrested for assisting a group of Jews in an attempt to escape to Switzerland. In July 1944 the hidden bomb meant for Hitler exploded, but Hitler was out of the room. Bonhoeffer was implicated in the plot and sentenced to death.

Bonhoeffer failed as a pacifist and as a militant. However, in prison he loved his captors. The guards smuggled his papers to the outside world. (They're now a published classic.) They would apologize to him at night for locking his door. He pastored congregations of men wherever he was imprisoned.

On April 8, 1945, at the conclusion of prayer, the prison worship service was interrupted. Two men entered and said, "Prisoner Bonhoeffer, come with us." Bonhoeffer whispered to a friend, "This is the end. But for me, it is the beginning of life." The next day he was hanged in Flossenburg (hours before the Allies arrived). It's said that as he approached the gallows, he broke free from the guards and ran to the tree on which he'd hang, shouting, "Oh death! You are the supreme festival on the road to Christian freedom! Jesus, I'm coming home."[2]

Bonhoeffer failed as a pacifist and failed as a militant. But he *did not fail* as a disciple of Jesus. He even looked like Jesus: the perfect image of the invisible God. I think Dietrich is completed.

You may ask, "What good did it do? What did it accomplish?"

Perhaps sacrificial love is not good for what it produces. Perhaps everything *else* is good for producing sacrificial love.

Perhaps this entire creation is like a crucible for trying gold, a furnace for manufacturing treasure. And that treasure is "sacrificial love," that is, sons and daughters in the image of their Father God. For perhaps God Himself is what we would call a stupid philanthropist. He gives Himself away for no other reason than because it is His nature and absolute pleasure, like a great artist who can't stop painting even if it kills him. And we are His masterpiece painted in His own blood: His self-portrait.

You know, parents are kind of stupid philanthropists. It *hurts* to give birth, and it hurts to raise children, yet they take great joy in doing it.

You know, artists are kind of stupid philanthropists. They create with passion even through pain. It's not necessity. They create out of an empty fullness, a hope, a longing—love. If necessity is the mother of invention, love is the father and mother of art, life, and creation.

At the end of his life, Renoir's arthritis was so bad they had to tape his paintbrush to his hand. He was wealthy and didn't need to paint. They said, "This is crazy! Stupid! Why do this?" He said, "Pain lasts a moment, but beauty lasts a lifetime."[3]

Paul writes, "For this slight momentary affliction is preparing for us an eternal weight of glory beyond all comparison" (2 Corinthians 4:17)—God's affliction and *our* affliction, God's glory and our glory. So when they slap you on the cheek, say, "Thanks! Could I have another? I'm being prepared for glory and life."

"We are his [masterpiece], created in Christ Jesus for good works, which God prepared beforehand, that we should walk in them" (Ephesians 2:10).[4]

But now, let me remind you: Jesus said, "I am the life." If it's to be "survival of the fittest," Jesus is most fit. The "survival of the fittest" doesn't explain life; it explains death. It explains how certain life forms are eliminated but not how they are created. Self-centeredness explains death. (One self takes the life of another self—that may sustain a life but not create it.) "Taking" explains death. "Giving" explains life. "The will to power" explains death. Sacrificial love explains life: one molecule surrenders to another molecule; one cell sacrifices for a body; one body part suffers for the whole.

Life is like one great dance of surrender, where individual entities surrender self to the good of the whole. Life is love.

God is building a body. We are the members. In a living body, each member sacrifices self for the whole. The body's life is love.

God is building His family. The family's life is love.

God is building the great society. *God* is. The New Jerusalem isn't made by us, but the New Jerusalem is made *of* us when we sacrifice self in love. That love is life. And that life is blessed—happy.

"Blessed are the poor in spirit; blessed are the persecuted for righteousness' sake, for of them," Jesus said, "is the kingdom of God." We are the New Jerusalem coming down. We are and will be the image of God, sons and daughters of our Father in heaven. He is blessed. He is happy.

And "blessed are the poor in spirit," for they'll receive the Spirit and give the Spirit. They will love, and they will live. "Blessed are the poor in spirit," for they lose themselves and find themselves dancing.

To sacrifice self in this world often looks like a cross or feels like a gallows, but in our Father's house, it must look like a dance and feel like a party.

When my kids were younger and the basement of my house was unfinished, we used to play ball in the basement (four square, basketball, catch football). When my youngest son, Coleman, was just a toddler, he'd watch us throw the ball around laughing and running . . . like a great dance. At two, he didn't understand the dance. He thought the life was in the ball. So he wanted the ball.

Every now and then I'd toss him the ball. I didn't have to, but I did. He'd grab it as if it were the greatest treasure in the world and then run off to a lonely place holding the ball. He wouldn't throw it back.

The other kids would yell, "Coleman, don't wreck the game!" Actually he couldn't really wreck the game. We had more balls, and I could take that ball from him if I wanted to. But I didn't want to. The game wasn't dependent on Coleman, but I wanted Coleman to join the game. So I'd say, "Coleman, throw it like this—like your father—like your dad." The first time he gave up the ball, it must have been painful, and he had to have done it in faith. In a two-year-old's mind, it must've felt like "surrendering your tunic or cloak." It must've felt like being crucified. And if I had taken the ball from him, he would've cried like he was crucified. But, you understand, the life, the joy, the fun wasn't in the ball but in the game.

Well, we had this in our favor: the longer he held the ball, the more boring the ball got; for apart from the game, the ball was just a piece of inflated plastic.

How long have you been hanging onto your stuff? How long have you been hanging onto your self? Do you ever feel like an inflated piece of plastic? a zombie? Maybe you could lose yourself and find yourself dancing. Maybe you could toss yourself away and find yourself in the game. It's the game that gives meaning to the ball. It's love that gives life to zombies. At first that life might feel like death and look like a cross. You'd have to give yourself away in faith to be like your Father, trusting your Father, but the day is coming when you will thoroughly enjoy the game.

As I write, my elbow aches and my shoulder is sore. I've been outside with Coleman throwing the football. He wants to be a quarterback. All quarterbacks do is throw the ball away.

In self-giving, if anywhere, we touch a rhythm not only of all creation but of all being. For the Eternal Word also gives Himself in sacrifice; and that not only on Calvary. For when He was crucified He "did that in the wild weather of His outlying provinces which He had done at home in glory and gladness."[5] From before the foundation of the world He surrenders begotten Deity back to begetting Deity in obedience. And as the Son glorifies the Father, so also the Father glorifies the Son" (see John 17:1, 4–5).

From the highest to the lowest, self exists to be abdicated and, by that abdication, becomes the more truly self, to be thereupon yet the more abdicated, and so forever. This is not a heavenly law which we can escape by remaining earthly, nor an earthly law which we can escape by being saved. What is outside the system of self-giving is not earth, nor nature, nor "ordinary life," but simply and solely hell . . .

The golden apple of selfhood, thrown among the false gods, became an apple of discord because they scrambled for it. They did not know the first rule of the holy game, which is that every player must by all means touch the ball and then immediately pass it on. To be found with it in your hands is a fault: to cling to it, death. But when it flies to and fro among the players too swift for eye to follow, and the great Master Himself leads the revelry, giving Himself eternally to His creatures in the generation, and back to Himself in the sacrifice, of the Word, then indeed the eternal dance "makes heaven drowsy with harmony." All pains and pleasures we have known on earth are early initiations in the movements of that dance, but the dance itself is strictly incomparable with the sufferings of this present time. As we draw nearer to its uncreated rhythm, pain and pleasure sink almost out of sight. There is joy in the dance, but it does not exist for the sake of joy. It does not even exist for the sake of good, or of love. It is Love Himself, and Good Himself, and therefore happy [blessed].[6]

8

DISCIPLINE TO DANCE

MATTHEW 5:48–6:6, 16–18

MATTHEW 5:48–6:6, 16–18 (NIV): *Be perfect, therefore, as your heavenly Father is perfect. Be careful not to do your 'acts of righteousness' before men, to be seen by them. If you do, you will have no reward from your Father in heaven. So when you give to the needy, do not announce it with trumpets, as the hypocrites do in the synagogues and on the streets, to be honored by men. I tell you the truth, they have received their reward in full. But when you give to the needy, do not let your left hand know what your right hand is doing, so that your giving may be in secret. Then your Father, who sees what is done in secret, will reward you. And when you pray, do not be like the hypocrites, for they love to pray standing in the synagogues and on the street corners to be seen by men. I tell you the truth, they have received their reward in full. But when you pray, go into your room, close the door and pray to your Father, who is unseen. Then your Father, who sees what is done in secret, will reward you. . . .*

When you fast, do not look somber as the hypocrites do, for they disfigure their faces to show men they are fasting. I tell you the truth, they have received their reward in full. But when you fast, put oil on your head and wash your face, so that it will not be obvious to men that you are fasting, but only to your Father, who is unseen; and your Father, who sees what is done in secret, will reward you.

Jesus just said in the last chapter (Matthew 5:16), "Let your light so shine before men, that they may see your good works and give glory to your Father who is in heaven." We tend to think those good works must be things like charity, prayer, fasting, and acts of religious devotion, but here Jesus tells us to do those things in secret.

In Matthew 5, we learned that the light we are to let shine is more like a *beatitude attitude*: poverty of spirit, mourning, meekness, a hunger for righteousness, mercy, purity of heart, peacemaking, and a willingness to be persecuted for righteousness' sake. That sounds more like Mother Teresa and less like Christian TV. And come to think of it, the world does give glory to God for people like Mother Teresa. Such people dance to another tune, so in them we begin to believe in music beyond our own head. Yet so much religion is just the same old sound, the sound of self-seeking glory—dead on the inside, like a whitewashed tomb, a zombie.

Now, having expounded the law, Jesus expounds the disciplines. In this section of His Sermon on the Mount, He points out three cardinal disciplines of the Jewish religious life and our religious life (charity, prayer, and fasting). And He says, "Do it in secret."

Even the rabbis taught this, and it's doubtful they ever really did blow an actual trumpet in the synagogue. While we don't blow trumpets, we toot our own horns. (We have donor banquets, plaques, Founders Clubs.) When we pray, we like to let people know: "Oh, I have prayed and prayed for this church, don't you know." When we fast—when we do without—we love to indicate our sacrifice.

Jesus says, "Don't do those things to be seen by men, or you already have your reward. Do it in secret, and your Father who sees in secret will reward you." *He* will reward you. Yet the concept of rewards is confusing, whether I get rewards from men or God.

First of all, if I think I *earn* rewards, what happens to grace?

Second, if folks have different and varying rewards in heaven, won't I be jealous of others' rewards for all eternity?

Third, when people do good deeds to get rewards, they usually end up hating the deeds they do. They're:

- no longer reading for fun but reading to pass a test;
- no longer singing for joy but working a gig;
- no longer sharing the good news but toiling in the ministry;
- no longer giving a gift to the Beloved but paying taxes to a welfare case;
- no longer dancing for joy but exercising to lose weight . . . doing aerobics.

Last, if you do good deeds to get some other reward, the deeds aren't good. If I give to the poor for some other reward, I'm a hypocrite (*hupokrites* in Greek). It means "actor." I'm *acting* like I love them, but I love the *reward*. I'm using them—defiling them—to get a reward, like a mercenary or prostitute. If I do loving things to get some other reward, the things I do aren't loving but evil.

Well, Jesus clearly says, "Don't do good deeds for some reward from men." I think He's also saying, "Don't do good deeds for some other reason." God will see and will reward. But don't do the deed to get some other reward, for in fact you shouldn't even know you're doing it! "Don't let your left hand know what your right hand is doing, so it will be done in secret." That is, even *you* won't know.

How can I do a good deed for a reward if I don't know I'm doing it?

Don't do it in order to be seen by men . . . or God, for that matter. "Be perfect like your Father, and don't be aware you're doing it." Now do it!

"When you give, don't even let your left hand know what your right hand is doing." I guess that means that when the offering plate comes around I should put my left hand in my coat pocket, take my wallet out with my right hand, hold it in my teeth while I remove some bills with the same hand, and place them in the plate. That way the left hand won't see or know. But that doesn't work. The left hand still knows, for both hands are controlled by my self-centered brain. To do this, I'd have to be out of myself, unaware of myself, dead to myself. I'd have to lose myself.

And that is a nice thought, for whenever people do good deeds and they're conscious of themselves, their good deeds stink. No wonder the poor resent our charity. No wonder some people resent our evangelism and witness. They can *smell* it. "You just went to some seminar, and now you're relieving your guilt using me to feel better about yourselves!" That's not love; it feels more like rape.

> Our self-consciousness
> makes our good deeds
> profoundly ugly.

Little children are so cute . . . until they become conscious that they're cute and, therefore, *try* to be cute. Then they're no longer cute, at least in the way they're striving to be cute. We call that *growing up*.

In the novel *Perelandra* by C. S. Lewis, the newly created Eve on Venus is tempted by the Evil One with a mirror with which she can see herself.[1] In the Garden, the newly created Eve on Earth was tempted with a tree of knowledge, so she could see herself and know if she was good or bad: judge herself.

Ever since then, we've been striving to be good, because we see we're bad. And Jesus said, "You must become like little children" (see Matthew 18:3). Paul writes, "It is a very small thing that I should be judged by you. . . . I do not even judge myself" (1 Corinthians 4:3).

Well, it's a nice idea to be non-self-consciously perfect, but it's a bit beyond us.

"Give without knowing it."

"Move in perfection without striving."

"Do the whole law—no greed, no lust, turning the other cheek—all without disciplining yourself to do so, a secret even to yourself."

That's quite a command! It reminds me of Hebrews 4:11: "Strive to enter [God's] rest." That sounds like, "Work to not be working. Discipline yourself to not be disciplined."

You know, God is at rest, yet Jesus said He's always working.

What kind of work is really rest?

What kind of perfection is absolute personal freedom?

Christ "sets us free," yet He also says, "Be perfect like your Father"—that is, everything in order, in perfect harmony, perfectly coordinated. How do I not let my right hand know what my left hand is doing without being totally uncoordinated?

I was thinking about all these things when I remembered an old movie clip and couldn't get it out of my mind. It's about an underprivileged, uncoordinated boy named Nevin whose family spends evenings singing songs on the porch. But no matter how hard he tries, he cannot coordinate his hands and feet with the music. The harder he tries, the worse it is, until one night, having given up, a miracle happens.

Lying in bed listening to his radio while eating a Twinkie, Nevin notices that his feet are moving to the music. He watches in wonder, because he couldn't make this happen before. Then the fingers on his right hand begin snapping to the beat. Soon he's dancing around the room in ecstasy. He yells, "Mom! Dad!" His parents run into the room, and Nevin exclaims, "Mom! Dad! This music speaks to me!"[2]

Nevin is played by Steve Martin, and the movie is *The Jerk*. The scene is a joke about black culture and white culture, and the movie isn't what you'd call wholesome, but it certainly illustrates the miracle we call dance. When the music spoke to Nevin, without trying, he began to dance. His entire body began to move in perfect order—harmony.

If you've studied music theory and physics, you know that music is extremely logical. It seems mysterious to us because there is more logic than the conscious mind can comprehend. Yet the conscious mind can recognize it as *good* and *beautiful*, and our bodies can be coordinated by its logic—its *logos* (in Greek).

Animals don't have the same capacity. But the logos may find a place in us, and we dance.

Nevin said, "This music speaks to me!" and he danced. Jesus said to some Jewish do-gooders, "My word (logos) finds no place in you" (John 8:37). "We piped . . . and you would not dance" (Matthew 11:17, Luke 7:32).

So how do I not let my left hand know what my right hand is doing yet be entirely coordinated? Well, I must lose myself and be coordinated by something else. When I dance, I surrender to the logic of the music. The more I surrender, the better I dance. But the more I stop and think about what I'm doing, the stiffer I get, the more uncoordinated I become—the more like a zombie.

A great dance is incredible order, yet it's also perfect freedom, for the *logos* (logic) bypasses my conscious brain—my self—and animates my body. And all the while, my conscious brain is just thinking, *I dig this funky music!*

What kind of perfect order is absolute freedom?
A great dance.
What kind of work is really rest?
We call it *play.*
Good dance is great play.

When little children play, they build things. They expend tremendous amounts of energy, and they suffer pain. But it's not work; it's play. They don't have to *make* themselves do it.

But if Dad comes out and says, "Listen up! If you build three Lego houses and run around the yard twelve times, I'll reward you. But if not, I'll spank you!" then it's no longer play but work, for the children are all at once extremely conscious of themselves.

But children are good at play, and their lives are like a dance because they lose themselves easily. And they lose themselves easily because everything is bigger than them.

The bigger *you* are, the harder it is to lose yourself. The less your world is filled with wonder, the less likely you are to be swept off your feet and caught up in a dance.

Children dance at the drop of a hat.
Proud people rarely dance,
And when they do dance, they don't dance well.

To be proud is to be self-absorbed and full of self, not poor of self and poor of spirit. The arrogant and the insecure are equally self-absorbed and equally proud. They feel equally responsible. They must be in control; that is, they must be constantly aware of what their left hand is doing and what their right hand is doing. They're very stiff. So they move like zombies. They're a drag to dance with! *No fun.*

To dance is to surrender to something bigger than yourself. So what do you believe in that's bigger than you?

Many people won't dance and won't believe in God, for He won't fit into their world. (I suppose that's true of all of us in some way.) But what if the biggest became smallest and entered our world?

. . . like a baby in a manger?

. . . like a Word from beyond?

. . . like a song sung through prison walls?

What if it found a place in us and we began to believe in life beyond? Well, maybe then we'd *dance*, even in this prison.

The Romanian pastor Richard Wurmbrand writes, "The Communists believe that happiness comes from material satisfaction, but alone in my cell, cold, hungry, and in rags, I danced for joy every night."[3] He was thinking of Jesus. And the guards gave him extra food because they thought he'd gone crazy.

Dancers only seem crazy to those who can't hear the music.

Well, God *is* bigger than you, but He became small to enter your world. He then gets large so that you might lose yourself and find yourself in Him; that you might *dance*.

Friedrich Nietzsche said he could only believe in a God who would dance.[4] That is a problem, for what music is larger than God, such that He could dance to it? To dance, He would have to *limit* Himself and dance in His own glory, like a Son surrendered to a Father.

Well, Friedrich, Christians not only believe that God dances, but we believe He *is* a dance. And the Dance has a name.

C. S. Lewis writes:

All sorts of people are fond of repeating the Christian statement that "God is love." But they seem not to notice that the words "God is love" have no real meaning unless God contains at least two Persons. Love is something that one person has for another person. If God was a single person, then before the world was made, He was not love. . . .

And that, by the way, is perhaps the most important difference between Christianity and all other religions: that in Christianity God is not a static thing—not even a person—but a dynamic, pulsating activity, a life, almost a kind of drama. Almost, if you will not think me irreverent, a kind of dance. . . .

And now, what does it all matter? It matters more than anything else in the world. The whole dance, or drama, or pattern of this three-Personal life is to be played out in each one of us: or (putting it the other way round) each one of us has got to enter that pattern, take his place in that dance. There is no other way to the happiness for which we were made.[5]

Above all else, writes Paul, "put on love, which binds everything together in perfect harmony" (Colossians 3:14). "Put on love"—that is, "put on Christ." "This is love, not that we loved God but that he loved us and sent his Son as an atoning sacrifice for our sins" (1 John 4:10 NIV). God is like a dance. We are invited to enter, for He has entered us and begun to sing.

I heard Walter Wangerin say that if a European wants to understand something, he takes it apart. If an African wants to understand something, he dances with it.

In European countries, God has been declared dead. That's what happens when you take something apart. In Africa God is dancing across the continent with His bride. The church is profoundly fruitful there.

Will Willimon writes:

You and I can give thanks that the locus of Christian thinking appears to be shifting from North America and northern Europe where people write rules and obey them, to places like Africa and Latin America where people still know how to dance.[6]

"Write rules and obey them"—that's what the Pharisees did! Remember that the religious people crucified Jesus. They took Him apart and tried to cut Him down to size, but they couldn't control Him. He's the Lord of the dance.

Pharisees hate the Dance. And Pharisees don't dance. The religious spirit doesn't dance. Oh, they'll tell you to dance, even *make* you dance. But their dance is exercise, it's no fun, it's work, and everyone is self-conscious the entire time. They'll say, "David danced and so should we."

They'll turn David's dance into a law. But David's dance was holy, precisely because it was *not* some law.

Remember the story in 2 Samuel? David stripped to a linen ephod (underwear) and danced with all his might before the Lord as the priests brought the ark of the covenant into Jerusalem. He was the man after God's own heart, and his dance was holy, precisely because it was not some law:

> He wasn't obeying a law.
> His left hand didn't know what his right hand was doing.
> He was "poor in spirit" and so, full of God's Spirit.
> He lost himself in God, became small and filled with wonder.
> He surrendered control.

When David got home, his wife Michal rebuked him. "How the king—the big king—dishonored himself, made himself small today. Undignified!" David was no longer acting (*hupokrites*) like a king but a child. And Queen Michal hated that; she lived for control and wanted to control David's dance.

An evil, religious spirit always seeks to control other dancers. But what Jesus says, Jesus does. He has a body, and we are His members.

And He doesn't let His right hand know what His left hand is doing. That is, I can't control your dance. And when I try, your dance becomes ugly. Yet when all members surrender to the music of the Father, mediated through the Head, which is the Son, we will see a great dance and recognize it as the perfect beauty it is: our Lord's finished bride.[7]

Well, Michal tried to *seize* control of the dance, and she was barren all her days.

Of course, in the new covenant, many are physically barren but profoundly fruitful. Abide in the dance, in Jesus, that you may bear much fruit. When bride and groom are fruitful, bearing life, it's because they are lost in a dance, making love to *each other.*

The Dance is incredibly fruitful, but the Dance is its own reward. In Matthew 25, Jesus says that on judgment day He'll say to the sheep on His right hand, "I was hungry and you gave me food to eat." And they'll say something like, "We don't remember that . . . we're not conscious of that . . . our right hand didn't know what the left was doing. We must have been . . . *dancing.*" And Jesus will say, "Yes. You were dancing with me, my bride." Their deeds bear life in this world and forever.

In Matthew 7:22–23, Jesus describes men on Judgment Day who are conscious of their deeds: "On that day many will say to me, 'Lord, Lord, did we not . . . do many mighty works in your name?' And then I will declare to them, 'I never knew you; depart from me, you evildoers.'" Their deeds bear evil and death. They practiced dance steps but didn't dance. They couldn't hear the music. They were zombies.

The Dance bears fruit, but the dance is its own reward. In the parable of the talents, the good stewards are rewarded with *more stewardship*. The good givers are rewarded with *more giving*. The good lovers are rewarded with *more loving*. "To him who has will more be given" (Luke 8:18).

The reward for dancing is the Dance!

If you love good deeds, you're loving love and you're loving God. C. S. Lewis writes:

Heaven offers nothing that a mercenary soul can desire. It is safe to tell the pure in heart that they shall see God, for only the pure in heart want to. There are rewards that do not sully motives. A man's love for a woman is not mercenary because he wants to marry her.[8]

You are the bride of Christ.

When you love, you're dancing with Him.

You are the children of God.

When you love, you are "becoming sons of your Father."

The dance is its own reward.

God gave us His only begotten Son. "Will he not also give us all things with him?" (Romans 8:32). God gives you all things. But here on earth you're acquiring a taste for the *best* thing: the very heart of God—Jesus.

And how could there be jealousy in heaven? All things are yours! So maybe your unique reward would be a unique perspective on Jesus and all things. If you thought you had more, your joy would be to give it away, to sing God's praises to your neighbor, to give yourself away. Everyone would be giving themselves away like Jesus. So instead of looking like a cross (one dancer, one giver in an evil world), it would look like a great dance! Heaven!

God is love, and the Father sings a song over this dead world. The song is Jesus—the Word—*Logos* (through whom all things are made)—the Rhythm of the Dance.

Does He find a place in you?

Does the Father's song speak to you?

Will you surrender to His tune—His Word?

Will you dance?

That is the judgment.

Some of you may say, "Great. That's nice. But seriously, how much should I give? How long should I pray? When I fast, can I drink liquids?" If that's you, perhaps . . .

- your play has become work;
- your love has become toil;
- your dance has become aerobics—an exercise in religion.

You're dancing because you *should*. But it's like someone turned off the stereo long ago. You've stopped worshiping. If you do all these good deeds but don't hear the music, the deeds are worthless, less than worthless—a lie. Then you're a zombie, a Pharisee, a noisy gong, a clanging symbol. You give away all you have and move mountains, but you have not love (see 1 Corinthians 13:1–3). You don't hear the music!

Now, some of you may say, "Well, I don't give, pray, *or* fast." Then you're certainly not dancing. Even if you hear the music, you haven't surrendered.

To start dancing is not to get all guilty and then just *try harder*, taking more control of every step. At some point, you must hear the music and surrender to it. The music is the love of God. "In this the love of God was made manifest among us, that God sent his only Son into the world, so that we might live through him" (1 John 4:9). Think of Jesus, listen to Jesus, believe Jesus, ingest Jesus, worship Jesus; and then take a step while you hear the music. One day you'll be amazed at your moves, what your right and left hands are doing.

I read that a hundred years ago the Presbyterian missionaries in Ghana, Africa, only allowed the African converts to worship in their native style during one part of the service—they danced during the offering. To this day, in some churches in Africa, I understand that they dance the offering. It's the only part of the service in which anyone smiles. And I bet they have a good offering.

Did you remember that when David danced before the Lord, he gave loaves of bread, raisin cakes, and date cakes to everyone in the crowd and blessed them all? I wonder if he even *knew* what he was doing. Well, his wife did. But David didn't calculate.

Remember the parable of the talents; it appears that the good stewards were not the conscientious, calculating types. The good stewards invested everything, trusting their master. The only one who is recorded as calculating is the evil steward, who buried his talents in fear for himself.

So do your deeds while you're dancing. That is, *always worship!* As St. Augustine put it, "Love God and do as you please."

> Well, should I even try to do good deeds?
> Should I even practice the disciplines—
> giving, quiet times, prayers, fasting?

The answer is yes, yes, yes.

- Yes, because they show you that you need to hear the music.
- Yes, because they describe certain movements of the dance— dance steps.
- Yes, because they are points at which we enter the dance.

We practice dance steps in the hope of dancing, unconscious of the steps because the dance has become our nature.

My son Coleman got an electric guitar for Christmas, and he's learning to play. But it's hard telling your left hand to form chords on the neck of the guitar while telling your right hand to strum a certain rhythm. But Coleman still disciplines himself to practice, because he loves electric guitar music. He's already *hearing* it in faith.

If you do the Christian disciplines to join the dance—to know Jesus, to know love, because you love Love—I think you're already hearing the music in faith. And you have faith because you already hear the music.

Well, Coleman and I got the score for an Elvis tune. I showed him where to put his fingers for the chords, and I described the strum. But it all sounded really bad until Coleman discovered a secret.

Now he says, "Dad, you sing and I'll play along." When I sing, his fingers begin to dance. His right hand strums in rhythm; his left hand changes chords at just the right times—all because he joyfully surrenders to the words of his father as I sing, "I'm just a hunk, a hunk of burning love." At that point his discipline turns to dance.

> *God the Father is singing.*
> *His Word is Jesus.*
> *He is burning love.*

Discipline yourself in such a way that you might forget your discipline, lose yourself, and find yourself playing along, a son of your Father, His Word in you making you dance. He makes old zombies dance.

The weekend I preached at my church on these verses, my friend Dale came forward and told me he'd seen another vision. Dale has had many visions in worship since the one I shared with you three chapters ago. Some are very personal for me, and some are specifically for our church. So I don't share them all, but this one you should hear:

Peter, as you were preaching, I saw a long double line of Christians going to church as the dutiful people they are. The procession went up a very long flight of steps that was lined with candles. The atmosphere was dark, and the ambience was as if this was a funeral procession. Each person was wearing a black hooded cloak with the hood covering most of his eyes. In front of them they held a large, ornate crucifix on top of a pole. As they went up the steps, I noticed the doorway they were entering was very similar to an Egyptian tomb, lots of rough stone and very dark inside.

After taking a few steps through the doorway, swords would come out from either side and cut off the head of each person, along with the crucifix he was holding. Immediately the cloak would fall off, and the person would drop the pole, but the body would keep walking. Several steps later the bodies were met by angels who started trying to teach them how to dance.

The bodies were very clumsy at first, but as they learned, they were transformed into very bright figures with new heads, that hardly even resembled the person who had walked in the doorway. Then the vision pulled back, and I saw that the inside of this place was actually a very large, beautiful, ornate grand ballroom with angels and transformed figures dancing all around. Right in the center of the room was the cross with Jesus standing in front of it, and through the roof came music. Then I saw above the roof the mouth of God and out of that came the music that was floating down through the roof for all the dancers to hear.

I suspect some of you have a hard time believing that some people see visions at all. That's okay (for now), but at least believe Scripture:

Thou hast turned for me my mourning into dancing;

thou hast loosed my sackcloth and girded me with gladness,

that my soul may praise thee and not be silent.

O LORD my God, I will give thanks to thee for ever.

(Psalm 30:11–12)

King David wrote that. It's the gospel! You must believe the gospel.

9

How to Pray

MATTHEW 6:5–14

In Monty Python's *The Meaning of Life*, the movie camera pans over rows of bored schoolboys listening to a sermon. A priest then steps to the podium and begins leading the boys in responsive prayer:

> Let us praise God
> O, Lord (boys echo: O, Lord)
> O, You are so big (O, You are so big)
> So absolutely huge (So absolutely huge)
> Gosh, we're all really impressed down here I can tell you
> (Gosh, we're all really impressed down here I can tell you)
> Forgive us, O Lord, for this our dreadful toadying
> (And barefaced flattery)
> But You're so strong and, well, just so super
> (Fantastic!)
> Amen (Amen)

I think they're mocking God . . . or us. Next they sing a hymn:

> O, Lord, please don't burn us,
> Don't kill or toast your flock.
> Don't put us on the barbeque

115

Or simmer us in stock.

Don't braise or bake or boil us

Or stir-fry us in a wok.

And please don't lightly poach us.[1]

That clip feels so sacrilegious (unholy). But it's sacrilegious because it's true . . . not true about God, but true about us and human religion. Our *hearts* are sacrilegious. We may pray and sing different words, but the world gets our meaning: God is distant, arrogant, and aloof. So we pray in faithlessness and fear.

At the start of the Sermon on the Mount, Jesus says, "Unless your righteousness exceeds that of the scribes and Pharisees, you will never enter the kingdom of heaven" (Matthew 5:20). The Pharisees were prayermongers. The ordinary Jew was required to recite the *Shema* (a collection of verses from Scripture) twice each day. They also were to pray the eighteen benedictions (*Shemoneh Esreh*) three times each day. I found it on the Internet. It is a beautiful prayer *five pages long!* Three times each day they were to pray it, plus a slew of other prayers for various occasions. There were prayers for everything from seeing a lake to the use of new furniture.

I find that amazing, for when Jesus teaches on prayer, He's talking to folks who would appear to us "entirely prayed up." He's talking to a religious environment that reminds me of some Christian college groups I was a part of long ago, where it seemed as if every talk was about having a quiet time. And the leader usually would say something like, "You know, Martin Luther used to say, 'I have so much to do this day, I must pray for four hours rather than two.'"

I always felt guilty about my prayer life. But, golly . . . after a half-hour, I'd run out of stuff to say! I'd literally be *bored to tears* with my many words, and I'd fall asleep. Then I'd wake up peeling those tear-stained, onionskin Bible pages off my greasy face, repent, and start over. (Oh, blessed communion, sweet hour of prayer!)

Well, it's into that environment—an environment of rigorous religious practices—Jesus speaks about the practice of piety. Our last chapter was titled "Discipline to Dance." God *is* a Dance, a Trinity called Love.

Does your prayer life feel like a dance?

Have you ever been to a church dance or a church party where you're having a great time, and someone (like the pastor) says, "Hey, everybody, let's just have a time of prayer"? Outside you smile, and inside your heart says, "Shoot! No more bean dip, and a half hour of standing in a circle with people impressing each other with their many and deep words."

Dance to discipline . . . happens in church all the time.

Jesus speaks to His church:

MATTHEW 6:5–8: *And when you pray [*proseuchomai *in Greek: "petitionary prayer"], you must not be like the hypocrites; for they love to stand and pray in the synagogues and at the street corners, that they may be seen by men. Truly, I say to you, they have received their reward. But when you pray, go into your room and shut the door and pray to your Father who is in secret; and your Father who sees in secret will reward you.*

And in praying do not heap up empty phrases as the Gentiles do; for they think that they will be heard for their many words. Do not be like them, for your Father knows what you need before you ask him.

Jesus teaches it's not about impressive words and public words. I don't think that means we can't pray in public (Jesus did), and I don't think that means we can't thoughtfully write out our prayers (David did). But Jesus says, "Don't be like the hypocrites"—the actors. "They act like they're talking to God, but they're not." It's impersonal.

"And when praying, don't keep babbling on like pagans." The verb in Greek is *battologe*—batta, batta, batta . . . on and on. You see, maybe I wasn't the only one bored with the words of my college quiet times. Maybe God was too!

Jesus says, "Don't keep babbling on like pagans. They think they will be heard for their many words" (*polylogia*— "much word"). It's as if Jesus is saying, "God heard you this morning. Do you think He's stupid? Do you think you have to twist His arm? Do you think He doesn't love you? Do you think this is magic like the pagans do? Do you think two more times before bed will make it work?" Jesus slams the religious system of His day.

Do you ever get Internet prayers? A couple of years ago I saw this one a lot: "The Lord has revealed to a prayer warrior that if one million people pray for Saddam Hussein to abdicate, we can avoid war. Pass this on to ten others." I thought that was a great prayer to pray. And I hoped that more than a million people prayed it. But I didn't pass it on. I may have been wrong, I really may have been, but to me it didn't smell like Jesus. It smelled like fear, shame, condemnation, and flesh. And I didn't want to perpetuate that religious system.

Pray, but not constrained by fear. We are to be constrained by something else. I don't think it's a matter of many words or a particular set of words. Perhaps it's a matter of many hearts. But hearts aren't redeemed by fear or many words, but by the one Word.

I don't know if Martin Luther ever said the thing about four hours of prayer, but I do know he wrote this:

> The gentile delusion [is] that prayer meant making both God and
> oneself tired with yelling and murmuring. . . . [Those] who make it

nothing but a work of drudgery can never pray with gladness or devotion. . . . Prayers ought to be brief, frequent, and intense.[2]

Scripture says, "Pray constantly." But Jesus says, "We won't be heard for our many words." Augustine writes, "Remove from prayers much speaking, but not much praying."[3]

"You won't be heard for your many words. Don't be like them, for your heavenly Father knows what you need before you ask Him." Prayer is not an information briefing for God.

And learning to pray is not about collecting a bunch of information or teaching. We have so many books, classes, and seminars on how to pray, just as the scribes, Pharisees, and rabbis did.

In Luke 11 (the parallel to Matthew 6), disciples come to Jesus and say, "Teach us to pray, like John taught His disciples to pray." And Jesus says: "Okay . . . when you pray say: 'Father, hallowed be Your name, Your kingdom come. Give us each day our daily bread. Forgive us our sins, as we forgive everyone who sins against us. And lead us not into temptation'" (vv. 2–4; paraphrased). *Period.*

They must have thought, *Are you mocking us? Surely it's more complicated than that! What about the prayer of Jabez and a bunch of Hail Mary's and the eighteen benedictions? Jesus, that only took* fifteen seconds!

In Matthew 6, Jesus says, "Not babbling words, not many words; your Father knows what you need before you ask Him, so then pray"—ask.

Your Father knows what you need before you ask Him. So why ask Him? Well, maybe *you* don't know what you need before you ask Him.

The earthly minded person thinks . . . that when he prays, the important thing . . . is that God should hear what he is praying for. And yet in the true, eternal sense it is just the reverse: the true relation in prayer is not when God hears what is prayed for, but when the person praying continues to pray until he is the one who hears, who hears what God is asking for.[4]

That's Kierkegaard. In the words of Madeleine L'Engle, "Until I tell God what I want, I have no way of knowing whether or not I truly want it."[5]

"Your Father knows what you need before you ask Him, so ask Him" . . . and in asking, maybe He'll tell you what you need.

Have you ever determined to say something to somebody (practiced your lines), but in their presence all your words changed? It happens to little children in the presence of their fathers.

For your Father knows what you need before you ask him. This, then,
is how you should pray:
"Our Father in heaven,
hallowed be your name,
your kingdom come,
your will be done
on earth as it is in heaven.
Give us today our daily bread.
Forgive us our debts,
as we also have forgiven our debtors.
And lead us not into temptation,
but deliver us from the evil one."
For if you forgive men when they sin against you, your heavenly
Father will also forgive you. But if you do not forgive men their sins,
your Father will not forgive your sins. (Matthew 6:8–15 NIV)

Jesus says, *"Pray, 'Our Father.'"* The way Jesus talked about God got Him killed. In John 5:18, the Jews sought to kill Jesus because He referred to God as His own Father. The Jews referred to God as the Father of Israel, but Jesus referred to Him as *Dad*. Because the word is preserved in the Epistles, we believe Jesus used His common, native, Aramaic tongue in prayer and called God *Abba* . . . like Papa, Daddy. He called God *Dad*.

Jesus says:

"Our Father."

"Our Dad."

"Your Daddy and my Daddy."

This lesson on prayer is a big brother teaching His little brothers and sisters how to talk to their Daddy. Jesus is the only begotten Son of God—the *only one*! Yet He says, "Pray 'Our Papa.'" How can that be?

"Our Father who art in heaven, hallowed be thy name." That is, "Let your name be hallowed"—respected—set apart.

In the temple in Jerusalem was the holy of holies. To enter spelled death. The Jews knew God was holy, distant, and other. But of what that holiness consisted, they just weren't too sure. The Jews believed, as Ezekiel prophesied, that when the Messiah came, *He* would make God's name hallowed among all peoples, and He would reveal the true nature of God's holiness.

"Thy kingdom come, thy will be done." What we think we need and what our flesh really prays in fear is, "Hallowed by *my* name. *My* kingdom come, *my* will be done." We don't know what we need, but praise God He doesn't give us what we ask for! For our flesh asks for hell:

My kingdom,

> *my* will,

> > forever alone,

> > > apart from the great dance.

The Jews rightfully believed the kingdom would come when the king came, when the Christ came.

"Thy will be done on earth as it is in heaven." In heaven His will is done faithfully, joyfully, freely; not constrained by fear but love . . . like a *dance*.

"Give us this day our daily bread"—*epiousian* bread. *Epiousian* is an extremely rare Greek word.

- Some people think it means "daily"—"this day daily." That's a bit redundant.
- Some think it means "bread for tomorrow," but in the next chapter, Jesus says, "Don't worry about tomorrow and what you are to eat."
- Some think it refers to manna, God's sustenance to Israel in the wilderness.
- Some have thought it refers to communion bread. *Epi*—above; and *ousian*—substance. Supersubstantial bread.
- Some argue it refers to heavenly bread, future bread, eschatological bread, bread of the messianic banquet.

"And forgive us our debts as we forgive our debtors." To forgive a debt is to make payment for a crime, so that restitution and vengeance are transformed into a gift—no longer wrath but grace. The Jews knew only God could forgive, but what was the gift, the payment, the sacrifice to fund all this forgiveness?

It's interesting that the sign of spirituality and efficacious prayer here is not fancy words, many words, or the length of your quiet time . . . not even miracles. It's your willingness to forgive.

If you won't forgive, don't think you're forgiven.

If you're forgiven much, you'll love much and you'll forgive.

"Lead us not into temptation." We hate praying that, for we love temptation. Still, what a strange thing to pray, as if God *would* lead us

into temptation. Commentators point out that *temptation* can also be translated "trials," and trials are inevitable. So Jesus is saying, "Pray that you might not fall into the temptation during your trials."

Whatever the case, remember that Jesus was led "by the Spirit" into the desert to be tempted by the "evil one" (Satan), yet He did not fall into temptation. He conquered the evil one. So stick with Jesus. On His cross He conquered Satan forever.

"Lead us not into temptation and deliver us from the evil one." Believe me, the evil one is not defeated with your impressive words, public words, fancy words, or magic, babbling words. He's only defeated with *the* Word.

In the words of Martin Luther's hymn "A Mighty Fortress Is Our God":

> The Prince of Darkness grim,
> we tremble not for him;
> His rage we can endure,
> for lo, his doom is sure,
> One little word shall fell him."[6]

It's true. I've seen it! One little word . . . but that Word is larger than all created reality, even though it's smaller than a standard Galilean manger. "In the beginning was the Word, and the Word was with God, and the Word was God" (John 1:1).

The Word is the One teaching His little brothers and sisters how to pray. They don't know what they need. Yet the Holy Father in heaven is now sitting on a hillside telling them what they need: Himself—the Word to speak. He is not distant, arrogant, or aloof.

> Jesus said, "I and the Father are one."
> Two persons, one substance,
> One dance, Father and Son.

Jesus says to pray, "Our Father."

He *is* the only begotten Son of God.

We are adopted into the family (the dance).

James Hewitt tells about a Sunday school teacher registering two brothers for class. She asked for their birthdays. The bolder of the two said, "We're both seven. My birthday is April 8, 1976, and my brother's is April 20, 1976." "But that's impossible!" answered the teacher. "No, it's not," answered the quieter brother. "One of us is adopted." "Which one?" asked the teacher before she could curb her tongue.

The boys looked at each other and smiled, and the bolder one said, "We asked Dad awhile ago, but he just said he loved us both, and he couldn't remember any more which one was adopted."[7]

We become flesh and blood. Jesus prayed saying, "Father, you have loved them as you loved me" (John 17:23 NAB). Wow! And here in the Sermon on the Mount, He teaches: when you pray, say, "Our Father."

So now we are to pray, *"Our Father in heaven, hallowed be thy name."* When Jesus was crucified, the curtain in the holy of holies ripped from top to bottom. Something got in: us. And something got out: the Spirit of Christ, the holiness of God. Speaking of His crucifixion Jesus said, "I, when I am lifted up from the earth, will draw all men to myself" (John 12:32).

Jesus from the bosom of the father

is the Holy One of God.

He is the Revelation of God's holiness,

the Love of God poured out on a cross.

Jesus is how God hallows His name.

"Thy kingdom come." Jesus came preaching, "The kingdom of heaven is *at hand.*"

"Thy kingdom come, thy will be done." "Thy Sermon on the Mount be done." That is, "Thy law upon Mount Sinai be done." Jesus came to fulfill the law in us. Emmanuel: God with us.

"Give us this day our daily bread." Bread for tomorrow, our manna, our communion bread, our messianic banquet bread. Give us all of the above; that is, give us Jesus this day and each day.

In John 6, Jesus says, "God gave them manna in the wilderness. But my Father gives you the true bread from Heaven. I am the bread of life. Unless you eat the flesh of the Son of man and drink his blood, you have no life in you." Give me bread; give me Jesus.

"And forgive us our debts as we forgive our debtors." When we pray for forgiveness, we're praying for the gift of God. We're praying for Jesus . . . for us, in us, and through us.

"Lead us not into temptation, but deliver us from the evil one." Deliver us, rescue us, help us! If I could sum up the Lord's Prayer in two words, it would be "God, help!" In Hebrew it became a name: *Yeshua* (God is salvation). In Greek it becomes *Iesous;* in English it's *Jesus.*

We call this the Lord's Prayer, yet it's *our* prayer for the Lord. We come to the Father with all these words—impressive words, public words, informative words, babbling words (*batta logos*), and many words (*poly logos*). And God is helping us say one Word with meaning.

The Word—the Meaning—the Logos—Jesus.

We come with all these needs, and speaking to God in His presence He helps us realize we have only one need—Himself. We think we need bread, house, family, world peace, and the knowledge of good and evil. But we really only have one need: the heart of God—Jesus.

You *should* pray for bread, house, family, world peace, and direction. Yet in all these things, He's showing you Jesus. He's helping you see Jesus, pray Jesus. And I'm not saying we should only pray the audible name Jesus. I'm saying that in Jesus are "hid all the treasures of wisdom and knowledge" (Colossians 2:3), and giving you Jesus, the Father will give you all things. "All things" come to us through Jesus. Yet Jesus is not merely a means for giving you all things. "All things" are a means of giving you Jesus. The "all things" are easy in and of themselves for God, but giving you His heart looks like a cross and costs Him all things.

I suspect "all things"— "all creation"—exists for you to help you pray "Jesus" and desire Jesus and trust Jesus . . . "in sickness and in health, in joy and in sorrow." You are His bride, and He is your Groom. He wants you to want Him. And you most need to *want* Him.

We come with all these needs, and God the Father in the Son helps us know and pray our true need—Jesus Himself. And we learn to pray by praying to Him, like a child learns to speak by speaking to his father. A first word, or *the* first word, is "Abba" addressed to Father, for the child knows his father saves and helps.

We get so stressed out about prayer and babble in fear wondering, "Does God help? Where is God? Can I hear Him? Can I speak to Him?" We're like babies in a womb wondering, "Where's Mother?" We're like an infant in his daddy's arms babbling into space.

I used to babble on in fear, working through lists and formulas, wondering where God was and did He hear me, and then I'd fall asleep. I bet He enjoyed it when I shut up and fell asleep . . . in His arms. But even more, He enjoyed it when every now and then, out of the babble, I'd mumble, "Abba . . . Dadda . . . Father . . . ."

We learn to speak from speaking to our Father, not from a class or seminar or book. Children of God, prayer is now your native tongue. We learn to pray by praying to our Father, present to us in Christ Jesus. Through Christ, God is not distant, and He never *was* arrogant or aloof. In Jesus' name, say, "Abba." Pray in Jesus' name. That's more than an audible word; it's His spiritual presence.

Jesus is how the Father gives meaning to your words.

Jesus is the Meaning—the Word—the Logos—the Truth—the Life.

He is how you pray.

He is the Word given to you and returning from you to the Father.

Paul writes in Galatians 4:6, "And because you are sons, God has sent the Spirit of his Son into our hearts crying, 'Abba! Father!'"

Richard Foster writes, "Hard as it may be for us to imagine, God is in everlasting communion with himself through our stumbling, bumbling prayers."[8]

P. T. Forsyth writes, "When we speak to God it is really the God who lives in us speaking through us to himself . . . in self-communing love."[9]

So the Lord's Prayer is our prayer for the Lord, but really it *is* the Lord's prayer for the Lord in us. We're being caught up in God's great dance of love: Father, Son, and Holy Spirit.

Jesus said, "If you've seen Me, you've seen the Father" (see John 14:9). God is not distant, arrogant, and aloof. He's here bleeding love for you.

In the Monty Python movie scene, they sang, "O, Lord, please don't burn us, don't kill or toast your flock." The tune sounded familiar. Then I remembered the words:

> The Church's one foundation
> Is Jesus Christ, her Lord;
> She is His new creation
> By water and the Word.
> From heaven He came and sought her

To be His holy bride;

With His own blood He bought her,

And for her life He died.[10]

Same tune, entirely different meaning.

May all your prayers have meaning, Word, way, truth, and life: Jesus.

Some of you might be saying, "You never answered my question. Should I pray every day?" The answer is, pray constantly. "No, I mean, should I have a quiet time every day? And is fifteen minutes long enough? Should I recite the Lord's Prayer verbatim, or use it as a pattern? Should I use the Lukan or Mathean version? And should I include the textual variant: 'For thine is the kingdom, and the power, and the glory'? While we're at it, preacher, you haven't answered my questions regarding this Sermon on the Mount . . .

- Should I join the military or not?
- Should I give money to every beggar?
- Should I fast?
- Can I divorce my adulterous wife?
- Should I turn the other cheek when my kids are in danger?"

Let me answer definitively: *I don't know* . . . hey, maybe you could ask your Father.

Ask in Jesus' name at the foot of the cross. Meditate on Him and speak through Him. You may say, "He doesn't answer me. He doesn't speak to me." Wrong. If you speak to Him, He has and does speak to you. If it doesn't seem that way to you, I suspect that's because when God speaks, all things move, even you, closer to Him.

10

TREASURE HUNTING

MATTHEW 6:16–24

MATTHEW 6:16: *And when you fast. . . .*

Apparently Jesus assumes His disciples will fast. There are different types of fasts: (1) religious fasts, (2) fasting from carbohydrates to lose weight, and (3) in much of the world, people fast because they have nothing to eat.

Perhaps we Americans ought to do some thinking about fasting, for we suffer from a national obsession with food, which takes the form of weight gain, bulimia, and anorexia.

It's important to remember that you really can't judge others on this topic very well, because you don't know their story or their body chemistry. Yet it seems strange that the church in America has made such a big deal out of smoking and drinking while at the same time serving *donuts* to people with *heart disease* on *Sunday morning!* (Okay . . . I confess.)

In Jesus' day, fasting wasn't about health but about focusing on God. But many of you aren't thinking about God. You're thinking about donuts. Just my talking about fasting makes you think about food—forbidden food!

Isn't it ironic that the growth of the American weight problem is directly parallel to the growth of the American diet industry? The more we try to diet, the bigger we get. The more we think about not eating, the more we do! The more I think, *No donuts, no donuts! No sweet, warm, fresh, Krispy Kreme donuts!* the hungrier I get for donuts.

It's almost as if when I want to do good, evil lies close at hand. And I don't understand my own actions, for I do not do what I want, but I do the very thing I hate (see Romans 7:15–21).

I think the diet industry and the religion industry have a lot in common.

The New Testament seems to be ambivalent about diets and fasting:

> Why do you submit to regulations, "Do not handle, Do not taste, Do not touch" (referring to things which all perish as they are used), according to human precepts and doctrines? These have indeed an appearance of wisdom in promoting rigor of devotion and self-abasement and severity to the body, but they are of no value in checking the indulgence of the flesh (Colossians 2:20–23).

That's the bad dieter's life verse! And we're all bad dieters. If you won't admit it, you're the worst.

Paul taught that there's a power within a diet or law to inspire *not* doing it. Law produces disobedience, shame, and addiction—zombies.

Folks do fast in the New Testament, but never as a law. Usually when *I* fast, I mostly just think about *food . . .* or worse, *myself.*

> MATTHEW 6:16–18: *And when you fast, do not look dismal, like the hypocrites, for they disfigure their faces that their fasting may be seen by men. Truly, I say to you, they have received their reward. But when you fast, anoint your head and wash your face, that your fasting may not be seen by men but by your Father who is in secret; and your Father who sees in secret will reward you.*

I *really* like donuts, but I have a far more dangerous addiction than that—approval. Some folks treasure food, and some treasure approval. If you beat your addiction to food with your addiction to approval, you're even more addicted.

Most people diet in order to look good, which is exactly why the Pharisees fasted: to look good religiously.

And we all fast, if not voluntarily, involuntarily. We all suffer loss. We all do without at times, so we're all tempted to use our fasting to get power over others and feed our ego. We use suffering in order to get sympathy and respect. It's a sweet treasure, but soon it rots and turns sour.

The problem with *acting* miserable is that you *become* miserable. The sympathy is sweet, but you can't dance, because it's not in the act. And besides—you're too aware of yourself to hear the music.

If you're religious like the Pharisees, it can really be sweet to let others know how much you suffer for Jesus.

"Oh, I'll bear my cross . . ."

"Oh, I'll just do without . . ."

"Oh, I suffer for Jesus . . ."

But then you're not really suffering for Jesus; you're suffering for your-*self* and making Jesus look like a drag. Your treasure is your*self*—your egotistical, religious, suffering *self.* And you need to fast from *that*, not food.

- Some people make a treasure of food.
- Some people make a treasure of not eating food.
- Some people make a treasure of feeling bad for eating food.
- Many make a treasure of all of the above, a cycle of addiction.

And all are poor dancers.

Here's the problem: If I say, "Don't think about food," you think about food. And if I say, "Don't think about your miserable self," you think about your miserable self. Then you think, *Gosh, I really* am *miserable . . . so miserable I can't stop thinking about my miserable self!*

Right now some of you can't stop thinking about your new car or your bank account, because you read ahead and realized Jesus was bringing up the topic of treasure in the Sermon on the Mount. And so your flesh cried out, "Batten down the hatches and guard the treasure!"

MATTHEW 6:19–21: *Do not lay up for yourselves treasures on earth, where moth and rust consume and where thieves break in and steal, but lay up for yourselves treasures in heaven, where neither moth nor rust consumes and where thieves do not break in and steal. For where your treasure is, there will your heart be also.*

The word *treasure* here is *thesauros*. Jesus says don't *"thesaurizo thesauros"* to yourself. "Don't treasure treasure to yourself." *Thesauros* is also translated "storehouse." *Thesauros* is the treasury and the treasure. The treasure is whatever you treasure in the treasury: food, clothes, money, image, ego.

When the average Jew heard "treasure," I imagine he thought of the gold and silver in the treasury in the temple. When the Israelites entered the Promised Land and when kings like David conquered enemies, much of the booty (gold and silver) was "dedicated" or "devoted" to the Lord and put in the treasury. When Solomon built the temple, all that devoted treasure was put in the temple treasury. Nobody seemed to understand *why* you put the treasure in the temple; they just knew the treasure was in the temple.

But the temple was destroyed in AD 70, just as Jesus said it would be. So where's the treasury now? What's the treasure? Jesus says, "Don't treasure to yourself treasure on earth. Treasure to yourself treasure in heaven."

Is earthly treasure the same as heavenly treasure? If so, then being godly is just good business—prudent selfishness; and heaven isn't full of new people but smart, selfish people. The world thinks that's true of our churches, and much of the time they may be right. But being a Christian must be more than just being a smart, selfish person as opposed to a dumb, selfish person.

"Treasure to yourself treasure in heaven." Where's heaven?

- Matthew 3:2: John the Baptist came preaching, "Repent, for the kingdom of heaven is at hand."
- Matthew 4:17: Jesus came preaching, "Repent, for the kingdom of heaven is at hand."
- Matthew 10:7: Jesus told the Twelve to preach, "The kingdom of heaven is at hand."
- Luke 17:21: Jesus says, "Behold, the kingdom of God is in the midst of you," or in the King James Version, "within you."
- Matthew 12: Jesus refers to the human heart as a treasury.

"The eye is the lamp of the body" [King James Version: "the light of the body"; New Living Translation: "lamp for your body"; The Message: "Your eyes are windows into your body"]. *So, if your eye is sound* [literally: "single" or "pure"—"Blessed are the pure in heart"] . . .

Jesus said, "Blessed are the pure in heart, for they shall see . . ." something.

MATTHEW 6:22–23: *So, if your eye is sound, your whole body will be full of light; but if your eye is not sound, your whole body will be full of darkness. If then the light in you is darkness, how great is the darkness!*

You could be totally blind!

Maybe the problem isn't our willpower but that we're blind. So it's not a matter of saying no to bad food but saying yes to good food (*really good food*, not tofu and bran muffins). It's not saying no to self as much as yes to somebody else.

Maybe the problem isn't saying no to earthly treasure but saying yes to heavenly treasure. Once you see it, you can drop earthly treasure like a bag of poop! Like Paul writes in Philippians 3, "I have suffered the loss of all things and count them as refuse [expletive, *skubula*] for the surpassing worth of knowing . . . (v. 8)" something else.

When Jesus fasted forty days and nights, and Satan tempted Him with bread, how did Jesus resist? "Bad, bad donut! I'm watching my figure." No! He said, "Man shall not live by bread alone, but by every word that proceeds from the mouth of God" (Matthew 4:4). *Every word.* Jesus had better comfort food than any Satan could offer.

In John 4, the disciples come to Jesus and say, "Rabbi, eat." In other words, "Jesus, you need to eat something." Jesus didn't say, "I'm a spiritual stud and I don't need to eat." He said, "I have some food you don't know about. My food is to do the will of My Father"—like He really could feast on heavenly food and see heavenly treasure *right here.*

So when Jesus loved lepers, Mary the Magdalene, Matthew the tax collector, the thief on the cross, and you and me, maybe it wasn't a discipline for Him. He could see *treasure* . . . treasure we can't see . . . hidden treasure.

Maybe *all of life* is like a *Highlights* Hidden Picture.

When I was a kid and my mom would take me to Dr. Shugart's office, the first thing I'd look for in the waiting room was the *Highlights* magazine, *not* because of Tommy Timber Toes but because of the Hidden Picture page.

The hidden pictures are treasure,
and you get to find them!

It didn't even matter what the picture page was:

- kids in a yard
- animals in a jungle
- someone sick or in prison
- even the last and the least of these

It didn't matter, because *Highlights* magazine revealed that there were hidden pictures—hidden meanings—treasure in whatever picture happened to be on that page. The joy was in finding the hidden pictures.

Some of you wonder why God doesn't give all the answers in life up front. I'm not sure, but I do know that if I turned to the Hidden Picture page and someone had already circled the pictures, I felt totally violated! The joy is in finding the treasure. And it's not just *kids* who love this.

Admit it. How many of you, when you take your kids to the doctor, see a *Highlights* magazine, and the first thing you do is turn to the Hidden Picture page? Admit it! Don't lie! The Hidden Picture page totally rocks! It's a treasure hunt!

Humans were made to hunt treasure. "It is the glory of God to conceal things, but the glory of kings is to search things out" (Proverbs 25:2). We're made to seek. Jesus also says that we're to seek something. "Seek ye first . . . ."

What if life is a *Highlights* Hidden Picture page?

You know, if you just have a *Highlights* Hidden Picture page, and you don't have a key, then you don't know what the treasure is that you're looking for. The picture will get boring really quickly.

This picture happens to be a teddy bear factory. Lots of religious people think the church is all about being a teddy bear factory: manufacturing uniform, happy, polyurethane-stuffed teddy bears.

Well, if you think that's the only meaning of the picture, the picture will get boring pretty quickly. But because you're a born treasure hunter, you might try to find meaning and treasure in the picture anyway, until you end up bored, angry, and addicted, trying to suck life out of a meaningless teddy bear factory, like an old Pharisee addicted to bad religion—the law.

But if someone comes along and shows you the key, then manufacturing teddy bears isn't the point. Finding treasure is the point.

Here's the irony: although the teddy bear factory is no longer the point, the teddy bear factory is far more interesting and valuable because it hides the point. The food is better, the gold is shinier, the sex is better, and church is more fun, because it's all about something else.

It's like "losing your life and finding your life,"
dying to one world and rising to another.

136

It's like finding a treasure in some old field,
and joyfully selling everything to get it.

I recently heard Henry Cloud share about a businessman he was counseling who was a developer. He said, "Dr. Cloud, all I do is build buildings, and it's all about money. I've got so much money and I'm so depressed. Maybe I should quit my job and go into the ministry . . . to find some meaning."

Soon after that Dr. Cloud counseled another businessman, also a developer. He said:

> Dr. Cloud, the only thing that keeps me going is my work. I find it so meaningful. I fly over an empty field, and do you know what I see? I see kids playing on playgrounds and families having picnics in the park that I'm going to build! I really don't care about the money, but when I design a house, I can picture Mom and Dad on the living room sofa. I care about getting all the angles just right, so they can see their daughter coming down the stairs dressed for her first prom. That's what keeps me going.[1]

Treasure.

Jesus said, "Treasure to yourself treasure in heaven." The kingdom of heaven is at hand. Our hearts are a treasury. In fact, we are the temple. So what's the treasure?

"In [Christ, the guy preaching the Sermon on the Mount] are hid all the treasures of wisdom and knowledge" (Colossians 2:3). What greater treasure could there be? Was there ever a more devoted, dedicated treasure than Jesus?

In Matthew 13:44, Jesus says, "The kingdom of heaven is like a treasure hidden in a field"—in dirt and ashes, like an earthen vessel. Listen closely to 2 Corinthians 4:3–7:

And even if our gospel is veiled [hidden], it is veiled [hidden] only to those who are perishing. In their case the god of this world has blinded the minds of the unbelievers, to keep them from seeing the light of the gospel of the glory of Christ, who is the likeness of God. For what we preach is not ourselves, but Jesus Christ as Lord, with ourselves as your servants for Jesus' sake. For it is the God who said, "Let light shine out of darkness," who has shone in our hearts to give the light of the knowledge of the glory of God in the face of Christ. But we have this treasure [this light] in earthen vessels. . . .

Jesus said, "I am the light" (John 8:12; 9:5). The light is in earthen vessels.

Can you see the treasure? If the eyes of your heart are pure, if the windows of your treasury are clear, the light shines in you. "Blessed are the pure in heart, for they shall see God."

> Jesus the Christ,
> perfect image of the Father,
> revelation of the Father,
> the light of the world,
> was sitting on the mount in front of the crowd.
>
> And they could not yet see Him,
> for they were not pure in heart;
> they were blind;
> they had not yet been cleansed by the blood;
> they had not yet seen the key.

What's the key?

Well, if all creation is a *Highlights* Hidden Picture page, then God is like the treasure, our hearts are the treasury, and God is in Christ, who is hiding in *all things.* He "fills all in all" (Ephesians 1:23).

Then wherever we looked, the key to finding God wouldn't be our discipline, our work; the key to treasure would be the cross of Christ. It would be the shape on the side of the paper that gave meaning to the whole picture, the shape that enlightened all things and revealed God, the treasure . . . almost as if God would "reconcile to himself all things . . . making peace by the blood of his cross" (Colossians 1:20), and that this was the "plan for the fulness of time" (Ephesians 1:10), ever since He drew the picture, creating all things through Him and for Him (Jesus)—the Word, the Meaning, the Key.

All life would be a treasure hunt. To live would be Christ, and "all things would be ours in Christ" (1 Corinthians 3:21; Philippians 1:21). Yet He (Jesus Christ and Him crucified) would be our treasure. We'd seek first Him, and "all these things shall be [ours]" (Matthew 6:33). And we could love all things without becoming addicted.

Robin Gunn writes:

We went to Open House tonight at the public elementary school. When Rachel's teacher met us, her eyebrows seemed to elevate slightly. She spoke kindly of our first grader but said she had some concerns. She then invited us to look at the artwork; we would see what she meant.

Dozens of brown paper treasure chests were tacked to the bulletin board. Each had a barreled top attached with a brad. On the front was printed, "A Real Treasure Would Be . . ." We walked over and began opening the lids to find Rachel's treasure and see why it so concerned the teacher.

As we peeked into each chest, we saw TVs and Nintendos, a few genies, heaps of gold coins, and a unicorn. Rachel's chest was in the very bottom corner. We had to stoop to open it. Inside, our daughter had drawn Christ, hanging on a cross with red drops of blood shaped like hearts dripping from his hands. She had completed the sentence, "A Real Treasure Would Be . . . Jesus."

"Do you see my concern?" the teacher asked, her arms folded across her chest.

"Yes," my husband agreed, "I see what you mean. The J is backward, isn't it?"[2]

Seeing Jesus and Him crucified turns the world upside down, turns the picture on its head. The better you see Him, the less important become TVs, Nintendos, heaps of gold coins, and even unicorns; the less important is food, yourself, and every other treasure in creation—less important yet even more interesting, because they hide Him Who already lives in your heart.

But now you know that even with the key it's sometimes hard to find the treasure in the Hidden Picture page. My mom was a genius at the *Highlights* Hidden Picture page. She'd always say, "Peter, when you can't find all the hidden pictures, turn the picture upside down."

When you turn the world upside down, it's not so easy to make out the old picture and old meanings. New meanings appear. So:

- Instead of eating so much, try not eating.
- Instead of exalting yourself, humble yourself.
- Instead of upward mobility, go for downward mobility.
- Instead of taking, start giving.
- Instead of rich in spirit, try poor in spirit. They're blessed.
- Instead of the pursuit of happiness, try mourning. Blessed are those who mourn.
- Instead of power, go for meekness.
- Instead of saving your life, try to lose it.

Pick up a cross. What could be more upside down than that? But maybe there you'll see Him. Maybe that's what the Christian disciplines are all about.

But remember: the treasure isn't an upside-down world. There are no points for just giving, praying, and fasting. There are a lot of old Pharisees, missionaries, do-gooders, and pastors who are cold and angry with God because they thought they got points for just turning their world upside down. But that's not the point. The point is seeing Jesus, the love of God poured out. That's the treasure. And that's the judgment.

What's your treasure?

MATTHEW 6:24: *No one can serve two masters; for either he will hate the one and love the other, or he will be devoted to the one and despise the other. You cannot serve God and mammon.*

A few years ago in Somalia, Jack Kelley, a reporter for *USA Today*, gave a starving boy a piece of grapefruit. Dead bodies lay all around. The boy was ravaged by worms, his belly distended, his skin wrinkled . . . he could barely stand. He was desperately hungry. Jack watched as he took the fruit and appeared to say thanks. He did not eat but began to walk toward his village. (They followed him in a way he couldn't see.)

When he entered his village, there on the ground was a smaller little boy. They figured he was dead. His eyes were completely glazed over. It turned out that this was the first boy's younger brother. The older brother knelt down, bit off a piece of grapefruit, chewed it, then opened up his brother's mouth, put the grapefruit in, and worked his brother's jaw up and down.

They learned the older brother had been doing this for two weeks. A couple days later the older brother died of malnutrition, and the younger brother lived.[3]

> Does that picture bother you?
> Do you want to turn the channel?
> Are you saying, "That's sick! It has no meaning . . .
> I can't look!"?
> *Hold on.* Take a look at the key.
> Do you see treasure?

If you really see treasure—not just in your mind, but where the light shines deep into your treasury (your heart)—if you really see treasure, you just might sell everything and go looking for more, looking for Jesus.

On the night He was betrayed, knowing that the Father had given all things into His hands, our Big Brother took bread. And having given thanks, He broke it saying, "This is my body given for you. Do this in remembrance of me." After supper He took the cup saying, "This is the cup of the new covenant in my blood, shed for the forgiveness of sins. Drink of it, all of you, in remembrance of me."

Treasure.

Now, some of you may be thinking, *I hate my life. I hate my picture. It feels like everything in my world has been turned upside down.* Well, sometimes my mom would take the *Highlights* Hidden Picture page out of my hand, turn it upside down, and say, "See?" God is willing to turn your world upside down to help you see Him.

The day will come when you receive everything back in and through Christ. I believe Jesus was all over that boy in Somalia—in him, around him, through him—and together they are dancing in eternity, because they know each other. They are treasure. Christ and His body, His bride, His little brother.

So if you're in the darkest of all places, don't shut down. Keep seeking. There is treasure! You are about to see the heart of the living God.

There will come a day when God will finally and ultimately turn your world upside down. You will die, and then you'll see Him, right side up.

You're a treasure hunter only because Jesus was a treasure hunter first. It is the glory of the King to search you out. He's treasuring treasure in heaven, and the treasure is *you.* He sold everything to get you.

11

PSYCHED OUT

MATTHEW 6:25–34

MATTHEW 6:25–34: *Therefore I tell you, do not be anxious about your life, what you shall eat or what you shall drink, nor about your body, what you shall put on. Is not life more than food, and the body more than clothing? Look at the birds of the air: they neither sow nor reap nor gather into barns, and yet your heavenly Father feeds them. Are you not of more value than they? And which of you by being anxious can add one cubit to his span of life? And why are you anxious about clothing? Consider the lilies of the field, how they grow; they neither toil nor spin; yet I tell you, even Solomon in all his glory was not arrayed like one of these. But if God so clothes the grass of the field, which today is alive and tomorrow is thrown into the oven, will he not much more clothe you, O men of little faith? Therefore do not be anxious, saying "What shall we eat?" or "What shall we drink?" or "What shall we wear?" For the Gentiles seek all these things; and your heavenly Father knows that you need them all. But seek first his kingdom and his righteousness, and all these things shall be yours as well. Therefore do not be anxious about tomorrow, for tomorrow will be anxious for itself. Let the day's own trouble be sufficient for the day.*

That sounds really encouraging . . . at first. You think, *I can just kick back and blow stuff off.* At first it's encouraging, yet I'm still supposed to "pick up a cross and follow."

At first it's encouraging,
but then you start worrying . . . about worrying.
At first it's encouraging,
but then you watch *Animal Planet.*

- "Consider the birds . . ."? Jesus, many species don't live too long, and they work really hard, and many that *do* live long suffer quite a bit. "Consider the birds . . ."? I immediately thought of the woodpecker I shot with a BB gun when I was a kid. I considered it (stared at it—its tongue was hanging out!) . . . it really made me anxious.
- "Consider the lilies of the field . . ." Okay, I just stepped on one. And did you notice deer eat the lilies of the field? Then it gets worse. It appears that Jesus *does* notice. He even says it:
- "Consider the grass, so beautifully clothed . . . before it's thrown into the oven and burned. Therefore don't be anxious." Gosh, Jesus, I don't want to be burned.

If I were a bird, a flower, or some grass, I'd be so stressed out about dying that I doubt I could do any living. To live in this world, to live in time, is to constantly die. Every moment we die to the last moment.

Jesus says, "Don't be anxious about your life, what you will eat, drink, and wear. Is not life more than food and the body more than clothing?"

For most of human history, that question was rhetorical. Folks would laugh and say, "Of *course* life is more than food!" For the first time, in the twentieth century, a significant portion of humanity began to say, "Well, actually, modern science has shown that life *isn't* much more than food. Actually, Jesus, we now understand that the only real things are things you can touch, feel, and measure with our advanced scientific instruments in a controlled environment."

That view is called empiricism or materialism. It's a corruption of science. In that view, birds exist not because of a loving Creator but because of a violent, desperate struggle not to die. Life is explained by death.

In the twentieth century, materialism gave birth to the Third Reich and communism. Theology was replaced by psychology. Theology has to do with powers beyond our control, powers that cannot be reduced and studied in a lab, and thus it has to do with powers that don't exist.

In the twentieth century, if you really had a problem, you wouldn't go to a theologian but a psychologist or psychiatrist.

In the twentieth century, pastors stopped studying theology and began studying psychology. That's an oversimplification, but maybe not as much as you think.

Someone said, "Modern man has so many psychological problems because they're the only kind of problems he's allowed to have."

Now, pre-modern man didn't deny psychiatry and the chemical functioning of the brain. (Every one of them knew that a couple pints of beer could change your psychic state.) Jesus knew that. He just believed there was much more than that.

A communist textbook defined *kiss* in the following way: "A kiss is the approach of two pairs of lips, with reciprocal transmission of microbes and carbon dioxide." Not that that's not true, but perhaps there's more to a kiss. Perhaps a kiss hides treasure. Perhaps life is more than food or drink.

Freud considered life and "the lilies"—the grass. "All flesh is grass, and all beauty is its glory, like the flower of the field. The grass withers, the flower fades." That's Isaiah 40:6–7. Jesus knew that verse when He said, "Consider the lilies." Freud considered and concluded that we're all secretly motivated by a repressed fear of death, and I think he's right.

Maybe abnormal psychology is just abnormal repression . . . and normal psychology is just socially acceptable repression.

Have you ever wondered, "What's a psychologist or one of those state-funded grief counselors supposed to say at the prospect of impending death?"

> "We now understand your grief cycle and the function of dopamine in your brain. Hope that helps."
>
> "Thanks, Doc. But *we're still gonna die!*"
>
> "Repress that thought! . . . or you won't be able to live."

Jesus says, "Don't be anxious about your life."
Several Greek words get translated as the English word *life:*

- *Bios,* from which we get *biology.*
- *Zoe,* from which we get *zoology.*
- *Psyche,* from which we get *psychology. Psyche* also is translated *soul* or *mind* or *being.*

Jesus says, "Is not your psyche more than food? Don't be anxious about your psyche (life). Stop taking your psyche so seriously!" What kind of psychologist would Jesus make? Imagine:

> "My goodness, you really *are* depressed. Well, stop taking your depression so seriously. You need to die, and I'll help you. This here is a cross; the nails go here and here."

We want to yell, "Stop it, Jesus! You could do severe psychic damage!"

Perhaps He'd say, "Yes . . . I'm aiming for *total* psychic damage. To quote Myself in Matthew 16:25, 'Whoever would save his life [psyche] will lose it, and whoever would lose his [psyche] for my sake will find it.'"

Yikes! Well, let's talk theology rather than psychology.

Jesus raises the question: "Why do we worry about life?"
Answer: Because long ago in a garden we lost it.
"Why do we worry about food?"
Answer: Because long ago in a garden we ate some bad food, and the day we ate it, we died.
"Why do we worry about clothes and fashion?" (That is a mystery psychologically.)
Answer: Because theologically, long ago in a garden we ate and died and lost our glory and tried to hide in shame. So we wear clothes.

Long ago in a garden we trusted a snake and traded the person who is good for the knowledge of the good. We wanted our own *logos* more than God's *Logos*. We wanted our own meaning more than God's Meaning. We wanted our psyche-*logos* more than the Theo-*Logos*—the God Word—the Word of God—Jesus.

Long ago in a garden we got *psyched out*, worrying, "Is God really good?" We got psyched out of life, heaven, and the great dance.

Maybe our anxieties are so strong and our addictions so powerful because they're:

- not really about food but *heavenly* food;
- not really about drink but *heavenly* wine;
- not really about clothes or fashion but *glory* that lasts forever and doesn't fade.

Maybe we really are motivated by and in bondage to a repressed fear of death, so scared we can barely live. Maybe we're already dead—zombies. Perhaps our anxieties are so strong and our addictions are so powerful because we're trying to get back to a garden. We're trying to find a kingdom—an eternal kingdom, but it is not of this world.

Jesus came preaching, "The kingdom of heaven is at hand." He has just said, "Store up treasure for yourselves in heaven." Now we read Matthew 6:25: "Therefore I tell you, do not be anxious about your life [psyche]." (We forgot to ask what the "therefore" is there for. It's there because of what came immediately before.)

In the last chapter, we postulated that all our reality is like the *Highlights* Hidden Picture page. It really doesn't matter what the picture is on the page: a teddy bear factory, kids in a yard, someone sick or in prison, the last and the least of these. What matters is that it hides treasure. The key on the side of the page tells you what the treasure is. At first you can't see the treasure in the picture, because it's a part of this other pattern, this other paradigm. You could call this picture or your initial perception of this picture your *psyche*.

When you lose your psyche (by turning the page upside down), other meanings appear. They were there all along, just hidden by your psyche.

If you have your psyche and no key, the picture gets boring and depressing, and you might become addicted to it, that is, desperately trying to suck meaning out of meaningless things. But if someone shows you the key (the meaning), then you can lose the picture and find the treasure in it. Here is the great irony: though you lose the old picture, you receive it back with new meaning. The food is better, the wine is better, the clothes are better . . . because they're all about something else. And you can love them without becoming addicted. You've "lost your psyche and found it with new meaning."

We postulated that all reality is like a *Highlights* Hidden Picture page. God and His kingdom are the treasure, and our hearts are the treasury. Jesus Christ crucified is the key. That is, His cross is the shape on the side of the picture that gives meaning to all things. Jesus is the light, the revelation of God. When the eyes of our heart are clear, He shines into our hearts and gives us the kingdom, and treasure is stored in heaven—heavenly treasure that does not rot or die.

Now, let's take that idea and apply time. Then your life, your psyche, is a string of *Highlights* Hidden Picture pages—a *movie*. Every picture, every frame, changes constantly, yet the key—the light that illumines the picture—is always the same.

The psyche changes, but the light remains the same. It's just like physicists tell us, "Time and even matter are somehow relative to light." Light is the constant. Jesus said, "I am the light." Paul writes, "When anything is exposed by the light it becomes visible, for anything that becomes visible is light" (Ephesians 5:13).

The light (Jesus) turns ordinary things into eternal treasures. In every temporal picture shines the eternal light. And if we don't close our eyes in fear or anxiety or shame, but let Jesus shine on our psyche (our lives) and into our hearts (our treasure), the treasures become eternal. We store up eternal treasure in heaven.

- We see a cup and a child. The light shines, we give the cup to the child in love, and the picture becomes eternal.
- We see a flower. The light shines, we give thanks, and it somehow becomes eternal.
- We're abandoned and confused. The light shines, we have faith, and faith is eternal.
- We despair. The light shines, and we have hope.
- We're beaten and persecuted for righteousness' sake. The light shines, and we learn to love like Jesus. Faith, hope, and love abide.
- We sin . . . really badly. We murder the only perfect man who ever lived. The light shines, we surrender, and we see the heart of God.

If you've ever wondered why space is so wide and time is so long—why there are so many moments—I suspect it is because God is so good and glorious that in order to show Himself to us—who are so limited and weak—He has to reveal bits and pieces of Himself spread throughout all space and time. Yet His glory in each moment is always revealed by His one light, Christ. As a movie is many frames revealed by one light (the projector bulb) revealing the story, so all space and time—every moment—is revealed by Christ proclaiming the glory of God: the greatest story ever told, the redemption of creation through the slaughtered Lamb on the throne.

Now we live in the story encountering one frame at a time. We have faith that the story is good because we've met the author and the plot: Jesus. One day, like the end of a movie, all the frames will come together and we'll "see" the whole story—provided that we've invited the light who is the meaning to shine on every frame. I imagine heaven is like an implosion of glory where all space and time come together in Jesus and reveal the glory of God. You realize the eternal city, the New Jerusalem, is literally constructed of treasure stored up in heaven while we walked on earth (twelve apostles, twelve tribes, the jewels on the priests' gowns . . . the nations gathered in). We must have seen the New Jerusalem when the light shone on the old Jerusalem. Perhaps we see the new world hidden in this old world whenever we let the light shine.

Well now, you see that this old material world—food, clothes, birds, grass—is always changing. To live in time is to constantly die. If all your life is no more than food and clothing, all your treasure will die, rot, and fade away. And *you* will die, rot, and fade away.

It's no wonder we're anxious! We were made to seek eternal treasure (the kingdom). But all our treasure dies, including ourselves. We confuse our temporal psyche with the eternal treasure and get neurotic, psychotic, and stuck in a moment—a temporal moment. We can't grow, we can't change, we can't live, and we can't die . . . because we're already dead. We've stopped dancing, paralyzed by fear.

Perhaps we can see treasure and miss the eternal somehow, because we make the treasure temporal. That is, we don't store it in heaven but yank it from heaven and treasure it (try to store it) here. But then the treasure rots. It has no "meaning." And then we stop dancing, for we've idolized one dance step, one moment in time, one frame of the picture. Then we lose faith in the story unfolding in all the pictures. We lose the dance, stuck on one dance step.

If you try to hang on to the treasure in time, you make it temporal and you miss the treasures God has in the next frame of the picture. We miss the treasure *now* trying to re-create treasures from the past in the future. When we're burdened by the past and worried about the past in our future, we miss the treasure *now*. We miss the story now, the plot now, the meaning now, eternity now.

Einstein said that if you traveled at the speed of light, all times, all pictures would be present in an eternal now. Jesus said, "I am the light." In His resurrected state, all pictures are eternally present to Him. "He who believes in the Son has eternal life" (John 3:36). *Now* is the point your time touches eternity; *now* you have faith; *now* you surrender to the plot; *now* you surrender to the meaning (the *logos*); *now* you enter the great dance; *now* you store up treasure in heaven.

The evil one tempts us to live in the past or the future, because that's not living. Eternal life is *now*. Sometimes we're stuck in the future with anxiety; sometimes we're stuck in the past with fear. In fact, ever since the Garden, we've been stuck in a bad picture. We've been *psyched out*.

When you first saw the *Highlights* Hidden Picture page, you saw a teddy bear factory, and you saw a teddy bear factory because pictures from the past gave meaning to the picture in the present. All those pictures in your past make up your life, that is, your psyche. Your psyche is how you, on your own, give meaning to every picture.

Have you ever met someone who responded to you in a totally bizarre manner so that you realized they're not even relating to you? They're relating to a picture in their past. They don't even *know* you. They can't *see* you.

Bono, from the music group U2, sings, "You've got to get yourself together; you got stuck in a moment and you can't get out of it."[1]

That's Satan's strategy: to get us "stuck in a moment" so we can't live *now*, can't dance *now*, can't have eternal life *now*. This is eternal life, knowing God and Jesus whom He sent. I can only know a person *now*. I can know *about* a person in the past or in the future, but I can only dance with a person *now*, trust a person *now*. I commune with Jesus *now*, and He makes me live *now*. The beast in Revelation 17:8 is he who "was and is not and is to come." Maybe that means he only has power in our past and our future. I'm convinced Satan's only real power is to psych us out so we won't look to Jesus *now*!

Jesus says, "Stop worrying about your psyche. Lose your psyche for my sake and you will find it. The good shepherd lays down his psyche for the sheep" (see John 10:11).

Jesus died and rose from the dead to give new meaning to all our pictures, to give us His psyche—His life. He can still give meaning to old pictures. The light can still illumine old frames. He makes "all things new" (Revelation 21:5).

When ritual abuse survivors are stuck in a past moment, they are so terrified they are often unwilling to look at the picture of that moment of abuse, and are too ashamed to invite Jesus into the picture. It's repressed, yet it controls all their present. In prayer they can go back to the memory and ask Jesus to reveal the true meaning, the hidden picture. Often He does it with visions, and the horrifying pictures are transformed into treasure and then stored in heaven. And the person is free to live in the moment now. Their psychology is transformed into theology, for it no longer has their meaning but God's meaning.

I've seen it in miraculous ways involving demons, angels, and visions, yet it's exactly what happens . . .

- whenever you forgive;
- whenever you confess;
- whenever you repent;
- whenever you receive forgiveness;
- whenever you surrender a moment to Jesus.

Jesus, the Theo-*Logos*, gives it new meaning. He transforms all our pictures and gives us new life.

Many of my friends are Christian psychologists whom I highly respect. I have no problems with them. I just think they should be called *theologists*, because what they do is take troubled psyches and help people apply Jesus.

They turn psychologies (self-meanings) into theologies (God-meanings).

They help people see treasure by helping people see Jesus. And so they help people live *now*.

Do you believe Jesus *now*?

If you're worried, anxious, and fearful, your psychology has a different meaning than Jesus, and you've been psyched out. Obviously, we've *all* been psyched out, for we worry about food and clothes and nourishment and covering our egos.

We worry about our lives.

Jesus came to give theo-*logos* to all our psycho-*logos*.

Worried about food?

Jesus says, "I am the bread of life broken for you. Take and eat."

Worried about drink?

Jesus says, "My blood is drink indeed. Drink of it all of you for the forgiveness of sins."

Worried about clothing?

Jesus clothes you in Himself, the glory of God.

Worried about your life—your psyche?

Jesus says, "Lose it and I'll give you mine—eternal life."

So He sat on the hillside two thousand years ago, and they didn't know Him. They all left Him when He was crucified. They were psyched out!

A cross is some pretty psycho-*logos*. Apply Jesus, and you have theo-*logos*—a whole new meaning and the glory of God. Jesus said to His disciples, "I am with you always" (Matthew 28:20). Can you see Him? I mean by that, do you believe? Or are you too psyched out?

If you give Jesus your life, you give Him your always. He shines on your past and your future and frees you to live now. He forgives your sins and transforms the meaning of your history from shame to grace. He's sovereign over your future, transforming fear into hope. He frees you to live now.

A monk was being chased by a man-eating tiger. He raced to the edge of a cliff and spotted a rope hanging over the edge of the cliff. He grabbed it and began climbing down the rope out of reach of the tiger.

He looked down and saw jagged rocks five hundred feet below. He looked up and saw the tiger waiting above. Just then, just beyond his reach, he saw two mice begin to nibble the rope. What to do? His past was chasing him, his future was death. He saw a strawberry within arm's reach, growing on the face of the cliff. He plucked it, ate it, and exclaimed, "That's the best strawberry I've ever tasted!"[2]

Stuck in his past or anxious about his future, he would have missed his treasure *now*. Your treasure is Jesus *now*. "Fine," you say. "But the monk on the cliff dies!" So? Is that a bad moment?

"'All flesh is like grass. . . . The grass withers, and the flower falls, but the word of the Lord abides for ever.' That word is the good news which was preached to you. . . . You have been born anew . . . through the living and abiding word of God" (1 Peter 1:24–25, 23).

"He . . . partook of [our] nature, that through death he might destroy him who has the power of death, that is, the devil, and deliver all those who through fear of death were subject to lifelong bondage" (Hebrews 2:14–15).

So consider the birds, the lilies, and the grass. They don't fear death! Birds toil and labor and die . . . but that doesn't stop them from singing. Lilies and grass get trampled and thrown into the fire, but that doesn't stop them from displaying God's glory. Birds, lilies, and grass don't get psyched out. They have no choice but to trust their Maker.

Jesus did have a choice—a psyche. Let's consider Jesus. There would come a day when He would die for the sins of the world, a day when He would be stripped of glory far greater than Solomon's, a day when He'd be cast into the fire. Yet He trusted His father and let "each day's trouble be sufficient for the day" (Matthew 6:34). I believe Jesus lived each moment.

- When someone told a joke, I bet He laughed loudest.
- When someone told a story, I bet He was the best listener.
- When the sun shone and the rains came, I bet He enjoyed them the most.
- When He ate a strawberry, I bet He tasted it with the greatest joy.
- When someone was injured, I bet He most fully felt their pain.
- When He went to a funeral, I bet He wept the deepest tears.
- When they danced in the courtyard of the temple, I bet His dance was the best.

- And when His Father whispered, "Son, today's the day," He poured out His heart, picked up His cross, and trusted His Father unto death. And now death is swallowed up in victory.

I had lunch with my dad about a year before he died. He was eighty-three then. He'd been burned and trampled, and his flower was falling. But he still sang his Maker's praise and displayed His glory. I know he'd been psyched out at times, but God is bigger than his psyche and used all of it anyway.

I asked Dad about a class he wanted to teach in church. It was entitled "How to Die." He said, "Oh, Peter, I don't know if I have anything to say." I said, "Dad, just that you're willing to talk! We're all so afraid of the day we die that we can't live *now.*" I said, "Just don't plan a graduation ceremony."

I think I know the lesson: how you die is how you live . . . without worry, trusting Jesus. In fact, the last frame, the last picture, is now the best picture, for all the picture is swallowed up by treasure and life! All our transient psychology becomes eternal theology. We are the fullness of Him who fills all in all.

On that day I'll be there and our family will be there. His grandkids and World War II buddies will be there. Bomb shelter Bible studies will be there, and folks that were sick and in prison will be there. Our cabin site in Frisco will be there. Birds will be there and lilies will be there and grass will be there. Bread and wine and the finest clothes and good strawberries . . . all those treasures he stored in heaven while on earth . . . he'll get them all back, and they'll all be in Jesus. They're all stories of Jesus, places he's seen Jesus.

He'll see Jesus and realize he's seen Jesus wherever he walked in faith . . . even here.

So what are you so worried about?

Some months later my father died (or began to really live). He never taught the course on dying. He *was* the course on dying. Everyone went to see him in the hospital, in the nursing home, and at his condominium where he died. Dying is hard, but Dad died in great faith. I served him his last meal. It was communion.

His funeral was a massive party. As the choir closed the service with the "Hallelujah Chorus," a few people had visions of Jesus standing at the front of the church, and next to Jesus stood my dad.

One friend saw huge gates appear behind Jesus and my dad. They opened, and she heard "all heaven" joining in with our choir (or maybe our choir joined them). Whatever the case, I believe all my dad's moments were coming together in a "weight of glory beyond all comparison." As the song came to a close, Jesus and my dad turned and walked through the gates behind them. Dad was home.

You may say: "That's some weird psychology."
Maybe so, but it's great theology.

So what do you want?
Psycho-*logos* or theo-*logos*?

In Jesus' name, don't get psyched out.

12

JUDGMENT AND PEARL CASTING

MATTHEW 7:1–6

MATTHEW 7:1: *Judge not, that you be not judged.*

I got a call from the stated clerk of our presbytery (the governing body for our local church). Cecil is a great guy and needed to talk to me about several things. At the end he said, "Ah, Peter, I suppose I should pass this on. I got a call from a man in North Carolina who was disturbed because the presbytery meeting is to be held at your church. His daughter had been to your church and heard you use a profanity [what he considered a "bad word"] in a sermon."

He called from North Carolina!

We religious people love to judge. If you see life or holiness as a competition (as did the scribes and Pharisees), judgment can be helpful, because the more fault you find in others, the better you look in comparison. If God grades on a curve, you should be pretty excited when someone else gets a bad grade!

Judging helps us compete, and it's a good way to get revenge. Just by telling you that story, I can get revenge and pass judgment on the man from North Carolina as a culturally conditioned and biblically immature Pharisee. I can judge him for judging me and use Scripture to justify a vengeful heart.

Competition, vengeance, and avoidance of pain.

Judgment is a great way to avoid pain. Why would I even *listen* to someone I've judged a Pharisee? Why would I even care? Sometimes, as in war, it really helps to judge a person as an evil enemy rather than a dad or husband before you shoot them.

Conflict in life is inevitable, but judgment helps you guard your own heart and avoid pain.

According to Paul Harvey, a young pastor was giving a sermon when he asked the rhetorical question, "Has anyone lived in such a manner that he now has no enemies?" Immediately an old guy in the back shot his hand up in the air. A little shocked, the pastor stopped and said, "Well, tell us, sir. How have you lived in such a way that you have no enemies?" The old guy stood up and said, "I outlived all them SOBs!"[1]

Well, that may work when the other people are dead. But it also works when they are alive. If you label all your enemies as SOBs, you may have to put up with some inconvenience, but you can guard your heart from pain. For why would you care what an SOB thinks of you anyway?

And now, if you're worried that this chapter will be convicting, you can guard your own heart from any painful truth that might be conveyed here by simply judging me as profane for using profanity or an abbreviation of a profanity.

The Jews were certainly taught to judge profane things. A pig was profane, and a dog was the most despised animal. Jews didn't think of Benji or Lassie when they thought of dogs. And a pig wasn't just sloppy, but unholy and demonic. To judge someone as a pig or dog was incredibly severe.

MATTHEW 7:1–6: *Judge not, that you be not judged. For with the judgment you pronounce you will be judged, and the measure you give will be the measure you get. Why do you see the speck that is in your brother's eye, but do not notice the log that is in your own eye? Or how can you say to your brother, "Let me take the speck out of your eye," when there is the log in your own eye? You hypocrite, first take the log out of your own eye, and then you will see clearly to take the speck out of your brother's eye. Do not give dogs what is holy; and do not throw your pearls before swine, lest they trample them under foot and turn to attack you.*

Does Jesus ever confuse you? He says, "Judge not," and then refers to certain people as pigs and dogs. In a few more verses, He says, "Beware of wolves in sheep's clothes," and He tells us how to know them, that is, discern them or judge them.

The word *judge* in Greek has a wide range of meaning and many different forms. This form alone, *krino*, is translated not only as *judge* but also *condemn, separate, consider, determine, decide* . . . even *esteem.* Most scholars would say the kind of judging Jesus refers to here is condemnation. "Condemn not that you may not be condemned." That's at least true, for there is no condemnation in Christ Jesus. So if you're in Christ, you won't condemn. It means at least that but maybe more.

In John 7:24, Jesus commands us to "judge with right judgment."

In Luke 7:43, Jesus tells a guy who answers a multiple-choice question, "You have judged rightly"—esteemed correctly.

In Matthew 7:1, He says, "Judge not, that you be not judged."

Has anybody ever *not* judged? Would anybody ever *want* to be judged?

When you pick a baby-sitter, you judge.

When you vote, you judge.

To live as a human being is to judge.

To say "I decided to follow Jesus" is to judge.

Søren Kierkegaard writes, "Decision is the awakening to the eternal . . . . In the end, the archenemy of decision is cowardice. Cowardice is constantly at work to break off the good agreement of decision with eternity."[2] That is, a good decision, a good judgment, is a surrender to eternity. A good judgment is a surrender to Jesus.

Well, that's a bit deep. But whatever the case, "the judgment you give is the judgment you get." Gosh, would anybody ever *want* to be judged—not condemned, but judged?

Psalm 7:8: David, the man after God's own heart, cries out, "Judge me, O LORD."

Psalm 67:4: "Let the nations be glad and sing for joy, for thou dost judge the peoples with equity."

I have a friend who was accused of a terrible crime. I believe he was innocent, but I was scared spitless for him. It was his word against another's, and a human judge had to decide. I *longed* for righteous judgment.

To an oppressed peasant in occupied Israel, the thought of God judging instead of some Roman must have been a thrilling idea.

I bet Paul actually *longed* for the judgments of Jesus when he wrote:

But with me it is a very small thing that I should be judged by you or by any human court. I do not even judge myself. I am not aware of anything against myself, but I am not thereby acquitted. It is the Lord who judges me. (1 Corinthians 4:3–4)

Do you hear Paul? "O Lord, I'm counting on You to judge me—sort me out." Paul acknowledges something tremendously important. He says, "I'm not aware of anything against me, but I'm not thereby acquitted." That is, "I'm blind to my own garbage."

People say, "What are your weaknesses?" and I struggle. It's not that I can't name some, but I take it as a matter of faith that my biggest weaknesses are the ones I can't see . . . like a big old *log* in my eye!

If you really had a log in your eye, it would hurt. But you couldn't see it. You'd be totally blind to it.

I have a good friend who almost drank himself to death a few weeks ago. He's wrecked his marriage and his business, abused his family and friends. I think he's miserable. But his heart can't see his addiction!

Psychologists say people develop defense mechanisms—neuroses, psychoses, personality disorders—all as a way of avoiding painful truth. I think they're right; I just think we all have them—bad psycho-logy to hide from good theo-logy. Mechanisms for avoiding the truth.

> *I AM is the truth.*
> *Jesus is the truth.*

He is a living and active Word that "cuts to the division of soul and spirit, joint and marrow, able to judge the thoughts and intentions of the heart" (see Hebrews 4:12).

He is the truth about truth.

He is truth crucified by us, the painful truth regarding us.

When I hide from truth, I hide from Christ and Him crucified. I hide from life, imprisoned in death and lies. And I *need* someone to judge me, for "the truth will set me free."

I think the meanest thing you can do to an alcoholic is not judge his alcoholism but enable it. Perhaps the meanest thing you can do to a sinner you love is not judge his sin but enable it. Certainly one of the meanest things a parent can ever do to a child is never judge him, never correct him, never discipline him. The Lord disciplines those He loves and will not leave their souls in hell.

In Stephen Lawhead's novel *Merlin*, Myrddin has lived for years in a cave in the woods, insane with fear and guilt. Finally a visitor arrives. Myrddin describes it:

"Myrddin," the voice was soft as a mother's crooning to her babe, "you will be healed. But first we must cut out the disease that poisons your soul."

"I am happy as I am," I gasped. Breath came hard to me. The wind howled now, and cold rain fell in stinging sheets upon us.

Annwas Adeniawc reached out his bony hand and touched my arm. "No one is happy in hell, Myrddin. You have carried your burden long enough. It is time to lay it down."[3]

If judgment is cutting a lie from my soul, I think I *want* to be judged. Humility is surrendering your heart to a just judgment.

In *The Chronicles of Narnia*, Eustace does some terrible things and turns into a dragon. He tries to scratch off the scales but can't scratch deep enough. A great lion appears, and Eustace describes what happens:

Then the lion said . . . "You will have to let me undress you." I was afraid of his claws, I can tell you, but I was pretty nearly desperate now. So I just lay flat down on my back to let him do it.

The very first tear he made was so deep that I thought it had gone right into my heart. And when he began pulling the skin off, it hurt worse than anything I've ever felt. The only thing that made me able to bear it was just the pleasure of feeling the stuff peel off. You know—if you've ever picked the scab of a sore place. It hurts like billy—oh but it is such fun to see it coming away.[4]

Once I was so judged it hurt like nothing I've ever felt. But if it was pain, it was the most exquisite pain I've ever experienced. If that's judgment, I'll scheme to avoid it, but I do want more, for I hate living in hell.

Let's put it this way: if I have a speck in my eye or a log in my eye, I want someone to take it out. But not just *anyone* . . . .

Jesus said, "First take the log out of your own eye, then you can see clearly to take the speck out of your brother's eye." I want the speck out of my eye. That is, I *do* want to be judged. Well then, *how* do I want to be judged? And by whom? I want to be judged by:

1. Someone who really knows me, not from a distance, but someone who has lived in my skin.
2. Someone who knows my sin. I want someone who has had a log in their eye, not now, but in the past. According to Jesus, the *only* way to take a speck out of another's eye is to admit you have or did have a log in your own eye. He assumes everybody has.

In his book *Church: Why Bother?*, Philip Yancey tells the story of the beginning of Alcoholics Anonymous. Bill Wilson had battled his alcoholism, staying sober for six months. One day in depression he walked into a bar thinking, *I need a drink.* Then it hit him: *No, I don't need a drink; I need another alcoholic.* That is, "I need a log eye." Yancey writes, "Church is a place I can say, unashamedly, 'I don't need to sin. I need another sinner.'"[5]

I want to be judged by someone who knows me and knows my sin and doesn't *want* to judge me, because they feel my pain.

3. Someone who doesn't condemn me. They judge me because they want to set me free. They want me to dance.
4. Someone willing to die for me. And if I were to die, they'd die with me.

Very few perfectly match these criteria. Some come closer than the rest: my wife Susan, my mom and dad, my small group, some close friends. I need them to judge me, and I need to confess to them.

"In the confession of concrete sins," writes Dietrich Bonhoeffer, "the old man dies a painful, shameful death before the eyes of a brother. Because this humiliation is so hard, we continually scheme to avoid it. Yet in the deep mental and physical pain of humiliation before a brother we experience our rescue and salvation."[6]

Next verse, Matthew 7:6: "Do not give dogs what is holy."

What is the holy thing?
And who are the dogs?

The deepest part of the temple was the holy of holies. *We* are the temple. And the sacrifices in the temple were holy. According to David in Psalm 51:17, the sacrifice the Lord desires is a broken spirit and contrite heart. That is, confession from the depths of our hearts. Perhaps the holy thing is logs and splinters removed from eyes and given to Jesus to be borne on His cross.

In Psalm 22:16, David prophesies the death of Jesus saying, "Dogs are round about me; . . . they have pierced my hands and feet. . . ." In Philippians 3:2, Paul writes, "Look out for the dogs, look out for the evil-workers, look out for those who mutilate the flesh." He's talking about circumcision and scribes and Pharisees: religious people who trust their religiosity. These people don't value your confession! Don't give them what's holy!

"Don't cast your pearls before swine." A pearl begins as a pain in an oyster's gut. It's a speck lodged in the depth of an oyster. But God wraps around the speck a treasure, so that what was a painful speck in the gut of an oyster, when taken out and surrendered, is a pearl.

Recently at our midweek service, my friend Kate saw a picture in worship and shared it with the congregation. She said:

I saw a huge oyster shell that was open; a piece of dirt then fell in. I then saw a drop of Jesus' blood fall on that piece of dirt. A pearl began to form that got bigger and bigger and bigger. It ended up a huge, pure, white pearl with no sign of the dirt that had started the process.

I believe the Lord is speaking to us about forgiveness, calling us to be reconciled to Him and to the people in our lives. My sense is He's saying, "These irritations as you rub each other are how I transform you into My pure pearls. As you allow My blood to cover the dirt in your own heart, I use the irritations, the conflicts in your life, to mold you and transform you. Receive My forgiveness so you can forgive each other and reveal the treasure in you: Jesus, My Pearl of Great Price."

Later in Matthew 13:45–46, Jesus says, "The kingdom of heaven is like a merchant in search of fine pearls, who, on finding one pearl of great value, went and sold all that he had and bought it." I believe the pearl merchant is Jesus, King of heaven, who sold all He had and surrendered His life to buy us—His church—His pearl.

Jesus is the pearl merchant, but He's also the pearl. His church is His body and His bride. The pearl is Christ in us.

We are the "fullness of him who fills all in all" (Ephesians 1:23)—the people of God who surround the wound of the cross on which the Prince of Glory bears our surrendered shame, our surrendered logs and specks. Perhaps we are that pearl.

And Jesus says we have pearls. I think the pearls must be our surrendered sins—confessed sins—that are wrapped in the grace of God—Jesus Himself—the blood of the Lamb.

Have you ever seen a pearl like that? A confession? Not just a vague "I'm sorry" (that's usually an evasion), but a real confession—that's a treasure.

A child who throws herself across your lap sobbing, "I'm sorry, Daddy!"

A prodigal boy saying, "I've sinned and don't deserve to be your son."

A tax collector beating his breast in the temple crying, "Have mercy on me, a sinner!" Remember the Pharisee saw him and prayed, "God, thank you that I'm not like him . . . that sorry man . . . that pearl."

"Don't cast your pearls before swine, lest they trample them underfoot and turn and attack you." Be careful to whom you confess your sins. Pigs can't see treasure, and Pharisees don't believe in pearls. All they see is mud and oysters.

Remember where pearls are found: in mud and oysters. We like them once they're cleaned up and packaged in a seminar or book. But we don't like mud and oysters in church. Oysters often don't feel welcome in church, nor do pearl hunters. To hunt for pearls is not easy, and often painful and messy. It requires "just judgments" and heartfelt confessions. Most of all, you have to believe there is a pearl when all you see is mud, oyster, and no treasure.

A pearl is a special kind of treasure. Jesus has been talking about "storing up treasure in heaven" by seeing with clear eyes (logless eyes) treasure on earth. The New Jerusalem is built of treasure stored up from earth. It has twelve gates, and each gate is a single pearl.

Perhaps whenever you confess a sin in Jesus' name, you make a pearl. And the very place where there was once an embedded sin (a splinter or log) . . . that very place becomes a door to the eternal city. You've seen those pearls, and we all enter by those gates: testimonies of amazing grace.

Whenever I preach flesh and law, I'm a pig. But whenever I preach "amazing grace, how sweet the sound that saved a wretch like me" and mean it, I'm an open door. The door is Jesus in me, the gate in me. He is the gate in the pearl!

In Revelation 21:25, we read that the "gates shall never be shut by day—and there shall be no night there." (The gates are always open. Are you always open?) "Yet outside are the dogs." I guess they don't want to enter. Swine hear a confession and trample it like dirt. Yet they don't enter; they don't believe. Jesus said, "Don't cast your pearls before swine." Swine can't see pearls as treasure. So don't confess your sins to just anyone. Perhaps once they're cleaned up and polished you can share them with the whole church, but first you need to confess to someone who can judge you well, that is, discern the mud and the pearl:

1. Someone who knows you and lives in your skin.
2. Someone who knows your sin and feels your pain.
3. Someone who will not condemn.
4. Someone who's willing to die for you.

I need to confess to my wife, Susan, a lot, and sometimes to my friend Andrew or my small group . . . but none of them matches perfectly my criteria for confessor or judge. Yet they are living vessels for the One who does. They are His body and His temple. And I need to confess to *Him*—Jesus. The "very few" who match those criteria is actually One.

1. He knows me. He wrapped Himself in flesh, and He even lives in my skin.
2. He knows my sin—a "high priest tempted in every way as I am." Even more, on His cross He became sin for me (see 2 Corinthians 5:21). He took my sin. He took the log from my eye and bore it all the way to hell. The log is my flesh, my self, my pride.
3. He does not condemn; He makes me His pearl.
4. He's not only *willing*; He *did* die for me.

He is the measure I want. He is my judgment. I am *His treasure* stored eternal in heaven. But now I'm being revealed in time. He's being revealed in me in time. He's making His pearl.

Once I was judged with perfect judgment. It was the sweetest pain I've ever felt. I was at a conference with Susan, and I was incredibly depressed. A huge, Native American, charismatic guy and a little, old, Roman Catholic lady asked if they could pray for me. To me they represented the spectrum of the church.

I don't know what they said, but the moment they started to pray, I heard these words in my mind. (I've never heard words from God so clearly before or since.) I heard, *Peter, you don't love My bride very much, do you?* And at that it was as if God ripped a scab off my heart, and I began to weep. All at once pictures, images, and ideas flowed from the depth of my heart: old wounds and hidden angers. In a flash, I realized I hated the church. In fact, I saw that I'd gone into the ministry for that reason. Of course, a fallen heart may have many reasons, but in that moment, I saw that I was driven by a desire to conquer my enemy— the church. I saw that:

I was angry over the way the church had judged my dad and lied about my dad at his pastorate in Colorado.

I was angry over the judgments of pastors in California, who had had affairs and lied to me.

I was angry over Pharisees who would call across the country to judge one word in a sermon.

I was angry at the church's bad judgments, and I had condemned her as mud.

I judged the church for all her bad judgments.

I judged "the church" . . . and I *was* the church.

What a hypocrite! I was a Pharisee! I was serving out of a heart full of bitterness and pride. And get this: I was totally blind to the log in my eye.

I was blind, I could not see it, and I could not get it out. But *Jesus could!* God judged me but did not condemn me. If it was pain, it was the sweetest pain I've ever felt. I wept and wept, yet it felt like Jesus weeping through me. So much pain . . . but pain washed down a river of tears— His tears. When I opened my eyes, the hotel staff had set up chairs around me, preparing for the next meeting. Everyone was gone, and it felt like a tumor was gone. But it was no longer a tumor; it was a pearl.

That was a unique, miraculous, seminal event in my life. Yet God is doing the same thing all the time through His people, when I confess my sins to them and believe God's judgment pronounced by them.

Jesus is the judgment of God for me.

"God judges the secrets of men by Christ Jesus" (Romans 2:16). Jesus, full of grace and truth. Jesus wraps Himself around the wound with forgiveness and grace, making a pearl, and washes away the mud to reveal the treasure.

Jesus is the measure we get. Jesus is the decision of God toward us. When we decide for truth, we decide for Jesus. It's not really *our* decision or choice but the decision of God in us. It's the judgment of God in us. It's the choice of God in us. For we were chosen in Jesus before the foundation of the world. And so with "faith, hope, and love" I can say, "Dear God, according to the gospel, by Jesus the Christ, judge me! Judge the *hell* out of me and make me Your pearl!"

And Jesus said, "Now is the judgment of this world, now shall the ruler of this world be cast out; and I, when I am lifted up from the earth [crucified], will draw all men to myself" (John 12:31–32).

"The measure you give is the measure you get." I think that's true for everybody, even God. He gives Jesus. What are you going to give God?

Maybe you feel like a thief on the cross: "God, what am I going to give you, other than myself?" He has given you Jesus. If you confess your sins (your *self*), you are wrapped in Jesus, His body and blood. And then in gratitude you give yourself wrapped in Jesus back to God.

"The measure you give is the measure you get." God gave Jesus, and God gets Jesus back, in you, on you, and all over you.

The pearl of great price.

13

THE GATE

MATTHEW 7:7–14

When you were a child, did you ever dream about other worlds? And did you dream of a gate whereby you entered that world?

- Alice enters Wonderland through a rabbit hole and a gate.
- Jack has a magic bean and a beanstalk.
- In *The Chronicles of Narnia*, the kids enter through a wardrobe, a picture, and a stable.
- In *The Matrix*, Neo takes a colored pill and enters the real world.
- In science-fiction movies, people go through black holes and star gates and use time machines.

Adults call those stories. "The things I believed most then, the things I believe most now, are the things called fairy tales. They seem to me to be the entirely reasonable things," writes G. K. Chesterton.[1]

Madeleine L'Engle writes, "The world of fairy tale, fantasy, myth, is inimical to the secular world, and in total opposition to it, for it is interested not in limited laboratory proofs but in truth."[2]

Fairy tales are not interested in things of this world but things *beyond* this world, like truth.

J. R. R. Tolkien was asked if his fantasies were "escapist" in that they shifted attention away from the "real world." Tolkien replied, "Everything depends on that from which one is escaping."[3]

Perhaps we're trying to escape
from the unreal *dead* world
into the real *living* world;
we're looking for a door.

Jesus came preaching, "The kingdom of heaven is at hand." In the Sermon on the Mount He's described hidden treasure and pearls, and now He mentions a gate—and a way that leads to eternal life.

MATTHEW 7:13–14: *Enter by the narrow gate; for the gate is wide and the way is easy, that leads to destruction, and those who enter by it are many. For the gate is narrow and the way is hard, that leads to life, and those who find it are few.*

"The gate is narrow." *How* narrow?

"Those who find it are few." *How* few?

At the start of the Sermon on the Mount, Jesus says, "Think not that I have come to abolish the law and the prophets" (Matthew 5:17), and then He expounds the law by saying, "You must be perfect as your heavenly Father is perfect."

God made a covenant with Israel. He gave the law and the prophets. If Israel obeyed, God would bless them, and they would enter the land. If Israel *didn't* obey, they would face death and exile.

As Joshua and Israel crossed the Jordan (the gateway into the Promised Land), they were met by an angel—a God-man—with a sword (the Lord of Hosts). He told Joshua to take off his shoes as Moses did at the burning bush. Joshua worshiped, and the God-man let him pass.

Well, you know the story: Israel breaks its covenant with God time and time again. It makes sacrifices to atone for sins, but none are sufficient.

In Jesus' day, the group that appears to have obeyed the law most fully was the Pharisees and their scribes. Yet Jesus has just said, "Unless your righteousness exceeds that of the scribes and Pharisees, you will never enter the kingdom of heaven."

That's a pretty narrow door! And we're pretty lax around here. Obviously we must need:

- more classes and better discipleship programs;
- classes on how to find God's will and how to guard your marriage and play it safe;
- ethics classes—instructions on right and wrong;
- lists of what's good and what's bad, what TV shows to watch and what TV shows you *can't* watch.

We must need more knowledge of good and evil! In the Garden of Eden stood the tree of the knowledge of good and evil, next to the tree of life. God told Adam, "The day that you eat of [the tree of the knowledge of good and evil] you shall die" (Genesis 2:17). Adam and Eve took the fruit from the tree and saw that they were dead.

"[God] drove out the man [the adam]; and at the east of the garden of Eden he placed the cherubim, and a flaming sword which turned every way, to guard the way to the tree of life" (Genesis 3:24).

> *How narrow is the gate?*
> *How narrow is the entrance for life?*
> *Well, it's so narrow it's shut, I guess.*

"None is righteous, no not one." "All have sinned and fall short of the glory of God." "The wages of sin is death." (Romans 3:10, 23; 6:23 respectively).

It is "narrow," and "few are those who find this gate." There are some three billion Christians in the world, but "few are those who find the gate." How do you measure up?

Jeremiah 29:13 says, "You will seek me and find me; when you seek me with all your heart." Are you seeking with all your heart? Have you ever met someone who sought God with all their heart; that is, someone without sin?

In Romans 3:10–11, Paul quotes the psalmist: "As it is written: 'None is righteous, no, not one; no one understands, no one seeks for God.'"

- How narrow is the door? It appears to be *closed.*
- How few find it? It appears to be *none.*
- How could we find it? According to Scripture, we're dead. And more than that, there is an angel-cherub, God-man kind of figure with a flaming sword guarding the way to the tree of life, just to make sure no zombies get in. It looks impossible!

And Jesus says, "Enter by the narrow gate that leads to life." Well, Jesus, what kind of gate *is* this?

In Walt Disney's animated fairy tale *Alice in Wonderland*, Alice follows a white rabbit, looking for a party. (The kingdom is a party.) She falls into a deep hole. Falling and falling, she remarks, "Oh, goodness! What if I should fall right through the center of the earth and come out on the other side, where people walk upside down?" "Curiouser and curiouser," she says. As she falls:

She turns on a light.

Jesus said, "I am the light of the world."

She looks in a mirror.

We look in the mirror of the law of liberty and persevere.

She reads a book.

Jesus is the Word who fulfills the law and prophets.

She hears a clock.

Jesus offers eternal life.

She lands in a rocking chair.

We strive to enter His rest.

She passes a fire, and her world is turned upside down.

When she lands, she follows the white rabbit into a room where she spots a little door—a little gate—behind a drawn curtain. She thinks it's *impossible*, but it's only *impassable*, because she is too large—there's too much of her. There's a table and a bottle labeled "Drink me."

When we drink from the Lord's table, we drink blood and wine. To some it's poison, yet to us it's life. It burns away what's bad and exposes what's good. It makes us small.

Alice drinks from the bottle labeled "Drink me" and grows small. The door is locked, but the door tells Alice she has the key. It's on the table. But now Alice is too small. She takes a bite of a wafer labeled "Eat me."

When we come to the Lord's table and eat of His broken body, we become large enough to see that we broke the body of Jesus—we crucified our Lord. And we weep over our sin.

Alice weeps saying, "Look what I've done. I'll never get home!" But the door *tells* her what to do. She drinks from the bottle again, and having become large, she becomes small again—a child. She grows small and floats through the door on a river of tears.

In the book, Alice sees a garden through the keyhole in the door. Well, *Alice in Wonderland* is a fairy tale full of all kinds of weird things, and I certainly don't know what it all means. But whatever the case, perhaps the gate (the gate Jesus is talking about) is like *that* one:

1. A gate to another world, not of this world, not comprehended by this world.

2. A gate that requires you to become small in one way and large in another. G. K. Chesterton writes, "One can hardly think too little of one's self. One can hardly think too much of one's soul."[4] We crucified the Savior, yet for us He died. Alice must grow small to enter Wonderland where everything is big, including Alice. Perhaps we must become like a child and grow down rather than up, in order to enter.

3. Perhaps the gate Jesus is talking about is *alive.* He tells us to "Enter by the narrow gate" ("the narrow door," as He puts it in Luke). "Narrow is the gate and there are few who find it" (Matthew 7:14 NKJV).

In John 10:2–3, Jesus says, "He who enters by the door is the shepherd of the sheep. To him the gatekeeper opens; the sheep hear his voice, and he calls his own sheep by name and leads them out." Jesus finds the door and leads others through. He says, "Truly, truly, I say to you, I am the door of the sheep. . . . I am the door; if any one enters by me, he will be saved, and will go in and out and find pasture" (vv. 7, 9). Jesus *finds* the door, and Jesus *is* the door.

So how narrow is the gate?

About as narrow as your standard Judean manger; about as wide as a Roman cross.

And how few are those who find it?

About *one . . .* just *one.*

Jesus finds the gate, and Jesus *is* the gate. Jesus has just said He came to fulfill the law and prophets. He perfectly obeyed all the old covenant law. He passed through that narrow gate and made Himself the sacrifice for *our* sin—the Lamb that is slain—the new covenant.

"He made him to be sin who knew no sin, so that in him we might become the righteousness of God" (2 Corinthians 5:21). He is the *eschatos* Adam, the last Adam, the "ultimate" man (see 1 Corinthians 15:22).

Jesus found and entered the old gate

(the old covenant),

and Jesus became and always is the new gate

(the new covenant).

He has become our gate as narrow as a manger and as wide as a cross.

In John 14:6 Jesus says, "I am the way, and the truth, and the life; no one comes to the Father, but by me"—the door, the way, the truth, the life. He is a living door, a living gate.

Jesus says, "On that day many will say to me, 'Lord, Lord, did we not prophesy in your name, and cast out demons in your name, and do many mighty works in your name?' And then will I declare to them, 'I never knew you; depart from me'" (Matthew 7:22–23).

You need to *know* Him, not just *about* Him. You can know *about* a person in the past or future, but you can only *know* a person *now*. You can only encounter a spirit *now*.

"All actual life is encounter," said Martin Buber.[5] Jesus is a living door leading to life *now*. How do we know Him? How can we find such a narrow gate?

MATTHEW 7:7–14: *Ask, and it will be given you; seek, and you will find; knock, and it will be opened to you. For every one who asks receives, and he who seeks finds, and to him who knocks it will be opened. Or what man of you, if his son asks him for bread, will give him a stone? Or if he asks for a fish, will give him a serpent? If you then, who are evil, know how to give good gifts to your children, how much more will your Father who is in heaven give good things to those who ask him! So whatever you wish that men would do to you, do so to them; for this is the law and the prophets.*

Enter by the narrow gate; for the gate is wide and the way is easy, that

*leads to destruction, and those who enter by it are many. For the gate is
narrow and the way is hard, that leads to life, and those who find it are few.*

In verse 7, without qualification Jesus says, "Seek, and you will
find." That's thrilling! . . . and also horrifying. I mean, what if we seek
the wrong thing? What if we don't seek Jesus but something else?

In *The Chronicles of Narnia*, a witch breaks into a garden rather than
entering by the gate. She steals fruit and wins her heart's desire. Aslan
the lion says, "Length of days with an evil heart is only length of misery
and already she begins to know it. All get what they want: they do not
always like it."[6] We get what we want but don't always want what we
get. We seek the wrong things in the wrong way.

The serpent said, "Eve, Eve, you'll become like God, knowing good
and evil" (see Genesis 3:5). That sounded good but tasted like death.
So it must have been the mercy of God then, that barred our way to the
tree of life, so we wouldn't live forever with an evil heart—like zombies.

Perhaps we've sought to *be like* God rather than to *know* God. Maybe
we've sought God's *things* rather than His *heart*. Bad religion is pursuing
God's stuff (like the knowledge of good and evil) without God. It's
pursuing our own selves in the name of God. Perhaps we've sought and
we've found. We've sought ourselves, and we're getting ourselves. Perhaps
in His mercy, He allows us to taste hell so we might seek something else.

When Jesus says, "Seek and you will find," it seems none so far had
found the gate. I guess they weren't seeking the gate.

In verse 12, Jesus says, "So whatever you wish that men would do to
you, do so to them; for this is the law and the prophets." That's the old
gate, and Jesus fills it. Jesus fulfills the law and the prophets. Jesus is the
manifest love of God, and that love is the fulfillment of the law. On the
cross, Jesus makes the love of God known. Jesus is the way, the truth,
and the life—the gate. He enters through the old gate, but we can only

enter *in Him.* We can only fulfill the law through Him. Apart from Him, we can do nothing. Yet in Him, and by His presence within us, we can begin to do to others as we wish they would do to us. We can begin to love and enter life through the gate, which is Christ.

Still, those disciples on the mountain that day couldn't see the gate. They can't truly see Him. They must have been blind. Jesus says they are evil. In verse 11, He says, "If you then, who are evil, know how to give good gifts to your children, how much more will your Father who is in heaven give good things to those who ask him?" In the parallel passage in Luke, He says, "How much more will the heavenly Father give the Holy Spirit to those who ask him?" (11:13). The Holy Spirit is the Spirit of Christ.

God is a very good Father.

In Matthew 18:3, Jesus says, "Truly, I say to you, unless you turn and become like children, you will never enter the kingdom of heaven." Children are born trusting—"poor in spirit" and "meek." They can't control their world. By necessity they must receive everything in their reality by grace. They're large in that they believe they're important to someone. But they're small in that they know they're dependent on someone. They themselves are small, and so their world is large and filled with wonder—hidden meaning. They seek and keep seeking, and they're curious about everything. They pay attention to the lilies of the field and the birds of the air. They're fascinated by things like an old manger and can easily believe it might just be a door to another world, its inside bigger than all the outside!

Jesus taught, "Become like children to enter." *Grow down.*

Alice must grow small to enter Wonderland. She must lose control. Jesus said you must become like a child. We idolize children but spend our whole lives trying not to *be* one—humble, dependent, and vulnerable. So we constantly eat the fruit of the tree of knowledge, trying to grow up, trying to find and control the gate. We try to become experts of the gate, like scribes and Pharisees. The law makes us big (at least in our own heads). Something *more powerful still* must make us small.

In Matthew 23:12–13 Jesus says, "Whoever exalts himself will be humbled, and whoever humbles himself will be exalted. But woe to you, scribes and Pharisees, hypocrites! because you shut the kingdom of heaven against men; for you neither enter yourselves, nor allow those who would enter to go in."

- They try to control the gate, regulate the gate, monitor the gate.
- They make all kinds of rules but don't enter themselves—don't confess their sins and surrender to God's grace. It's not impossible but im*pass*able (like a camel through the eye of a needle).
- They don't fit and won't get small.
- They don't seek because that means they don't know.
- They don't ask because that means they don't have.
- They don't knock because that means they're on the outside.

Someone said, "You *can* get a camel through the eye of a needle. It's just very hard on the camel." Maybe you can get a Pharisee through the narrow door; it's just hard on the Pharisee. It's like you have to *die* to self and be born again. Who would seek that?

Well, Jesus says, "Seek"—present active imperative form. "Seek and keep seeking. Don't stop seeking." There is always more wonder in Wonderland. Books, degrees, classes, and knowledge are wonderful as long as they help you seek and are not the thing you seek. But books, degrees, and classes all come to an end. Jesus is the one you seek, and there is always more of Him. He is the meaning of all things.

Sometimes we're born again and then think we've arrived: grown up.

Sometimes we read a book or get a degree and think we've arrived; sometimes we act like Pharisees.

"Seek and you will find." What a promise! That entirely undercuts the monopoly of the religion industry.

- He doesn't say you need some scribes and Pharisees.
- He doesn't say you need an accredited seminary.
- He doesn't say you need a workbook or tape series or some special knowledge.
- He doesn't even say you have to be a "Christian." These folks on the hill listening aren't what we'd technically call "Christian."

Jesus just says, "Seek and you will find."

So if a little abused girl in a faraway country seeks love, she'll find Him. God is love. And if some Iraqi soldier lies dying in a field this day and cries, "Allah! God! Jesus! Whatever Your name is, I want the truth!" . . . if he seeks truth, he'll find it. And the truth is Jesus (not Allah, but Jesus—they are different). If you seek truth, seek the way, seek real life, you are seeking the gate, you are seeking Jesus. And you will find Him.

How can that be?
How can the gate be in all those places?

For one, in Matthew 25:40: Jesus says, "As you did it to one of the least of these my brethren, you did it to me." Perhaps the gate is in the last and least of these. Perhaps the true gate is in Lazarus lying by the rich man's gate. Perhaps the gate is in every pearl surrounding the eternal city; in every confession of every believer. Perhaps the gate is in all those people.

185

Perhaps the gate is in us and travels with us and is all around us, like doorways to the kingdom—narrow yet everywhere—as narrow as Jesus and as present as Jesus. After all, every particle in our universe is continually upheld by Him, the Word. The "kingdom of heaven is at hand," and the Gate promised His followers, "I will never leave you nor forsake you" (Hebrews 13:5 NKJV).

So we should never go anywhere or any-when in fear and trepidation, but always "curiouser and curiouser" seeking in faith, hope, and love. "Seek and you will find." Still, there's this tremendous problem: will anyone seek the gate?

Will anyone seek God? Or will they only seek their own selves in the name of God? Remember what Paul said, quoting King David in Romans 3:11: "No one understands, no one seeks for God." Jesus says, "Many are called, but few are chosen." How few? I think only one. Paul writes in Ephesians 1:4 that we have been chosen in Christ Jesus, and Jesus tells His disciples, "You did not choose me, but I chose you" (John 15:16).

No one seeks God, but Jesus does. If you seek God, it's the Spirit of Jesus in you seeking God. If you long to be chosen by God, it's the Spirit of Jesus in you being chosen by God.[7]

No one seeks God, but God seeks us. So "God has sent the Spirit of his Son into our hearts, crying, 'Abba! Father!'" (Galatians 4:6).

There are great mysteries here, but God wishes that none should perish (see 2 Peter 3:9). And no one seeks God, but God seeks us. I believe:

- God seeks little abused girls in faraway lands as they long for love. To seek love is to have been sought by love. God is love.
- He seeks Iraqi soldiers dying in the desert as they long for truth. To seek truth is to have been sought by truth. Jesus is the truth.
- He seeks you and He seeks me.
- He seeks worshipers who will worship in spirit and truth.

Jesus found the narrow gate and Jesus *is* the narrow gate. I suspect that Jesus is the "flaming sword" in the hands of the cherubim east of Eden.[8] I suspect Jesus is the Lord of hosts with the drawn sword at the River Jordan.

I'm convinced Jesus is the gate to the eternal city. He appears to John in the Revelation, shining and brilliant, and a two-edged sword issues from His mouth. He says, "Come up here," and John goes through a doorway in heaven. He sees the city and the gate. Jesus says, "Blessed are those who wash their robes [remember that they're washed in blood], that they may have the right to the tree of life and that they may enter the city by the gates" (Revelation 22:14).

> *Jesus is the gate.*
> *He finds us.*

That's why He came. Romans 10:20 says, "I have been found by those who did not seek me; I have shown myself to those who did not ask for me."

The God-man with the double-edged sword—the gate—sits on a hillside saying, "Children, seek. The kingdom is at hand. Time to come home." But they don't see Him truly or seek Him truly. Soon they'll abandon Him and crucify Him. And then they'll seek Him.

On the night before He was crucified, Jesus said to His disciples, "You will seek me. . . you will see me . . . and if I go, I will send the Spirit of truth. He will be in you . . . and he will convince the world."

Jesus sends His Spirit into our hearts crying, "Abba Father!" He seeks us and makes us seek Him.

So always and everywhere seek the gate, for Jesus has sought you. Stop fearing, hiding, running, controlling, manipulating. Stop playing it safe and surrender to the Seeker *now.* Live in faith, hope, and love *now*, always "curiouser and curiouser." For wherever you go, there is this God-man, the Lord of hosts, with a bright, flaming sword, Jesus the Word—the Meaning—the narrow door leading to life. Always look through the door.

Come to the table of the Lord, and you're beginning to live in Wonderland.

MATTHEW 26:26–28: *Now as they were eating, Jesus took bread, and blessed, and broke it, and gave it to the disciples and said, "Take, eat; this is my body." And he took a cup, and when he had given thanks he gave it to them, saying, "Drink of it, all of you; for this is my blood of the covenant, which is poured out for many for the forgiveness of sins."*

"Drink me."
"Eat me."
"Enter my Father's kingdom."

If you hang around the religion industry (of which I'm a part), you'll find a million books, seminars, formulas, classes, and manuals on "How to find God." They all have to do with things we should do to enter. I suspect that the gate is narrower than that, more present than that, and far more beautiful, wondrous, and good than that.

When I preached on this text, my friend Dale had a vision:

I saw a young, vagabond little girl [like the last and least], and she was standing in the midst of an immense crowd, all moving past her but no one was paying any attention to her. I looked up to see where they were all going, and I saw this huge, brand-new, beautiful arena-type building that they were filing into. A large sign outside the building read "How to Find God." Then I noticed that I was standing in the middle of an enormous courtyard, and around it were many similar buildings, all with their own large signs, announcing things like "How to Find God in Science," "How to Find God in the Earth," "How to Find God in You." I watched and the multitude lined up for every one of these, and I found myself kneeling down and lifting my hands toward the sky and asking, "God, where are You?" Then the little girl came over to me and gave me a big hug. [She found him.] She said, "Look over there." She pointed to a tiny, dilapidated shack squeezed in between two of the other buildings. It had a sign which read, "Are You Thirsty? Free Blood."

It was church. Dale told me that inside were people he knew passing out drinks in little cups.

Make what you will of that, but stake your life on this: "God so loved the world that He gave His only begotten Son, that whoever believes in Him should not perish but have everlasting life" (John 3:16 NKJV).

How narrow and present and beautiful;
wondrous, good, and gracious is The Gate!

14

TREE STORY

MATTHEW 7:16–17

After Jesus talks about entering by the gate, He begins to talk about trees and fruit. Trees play an amazing role in Scripture.

On Easter last year, I brought four trees to worship to show the congregation. The first was a bristlecone pine. The oldest living thing on earth is a bristlecone pine named Methuselah. It's 4,767 years old. So when it was 673 years old, God said, "Abram, I'm going to bless the nations through you"—the seed of Abraham. When it was 1,714 years old, King David was born. It was 2,731 years old when Jesus hung on the cross.

The second tree was a giant sequoia—just a seedling. I said, "I'm going to plant this in my yard so that in three thousand years my progeny can drive a bus through its trunk. It will weigh 2.7 million pounds, and it grows from a seed the size of an oat flake." Jesus said the kingdom of God is like that.

The third tree was my schefflera tree. I got it from my grandpa Ralph in 1978 just before he died. The bends and turns in the trunk tell a story . . . like when my college roommate dropped his bike on it, and when I grew it on my shelf, and when my parents tried to throw it away. For the last ten years, it's been in six different offices at the church. It's like my *life tree*, and it tells a story (like the rings in a bristlecone or redwood tell a story). Trees tell a story and often come up from a root—an even deeper story. Scripture says Jesus is the root of David.

The fourth tree was a fruit tree. I said, "I'm going to plant it in my yard so it will tell a story and also give life to my kids. My children will eat the fruit from this cherry tree for years to come. Through photosynthesis, the leaves of this tree absorb light, and then mysteriously the tree mixes light with dirt and steer manure, absorbed by the roots, making *life*: cherries, fruit, and seed."

Just as God breathed into dirt and made a human soul, so trees put light into dirt and make life. A tree is a long story of life, life that is dirt redeemed by light.

The Bible is a long story too. In Genesis 1, Scripture records that God created everything in six days and rested on the seventh. On the sixth day He says, "Let us make man in Our own image."

A few years ago a physicist from MIT named Gerald Schroeder calculated the age of the universe, factoring in the mass of the universe and the rate of expansion since the Big Bang. Schroeder figured that the universe is roughly fifteen billion years old . . . from the standpoint of earth. But time is relative to where you're standing. So he calculated from the standpoint of the Big Bang, looking at earth, and found the universe to be not quite seven days old.[1] In that case we'd still be living in the sixth day, still *being* made in God's image.

Well, no matter what, by Genesis 2, Scripture is back to describing the sixth day, for God is making man and woman in His own image. And then the first thing He does is plant trees.

In the middle of paradise, He plants *the* tree—the tree of life. I wonder what it looked like?

What kind of tree would make you live forever, or give you eternal life? That is, what tree would make you born again if you ate its fruit?

And then, right next to it in the very middle of the paradise garden, God plants the strangest tree of all—the tree of the knowledge of good and evil. I wonder what it looked like?

What kind of tree would make you know what is good and what is evil, and at the same time would kill you if you partook of it?

God said, "The day you eat of this tree, you will die. Don't do it." The tree of *knowledge*—He puts it in the *very middle* of the Garden!

There are different ways of knowing.

Until 1964 Methuselah, the bristlecone pine, was only the second oldest living thing on earth. Another bristlecone pine was named Prometheus. (Prometheus was the Greek god who brought fire and art to mankind and suffered for it.) In 1964 a grad student named Donald Curry wanted to know how old Prometheus was. So he cut Prometheus down in order to count his rings—4,862.

So did Donald Curry *know* Prometheus the tree? Yes and no. He knew *about* Prometheus, that he had 4,862 rings, yet he did not *know* Prometheus, for Prometheus was dead. And when Donald Curry counted the rings, I bet a piece of him died, too, because he knew that he had just *killed* the oldest living thing on earth. He killed what he wanted to know.

I can know about my wife by cutting her down and dissecting her parts ("there's her liver . . . there's her spleen"), or I can know my wife by surrendering to her love and loving her in return. But love hurts, yet love bears fruit . . . even babies. When Adam *knows* Eve in Genesis 4, she becomes pregnant. There really are different ways of knowing.

The snake tempts Adam and Eve saying, "Take the fruit, steal the fruit, conquer the tree; you'll be like God, knowing good and evil."

The "knowledge of good and evil"—what is that?

Well, first, it's the law—God's law—what is good and what is evil.

Well, isn't the law good? Isn't the tree good?
Yes!

Then what's bad?
I guess the way you *take* it.

Eve takes it to be *like* God, to get power over God. Adam and Eve want to make God part of their story rather than entrusting themselves to God's story. So they eat, and all at once they *know*. They know they are evil, for they cut down the One who is good—"the good" they most truly wanted to know.

The evil serpent hates people and trees; that is, stories of life.

So God curses the snake and the world, and Adam and Eve are driven from the Garden. God places cherubim and a flaming sword at the east of Eden, as a gate to bar the way to the tree of life lest they eat of it and live forever as they are, unable to love: *hell.*

Most folks act as if God didn't see that one coming . . . so this fallen world is beyond His plan; that is, Satan won and wrecked the story right at the start, so God had to scramble and come up with Jesus and the cross. They would say that's why evil things happen—because Satan tempted us, and we screwed the whole thing up! That's true. But is it all the truth? Did God write the story of salvation as plan B or plan A?

Speaking of evil, Elie Wiesel told a story of his time in Hitler's death camp at Auschwitz. He was watching three men hanging from a gallows. One of them was an innocent boy whom he called the "sad-eyed angel." The boy wasn't heavy enough to die quickly, so he hung on the gallows twitching for half an hour. The Nazis made the prisoners file past. The man behind Wiesel muttered, "Where is God? Where is God now?" Wiesel writes, "I heard a voice within me answer him. 'Where is He? Here He is. He is hanging here on this gallows.'"[2]

Is that part of plan A?

Is God still the storyteller?

Where is the plot—the meaning?

Is it a gallows without meaning, a gallows without plot?

Is life a story, a good story, a gospel?

I saw *The Lord of the Rings* at the movie theater. When Gandalf fell into the abyss as Sauron and Saruman rose in power and the fellowship was broken . . . well, I didn't stand up and yell out in the theater, "Oh no! How can it be?" Instead, I leaned forward in hope, because it's a *good* story—a gospel. And every evil in a good story gets redeemed in glory, because a good author infuses every detail with his meaning, the plot.

Whether you scream in terror or lean forward in hope, whether you are paralyzed with fear or dance with joy all depends on who you believe is writing the story.

Scripture says God accomplishes all things according to the counsel of His will (Ephesians 1:11). God creates and upholds all things by His Word—the Word—the Plot.

What gives me great hope is that *before* the Fall, right after God formed man, He planted a tree.

In the old days in the Deep South, when a slave baby was born, the women would sneak out into the woods and bury the placenta and birth waters at the base of a tree. Then when that young child was sold into slavery, the momma would go sit by the tree, hoping to commune with the spirit of her child. And wherever that child was, he knew there was this tree—his story tree.

We sold ourselves into slavery, but God had already planted a tree. I wonder if He would go sit by it?

In the Old Testament, wild and weird stuff happens with trees. The Hebrew word for tree is *ates*. It's also translated "wood," "staff," "gallows" (the wood on which you would kill a man). When combined with another Hebrew word, it's translated "carpenter."

In the Old Testament:

- Noah and his family get saved by an ark made of wood.
- Moses parts the Red Sea with his staff of wood.
- The Israelites are saved at Mara when Moses throws a special tree into the poison water, which becomes sweet.
- They conquer in battle because God is somehow present in the ark of the covenant made of wood.

The New Testament is written in Greek, and when the Old Testament was translated into Greek, *ates* was translated as *xoolon*. The Greeks had other words for trees, but *xoolon* carried the range of meaning to best translate *ates*.

Like *ates*, *xoolon* means "tree," "wood," "staff," "gallows," and "cross."

- When Jesus is born, He's placed in a manger of wood.
- He grows up as a carpenter (*ates* worker).
- He spends a lot of time in wooden boats.
- He has a bizarre relationship with trees.

A few days before He dies, Jesus curses a fig tree because it's not bearing fruit, and the tree dies. Fig trees are a symbol of Israel. A few days later, the religious people—Israel—curse Jesus. They cut Him down and nail Him to the tree. Although He's the only sinless man who ever lived, the One who is good, they crucify Him to guard their religion—their story—their knowledge of good and evil (the law). They crucify Him on a *xoolon*—the cross.

In Matthew 7, Jesus teaches us to know a tree by the fruit it bears.

What kind of tree is the cross? Well, when we come to this tree, we do know something:

1. We know what is good . . . not really *what* but *who*. The good is the bleeding heart of a lover. The good is Jesus from the bosom of the Father. The good is our Maker not just waiting by a tree but nailed to His own tree for the love of us.

2. And we know what is evil . . . or perhaps *who*. Who nailed Jesus to the tree? *We* nailed Him to the tree. Every time we sin, we nail Him to His tree—the law. Even before He planted the tree, He chose to die in our place. It was His plan. He was "slain from the foundation of the world" (Revelation 13:8 KJV).

Peter writes, "He himself bore our sins in his body on the tree, that we might die to sin and live to righteousness. By his wounds you have been healed" (1 Peter 2:24).

Paul writes, "Christ redeemed us from the curse of the law, having become a curse for us—for it is written, 'Cursed be everyone who hangs on a tree'" (Galatians 3:13).

So now we go to the tree longing for the good, confessing we're dead. We know evil, because we killed the Good. We cut Him down and tried to count His rings, tried to steal His kingdom and make ourselves into gods. We *know* evil.

But when we look to the tree longing for good, there's a man hanging on it! We can't steal the fruit, for now He gives us the fruit saying, "Take and eat my body broken, blood shed. Unless you eat my body and drink my blood, you have no life in you." We *know* good.

We know good and evil not simply because we broke the law but because we have surrendered to God's grace. We stole the fruit, but now He gives us the fruit: body broken and blood shed.

Jesus is the fruit: not taken but given. We took but God gave. Even before we took He *for*gave. It's sin to take Jesus' life. It's redemption to receive it.

Jesus is "the life" crucified on the tree of knowledge (the law) but resurrected from the dead by the power of God as a gift to us.

Jesus is the good, but not the *dead* good; not the *dead* word (a theory or law or religion). He is the *Living* Good, the *Living* Word (the Great Lover of our souls).

I believe He is the fruit of the tree of knowledge. (We are "joined with Him in a death like His" when we see that we killed Him.) Do you know Him?

I believe He is also the fruit of the tree of life. (We are "joined with Him in a resurrection like His" when we believe His love.) Do you know Him?

Jesus said, "I am the way, the truth, and the life." He is "the way." He is "the truth" (about good and evil), and He is "the life."

The way is the truth is the life. There is one way, and in the end there is one tree, and that tree is His cross. His cross is the way. This is the "plan for the fulness of time, to unite all things in him," "to reconcile to himself all things . . . making peace by the blood of his cross" (Ephesians 1:10; Colossians 1:20 respectively).

If I lost you, listen now: God is still telling His story: *History.* He is the best author, and it is the very best story—a tree story. The new creation is the fruit of the tree. (In Christ all things hold together and are made new [Colossians 1:17, Revelation 21:5].) The resurrection of Jesus Christ is the revelation of the plot, the first fruit of the new creation.

In the Revelation, John sees the eternal city, the New Jerusalem, the paradise of God, the seventh day—heaven. In the midst of the city, he sees the *xoolon*—the tree—the cross of life. It bears twelve kinds of fruit

(fruit for each month and tribe). The leaves are for the "healing of the nations."

Leaves take light and mix it with dirt and manure absorbed through the root, and the tree turns it into life and fruit. We surrender our dirt and manure to the light at the cross, and He turns our sin and sorrow into life—the fruit of His grace. He changes the meaning with Himself, the Plot. The tree is for the healing of the nations, the salvation of the world. On His cross, He redeems everything that is anything.

When Elie Wiesel stared at the boy hanging on the gallows (the *xoolon*) and heard, "Here is God, He's hanging on this gallows," I think he heard *truth*. Perhaps Jesus hangs on every gallows, for He is the meaning of every cross. (If Elie Wiesel was longing for meaning, he was longing to believe in Jesus.)

I believe Jesus hangs on the gallows with that boy and before that boy in space and time, and catches him when he falls. And I suspect Jesus takes that boy to glory. Then that sad-eyed boy has tasted the love of God poured out for him on the gallows of Calvary—the cross of Christ. That taste is treasure forever.

In the beginning, God willed to make man in His own image. His image is Jesus, His heart is Jesus, and Jesus is the love of God poured out, love willing to die the ultimate death for the ones He loves. His story is *the* love story. We each taste a minute fraction of His suffering borne for love of us. For He not only bears our sufferings, He bears our hell.

In the beginning, God willed to make man in His own image, and then He planted a tree, knowing full well He would be nailed to that tree once and for all, for all people in all time, bearing our hell so we wouldn't have to, yet allowing us to taste His pain so we would know His love. He bears the pain of all time . . . to make us in His image for all eternity.

The night I preached to the congregation about seeing treasure and not allowing yourself to be "psyched out" by the evil one, my friend had another vision. He wrote:

At the beginning of the evening God took a sword and cut my chest open and asked me for my heart. . . . Once He got me out of the way so I could see, He said, "Come up here with Me and I will show you." He was on the cross and so He crucified me on the cross with Him.

As I looked out over the room, I saw many different people doing many different things. I saw people praying, worshiping, crying, scared, anxious, children running around . . . Next I started seeing a lot of suffering. I saw people with cancer, enduring horrible abuse, involved in ritualistic sacrifice. I also saw a person executed while on their knees, face and hands uplifted as their body was riddled with bullets. I saw people die in the German concentration camps, and I saw Peter (from the Bible) get stoned.

At that point the vision just ended and I told God, "This is [supposed to be] a message of hope. That can't be it. There must be more." He told me to be patient and to come up a little bit higher and then to look closer. When I did [as if the cross that he was hanging on grew], I saw that all of this was happening all at once within the walls of the New Jerusalem, the gleaming white walls with flags flying in the wind. "This is heaven," He said. "This is what the New Jerusalem is made of."

In the midst of the New Jerusalem stands a tree . . . a *xoolon*. In the New Jerusalem, there shall be no more mourning or crying or pain. Yet the New Jerusalem is made up of:

- people who know "the good" and have known "the evil" yet "live;"

- people who freely choose to love even if it hurts;
- people in God's image. Jesus is God's image.

Remember that at the start of His sermon, Jesus said, "Blessed are the poor in spirit, for theirs [literally: "of them"] is the kingdom of heaven. Blessed are those persecuted for righteousness' sake, for theirs [literally: "of them"] is the kingdom of heaven." The kingdom of heaven consists of those made in God's image. God's image is Jesus. The cross makes us in God's image. We are the fruit of that tree, and Jesus is the "first fruits" (1 Corinthians 15:23).

That's the plot, the story—the tree story.

Are you part of that story? In one sense, everyone is. You can't *not* be. So what I'm asking is: are you surrendered to the plot, or are you just an extra?

An extra is just a backdrop for the real characters in a story. Extras have no character development, no meaning in themselves, no heart— the light shines on them but not through them. I believe Paul called them "vessels of wrath" whom God endures "in order to make known the riches of his glory for the vessels of mercy" (Romans 9:22–23).

It appears you *can* go to hell . . . if you want to.

I hope this illustration isn't too much of a stretch for you: in the movie *Toy Story 2*, thousands of Buzz Lightyears are packed in boxes, existing in a delusional state on toy-store shelves. It's a picture of zombies in hell. The real Buzz Lightyear has the mark of Andy on the sole of his space boot. Andy is the boy who has loved him and made him real.

Paul writes, "I bear on my body the marks of Jesus" (Galatians 6:17). They were scars born in love, the marks of Christ's cross (the *xoolon,* the tree). That is, Paul was rather "woody."

Woody is the other toy in the movie. He finds out that he'd been the star of his own TV show in the fifties. The real Woody is tempted to forget about Andy, the boy who loves him. He is tempted, because sometimes love hurts. He thinks he'll *die*. Woody's tempted to exist forever in a glass box on a museum shelf as the star of his own show. He's tempted to save his life so he won't lose it.

When Buzz comes to rescue Woody from himself, he says, "Somewhere in that pad of stuffing is a toy that taught me life is only worth living if you're being loved by a kid."[3]

So they choose love. They surrender to Andy's story, the "toy story"—the mark of Andy.

Surrender to the "tree story." Surrender to being loved by God, even if it hurts. His love makes us real.

God planted the tree in the middle of the Garden so that one day you would see the depths of His love and surrender to His love, so He could write His signature upon your heart—make His mark upon your soul—so that you would be made in His image: that is, look like Jesus.

15

WOLVES IN SHEEP'S CLOTHING

MATTHEW 7:15–23

One morning I came to worship with a bucket of wet sheep poop and mud (not figurative but literal). I was giving the children's sermon.

I asked the kids, "Would anyone like an apple?" Several hands went up. I said, "Oh, I'll make one." I reached into the bucket, grabbed a handful of goop, formed it into the shape of an apple, put a fake leaf on top, and handed it to my volunteers.

They didn't look pleased, so I said, "What's wrong? Apples are made of sheep poop and dirt, aren't they?" They said, "No way!" I said, "Yeah way . . . I have a tree in my back yard. It takes sheep poop and dirt and turns them into delicious apples . . . but, you know, this apple I made doesn't smell like those apples. I guess I'm not a very good tree, and that's a problem.

"The Bible says we're supposed to bear fruit; that our good deeds are supposed to be like fruit. I think we normally just take our dirt and garbage and try to make apples, but that's not really apples, just apple-shaped poop. We need a tree to turn dirt and poop into fruit.

"Jesus has a tree and is kind of like a tree. We give Him our dirt; He mixes it with light and turns it into fruit. That's why we confess our sins."

We prayed. The kids went downstairs, wondering if I was insane or maybe bad for bringing my poop to church. Shouldn't you hide the poop when you go to church?[1]

In the movie *Dogma*, the fictional Cardinal Glick unveils the church's new image at a press conference on the steps of a cathedral. In his speech he recognizes that people have become uncomfortable with the image of Jesus on the cross:

> While it has been a time-honored symbol of our faith, Holy Mother Church has decided to retire this highly recognizable yet wholly depressing image of our Lord, crucified. Christ didn't come to earth to give us the willies. He came to help us out. He was a booster.[2]

Then, as part of the new "Catholicism Wow Campaign," he unveils a new statue—the "Buddy Christ"—a handsome, Caucasian Jesus winking and giving a big thumbs-up. The choir breaks into an anthem: "Hallelujah, amen."

I don't recommend this movie for casual family viewing. But that scene is a pretty accurate description of much of today's American Christianity. Sometimes I think the "Catholicism Wow Campaign" is also called the American evangelical Protestant church.

"Jesus Christ and Him crucified" is pretty hard to reconcile with a lot of what you see on TV, buy at the bookstore, or hear in our churches. He's supposed to be a *booster* . . . help us feel good about ourselves, right?

Most people love Jesus the teacher, the philosopher, the role model, the outstanding moral example; they even love the prophet, the exorcist, and the miracle worker. Yet His defining moment, what we're called "to know" ("Jesus Christ and Him crucified") doesn't quite *fit*. So we've got Jesus on the outside but not the heart of Jesus—the heart of God—on the inside.

MATTHEW 7:15: *Beware of false prophets, who come to you in sheep's clothing but inwardly are ravenous wolves.*

A wolf is a predator, and if it has sheep's clothing, it probably got them by consuming sheep. A wolf is also a very *smart* predator. If a wolf ever got sheep's clothing, I doubt it would give itself away by saying, "I hate sheep" or "I'm no longer into Jesus Christ and Him crucified."

So folks like Cardinal Glick in the movie, or liberal theologians from liberal churches, probably aren't the wolves Jesus is talking about. There may be jackasses in sheep's clothing, but wolves don't give themselves away. Maybe we need to stop worrying so much about jackasses in sheep's clothing, but wolves are another matter.

In Matthew 7:15, Jesus says to beware of "false prophets." Prophecy has a broad definition as something that all believers do. "The testimony of Jesus is the spirit of prophecy" (Revelation 19:10). Prophecy also has a narrower definition as a spiritual gift, like a vision or word of knowledge. But prophecy is always to be a testimony of Jesus.

MATTHEW 7:15–20: *Beware of false prophets, who come to you in sheep's clothing but inwardly are ravenous wolves. You will know them by their fruits. Are grapes gathered from thorns, or figs from thistles? So, every sound tree bears good fruit, but the bad tree bears evil fruit. A sound tree cannot bear evil fruit, nor can a bad [rotten] tree bear good fruit. Every tree that does not bear good fruit is cut down and thrown into the fire. Thus you will know them by their fruits.*

The last two churches where I worked were pastored by high-profile pastors residing over large budgets, big buildings, and extensive growth. At my church, we have a beautiful, new building, and at times we've seen dramatic growth.

Sometimes people will say, "Well, you must be doing something right, Peter. Just look at all these people!" I don't mean to be rude, but sometimes I'll answer, "Well, Hitler was pretty popular too. And Hitler had a lot of converts." Is that fruit?

At both of my past churches, the senior pastors were living bold-faced lies and then caught in sexual immorality. That's not good fruit.

But at my current church:

- We don't only have a big crowd and new building, we have an Orthodox confession: "Lord, Lord."
- We also have a remarkable prophetic ministry team, and people have told me I preach prophetically.
- We've cast out demons.
- We've seen miracles, visions, and even some bona fide healings.

That's got to be some *good fruit* . . . from a *good tree!* Yet . . . next verse:

MATTHEW 7:21–23: *Not every one who says to me, "Lord, Lord," shall enter the kingdom of heaven, but he who does the will of my Father who is in heaven. On that day many will say to me, "Lord, Lord, did we not prophesy in your name, and cast out demons in your name, and do many mighty works in your name?" And then will I declare to them, "I never knew you; depart from me, you evildoers."*

Yikes!

Maybe "lots of people" . . .
"a good confession" . . .
"prophecy" . . .
"casting out demons" . . .
"mighty works in Jesus' name" . . .

maybe that's not the fruit Jesus is talking about.

Maybe it's not fruit at all.

In Galatians 5:22–23 Paul lists some "fruit"—the fruit of the Spirit: love, joy, peace, patience, kindness, goodness, gentleness, faithfulness, and self-control (that is, control of self or temperance).

Then Paul lists some "works of the flesh"—our self, our old sin nature: adultery, fornication, debauchery, idolatry, witchcraft . . . then hatred, strife, jealousy, anger, selfishness, dissension, factionalism, envy, drunkenness, orgies. He just lumps them *all together*, from envy to orgies, from witchcraft to selfishness.

Witchcraft is rather obvious, but gosh, you could build a church, write a book, run a mission, and do "many mighty works" all out of selfishness, envy, or a competitive spirit. You could be, like, alive on the outside and dead on the inside . . . like a zombie . . . like a whitewashed tomb. Worse than dead on the inside, you could be a wolf on the inside.

Sheep on the outside, wolf on the inside—a Pharisee!

In Galatians 5, Paul argues that all those "works of the flesh" come from those under the law, those who "bite and devour one another" (those who compete and compare). Here in the Sermon on the Mount, Jesus has been talking about Pharisees in Israel. In Galatians, Paul is talking about Pharisees in the church.

Remember, out of all the groups in Jesus' day, it can be argued that the Pharisees bear the most striking resemblance to today's mainline evangelical church. They were the good religious folks of their day. And the people in Jesus' little story of the judgment appear to be Pharisees . . . but Pharisees in *Jesus' name!*

The right confession,

the right words,

the right deeds,

yet Jesus doesn't know them.

"You will know them by their fruit." Jesus doesn't see fruit (love, joy, peace . . .) in them. Jesus can judge that fruit. (He can see into a heart.) But how can we judge that fruit? (We can't see inside another's heart.)

From a distance, the pastors in my old churches appeared to have a lot of fruit. I don't know what they had in their hearts, but people are good actors (*hupokrites*).

- People can perform dance steps without ever hearing the music.
- They can act gracious yet be very legalistic about grace.
- They can act faithful and be entirely motivated by fear.
- They can act humble and be extremely proud of it.
- They can pretend to serve, yet it's all a means of control.
- They can affirm with their lips while they bite and devour with their soul.

People are good actors. It's extremely hard to tell what's fruit and what's flesh in others. It's hard to tell what's fruit and what's flesh in *me*. If I'm honest, I'd have to confess it's almost as if there are two trees in me. One grows the fruit of the Spirit, and one produces the works of the flesh.

I have to die to one and live to the other. I can do that, because by God's grace I'm beginning to discern the fruit and the flesh in *me* . . . not really in others, but in *me*.

Jesus says, "You'll know a tree by its fruit." Maybe I'm to know a tree by the fruit or flesh it produces in *me*.

Have you ever had someone pray for you because they said they wanted to "bless you"? They used a lot of religious words and proper confessions, yet when they were done, you felt more envious, angry, factional, frightened, or competitive than before. You became very conscious of your dance steps and forgot the music. You felt a lot of flesh—a lot of *you*.

Well, maybe you've been slimed; maybe you've been leavened by a Pharisee. Leaven makes more leaven; flesh breeds flesh. Jesus is saying, "Beware—take note—don't confuse that tree with Me."

Yet have you ever been prayed for and when it was over you felt love, joy, peace . . . fleshlessness? You were less self-conscious and more Jesus conscious. You forgot your dance steps, swept away by the music. Well, then, that's a good tree.

Now, I imagine you may be asking yourself, "What kind of tree is *me?*" I doubt that many people intentionally try to be wolves; it's just that they find that they have a taste for sheep flesh. They deny it, but they feed on sheep. It's called competition—survival of the fittest—self-preservation—the way of the world—control. And it's the opposite of love, joy, peace, patience, kindness, goodness, gentleness, faithfulness, and control of self (the fruit of the Spirit).

> *So what kind of tree are you?*
> *How fruitful are you?*
> *How do you compare?*

If you answered those questions, I guess you're competing for fruit. If you answered those questions, I bet you're trying to love *best*, sacrifice *best*.

- You're trying to exalt yourself by being best at not exalting yourself.
- You're trying to be first at being last.

- You're trying to grow fruit with your flesh.
- You're trying to make apples out of sheep dung and dirt, and that won't do.

So try harder! Get your butt in gear and grow some *peace!* Do it *now!* Grow some patience. Get serious, you bunch of losers; grow some kindness and gentleness! Grow some fruit!

You see the problem, don't you? You can't grow fruit by *trying,* because you can't make fruit with your *self.* You can't turn sheep dung and dirt into apples. You need a tree. I need a tree in me.

In the last chapter we saw that in the end, the one tree is the *xoolon* (the cross). Jesus hangs on that tree and is the fruit of that tree, and in Him is an entire new creation. I conjectured that the tree of the knowledge of good and evil, like the tree of life, was actually the cross. Jesus said, "You'll know a tree by its fruit." From a good tree you get good fruit; from a bad tree you get bad fruit.

I've just about given myself an aneurysm trying to figure out if the tree of the knowledge of good and evil is *good* or *evil.*

God knows good and evil, and God is good. God planted that tree, so it must be good.

Yet Adam and Eve had a serious reaction to the fruit: shame and death. So what's the tree?

Furthermore, how would you know if the tree of the knowledge of good and evil was good or evil unless you tasted the fruit so you could know good and evil? For even if God warned you beforehand, how would you know His advice was *good?* or that *God* was good?

Well, in Matthew 12 Jesus says to some Pharisees who are trying to judge Him, "Make the tree good and the fruit good, or make the tree bad and the fruit bad."

. . . kind of like He was a tree, and for those to whom the fruit tasted bad, He was a bad tree; for those to whom the fruit tasted good, He was a good tree.

. . . kind of like He was an aroma of "life to life" for some and of "death to death" for others.

. . . kind of like He was *their* judgment. Their judgment was how they judged Him. He said, "Now is this world judged," speaking of the moment He would be lifted from the earth on a tree.

Maybe the tree of the knowledge of good and evil is like your judgment: good or evil depending on what you do with the fruit, or better, what the fruit does to you. To some it leads to condemnation; to some it leads to life, so for them that tree becomes the tree of life.

So, I about got an aneurysm . . . and then I read Romans. And wherever Paul wrote "law," I read "the knowledge of good and evil." That's what the law *is*.

> What then shall we say? That the law [the knowledge of good and evil] is sin? By no means! Yet, if it had not been for the law [the knowledge of good and evil], I should not have known sin. . . . For sin, finding opportunity in the commandment, deceived me and by it killed me. So the law [the knowledge of good and evil] is holy, and the commandment is holy and just and good. Did that which is good, then, bring death to me? By no means! It was sin, working death in me through what is good, in order that sin might be shown to be sin, and through the commandment might become sinful beyond measure. (Romans 7:7, 11–13)

Maybe God knew man had sin in him when He planted the tree, and the purpose of the tree (the law, the knowledge of good and evil) is first of all to kill us—to show us that we alone are incomplete, guilty, condemned, and dead. Paul keeps writing:

There is therefore now no condemnation for those who are in Christ Jesus. For the law [the knowledge of good and evil] of the Spirit of life in Christ Jesus has set me free from the law [the knowledge of good and evil] of sin and death. (Romans 8:1–2)

The law of the Spirit is the *new* law—the *complete* law—as James calls it, "the perfect law of liberty" (James 1:25 NKJV), that is, the "completed law of freedom."

For God has done what the law [the knowledge of good and evil], weakened by the flesh, could not do: sending his own Son in the likeness of sinful flesh and for sin, he condemned sin in the flesh, in order that the just requirement of the law [the knowledge of good and evil] might be fulfilled in us, who walk not according to the flesh but according to the Spirit. (Romans 8:3–4)

Remember at the start of the Sermon on the Mount, Jesus said He came to "fulfill" the Law. He came to fully fill that old tree, to bear its curse for us and give it new meaning.

If the Law of Moses on Mount Sinai was the *fill*ment of the law, then Jesus on Mount Calvary was the *full*fillment of the law—the tree—the ripe fruit.

Now we look to the tree and see the good—not just ten commandments; the good is Jesus, God's love. And the evil is us, who nailed Him to the tree.

The good purpose of the tree of knowledge is to kill us, that sin might become "sinful beyond measure" (Romans 7:13), and that we would see sin for what it is: the murder of God! The good purpose of the tree is that we would die to ourselves—our flesh, our self-righteousness. So instead of stealing the fruit, trying to be good with our own power, we'd surrender to

God's grace and receive Christ's life as the lavish gift it is: "the good" that is *God*. Christ's life, His body broken and blood shed, is the knowledge of good and evil, and when received by grace in faith it is life: the fruit of the one tree. The good purpose of the tree is that we'd die and be born again. A tree in me. A tree of life that knows the evil but grows the good.

"Jesus didn't come to give us the willies; He came to help us out." Actually, He came to fulfill the Law and finish the job, crucify our old man and give us His very life. The cross is how He does it.

The problem with a zombie—a Pharisee—is that he doesn't really believe the law. He hasn't thoroughly digested the law. The fruit is undigested and has not yet killed him, or he does not yet believe he's dead. He thinks that he can be good in the power of his own flesh. So he's a bad tree bearing the works of his own flesh and lying to himself that those works are good. Yet . . .

. . . he doesn't even *know* the good.

. . . he hasn't surrendered to the good.

. . . he hasn't ever *tasted* the good.

. . . he's hiding from the good like Adam and Eve.

. . . he's hiding in the trees, the law.

. . . he thinks his dance steps are dancing, but he hasn't even heard the music.

. . . he thinks fruit is just apple-shaped sheep dung and mud.

. . . he's wearing sheep's clothing, but he can't help being a wolf.

He can't help feeding on other wolves or sheep. He can't help it because he thinks that's all there is. He's never tasted real fruit or digested it if he consumed it. He can't see love. For him love is just a category of competition, a way to exalt himself. Love is a sophisticated selfishness. Love is just one more way the strong survive. At best, love is when you really like something (like a steak or a woman), so you consume it and bite it and devour it.

So when a sheep says, "I love you," the wolf can't really believe it, as he doesn't really know what "it" is. "It" is God. And God is love.

A wolf has no clue who God is!

But, if you're a believer, you *do*. You've come to the tree and seen that you're dead. You've surrendered your life, your heart, your knowledge, your self; and you've seen (if only for an instant) that God is love and He loves you, for He hangs on the tree for you. You took His life, yet now He gives His life to you. You can't take His life—He *for*gave it to you!

> *He gives you His life, the good, the fruit, the seed.*
> *Eve, He is the promised seed. And fruit is seed.*
> *Eve, He gives you the fruit as a gift.*
> *Eve, He enters you with His body and His blood, His seed.*

Seed is *sperma* in Greek. In that culture, children were referred to as fruit. And in that culture, "to know" was a euphemism for making love. Jesus says to those who did the mighty works, "Depart from Me. I never knew you. I don't know where you come from. You never surrendered yourself, that is, your naked shame, to Me. So it's not *My* life that you're bearing now."

You realize it's called the fruit of the *Spirit*; and the *Spirit* is Jesus' Spirit, and the life is Jesus' life.

"Love, joy, peace,
    patience, kindness, goodness,
        gentleness, faithfulness, self control"
            is Jesus in you.

Perhaps you thought Christianity was about trying to be good and hide the dirt. No, that's what every other religion is about. Christianity is the bride of Christ—the church—allowing herself to be known by her Groom, allowing Jesus to make love to her, even in her place of shame and emptiness—especially in her place of shame and emptiness—the very place she covered in fear so long ago in the Garden. Jesus makes love to her there. It's called grace. And fruit happens!

She bears the fruit that "befits repentance" (Matthew 3:8). Surrendered shame—sheep dung and dirt exposed to the light through the one tree—turns into the fruit of His kingdom.

One last thing . . .

Perhaps you know a tree by its fruit in you. Jesus bears Jesus in me. And Jesus in others bears Jesus in me. And so I can "beware of false prophets and wolves in sheep's clothing," for they *don't* bear Jesus in me. They bear *me* in me. Zombies turn me into a zombie.

I've learned to check the fruit in me. A good tree produces Christ in me, and I forget me and think about Him. I dance. A bad tree produces me and the power of me—my flesh, so I think about me. I'm zombified.

Jesus says, "Beware of false prophets." It's imperative tense—a command, not an option. So I'm learning to beware, and I made a little list of when *I* get wary:

1. *When preachers and prophets make deals.* "If you do this, then God will do that." Prophets in the old covenant make deals, but on His tree Jesus said, "It is finished"—perfected. There's one deal, one covenant, one tree.

2. *When prophets compare.* "Oh, Peter, God wants you to be like so and so, like this church or that church." My flesh competes and compares.

3. *When prophets preach a system, a program, a deed they did.* Then it's what *they* did. *Flesh.*

4. *When prophets don't speak in absolutes.* Muhammad says, "I can divorce my wife twice but not thrice" (and remarry her). "I should give some of my money but not all." Jesus says God requires *all.* He requires absolute love, and I am absolutely guilty. So He is absolutely gracious, and I am absolutely saved absolutely and forever. He did it, it's done, it's finished.

5. *When prophets speak shame but not conviction.* That is, prophets who shame me with vague statements of guilt so I'm in their control, but they don't convict me with truth in the light so I can die to sin and live to God.

6. *When prophets prophesy fear—just* some *fear.* Either scare me to death so I can live, or don't scare me at all! Perfect love drives out fear . . . crucifies it and resurrects it as faith (1 John 4:18).

7. *When prophets understand everything they say.* If they understand everything they say, they're probably not saying Jesus and certainly not His Spirit.

Well, that's a list and not a law. Some of it may be wrong. I'm just saying that these kinds of prophets and preachers produce *flesh* in me. But good prophets and preachers produce *Jesus* in me—the fruit of the tree.

A true prophet paints a picture of Jesus and His tree, and when the prophet is finished, there's no *them* and no *me.* I forget them and me, and find myself worshiping at the tree. I find His fruit in me. I've lost myself, and I'm dancing.

"You'll know a tree by its fruit," and Jesus is the fruit. And all around you grow His trees. So Adam (man), don't hide in the law. Hide in these trees—His tree:

They may not write a book.

They may never win a convert (only Jesus does).

They may never cast out a demon.

They may be the last and the least.

They may be poor in spirit.

They may be mourning.

They may be meek.

They may be hungering and thirsting for righteousness themselves.

But if they testify to Jesus, they are His trees. For there He is crucified, rises from the dead, and grows His fruit . . . where He "knows" them.

At the beginning of Matthew, John preached to the Pharisees, "Repent! Bear the fruit that befits repentance." That's where fruit comes from: repentance at Jesus' tree.

Chuck Colson works with prison reform. A few years ago he told about a prison he visited in Brazil named Humaita:

When I visited Humaita, I found the inmates smiling—particularly the murderer who held the keys, opened the gates, and let me in. Wherever I walked I saw men at peace. I saw clean living areas, people working industriously. The walls were decorated with biblical sayings from Psalms and Proverbs. Humaita has an astonishing record. Its recidivism rate is 4 percent compared to 75 percent in the rest of Brazil and the United States. How is all this possible?"[3]

He's asking, "How can there be such fruit: 'love, joy, peace, . . . kindness, goodness, faithfulness, gentleness, self-control, against such there is no law'? (see Galatians 5:21–22). How is all this possible?"

I saw the answer when my guide escorted me to the notorious punishment cell once used for torture. Today, he told me, that block houses a single inmate. As we reached the end of a long concrete corridor and he put the key into the lock, he paused and asked, "Are you sure you want to go in?"

"Of course," I replied impatiently. "I've been in isolation cells all over the world." Slowly he swung open the massive door, and I saw the prisoner in that punishment cell: a crucifix, beautifully carved by the Humaita inmates—the prisoner Jesus hanging on the cross.

"He's doing time for all the rest of us," my guide said softly.[4]

Yes. He bears the pain of all time to make us in His image for all eternity. He's the good tree and the good fruit. And you are what you eat.

16

ROCK ON

MATTHEW 7:24–29

On Tuesday, October 17, 1989, at 5:04 p.m., I was bending over trying to put my key in the trunk of my '67 Ford Mustang, and I missed the keyhole. So I tried again and missed the keyhole again. I figured some high school kid was shaking my car, because the trunk was moving. I looked up, and the house was moving, the trees were moving, the street was moving, the mountains were moving, and *I* was moving. I could see waves coming down El Pintado Boulevard.

It was the Loma Prieta earthquake.

Earthquakes are incredibly unnerving, because everything moves and you feel entirely out of control.

When it was over, Susan, Jonathan, four-day-old Elizabeth, and I all sat in the front yard and listened to our radio as damage reports came in. The Cypress Freeway had collapsed . . . the Embarcadero was crumbling . . . in the Marina district, buildings fell like cards and burned. It was strange: the same earthquake—one block unscathed and the next obliterated.

In fact, if you were to draw a line around the areas of devastation, you would produce a geologic map exhibiting areas of bedrock and areas of unconsolidated sand and landfill. The Cypress structure, the Embarcadero, and the Marina district were all built on man-made landfills. The sand and mud shook like Jell-O in a bowl (liquefaction), so those great structures fell. "And great was the fall of them." The earthquake—the earth-storm—revealed the rock and exposed the foundations.

> MATTHEW 7:24–29: *"Every one then who hears these words of mine and does them will be like a wise man who built his house upon the rock; and the rain fell, and the floods came, and the winds blew and beat upon that house, but it did not fall, because it had been founded on the rock. And every one who hears these words of mine and does not do them will be like a foolish man who built his house upon the sand; and the rain fell, and the floods came, and the winds blew and beat against that house, and it fell; and great was the fall of it."*
>
> *And when Jesus finished these sayings, the crowds were astonished at his teaching, for he taught them as one who had authority, and not as their scribes.*

Both men built a house. Whatever you build on is what you have faith in. Everybody has faith in something: God, self, science, atheism, religion. People may profess faith in one thing (like Jesus) but actually build on something else (like public opinion or religious deeds and statements). And all houses may look alike. All may say, "Lord, Lord" above the entryway, but the storm exposes their true foundation—sand or rock.

Why, then, would a person build on sand instead of rock? Well, sand is easy to push around.

- If you build your house on rock, you have to conform your house to the foundation.
- If you build your house on sand, you can conform the foundation to your house . . . control the foundation.

Jesus says, "Every one then who hears these words of mine and does them will be like a wise man who built his house upon the rock"—not *a* rock but *the* rock.

What is the rock?

Well, we know building on this rock is like "doing these words of Jesus": that is, the Sermon on the Mount.

Moses received the Law on Mount Sinai at the start of Israel's journey through the wilderness. Now on this mount Jesus expounds the Law and begins to lead His disciples on a journey. Clearly Jesus' words are more foundational than the Law, like His mountain is more solid than Sinai.

I hope you work to conform your life to His words, that you dig down and study Scripture and obey. It's frightening how often we don't. For instance, so many couples profess faith in Christ and then live together—sleeping together—outside of marriage. That's, like, not even *trying*. I want to say, Don't we get it? You can't conform His words to your preferred lifestyle. You must conform your lifestyle to His Word. It's not simply my opinion; it's *solid rock*. You're slamming your head into solid rock, and the rock can crush you.

"But he who hears these words of mine and does them," says Jesus, "will be like a wise man who built his house *on* the rock." "These words of mine" are the Sermon on the Mount, and it begins with the Beatitudes: "Blessed are the poor in spirit, those who mourn, the meek, those hungering for righteousness." They are *blessed* . . . and you wonder, "How can I be more like that?"

- Then Jesus starts expounding the Law.
- Then Jesus talks about spiritual disciplines.
- Then Jesus discusses treasure, gates, and pearls.

The Sermon on the Mount itself is like a journey. And Jesus' words are incredibly *hard* in places. I wonder if I've even *tried.* He sums up the Law by saying, "You must be perfect as my heavenly Father is perfect." And then, "Practice perfection without your right hand knowing what the left is doing." Like, "Love to perfection and do it without consciously trying."

It's easy to think, *Well, I'm obviously going to fail. I can't give without knowing it. Why even try? Lust, anger, turn the other cheek? Every time I look at my girlfriend I commit adultery in my heart. I might as well do it in my bedroom. Why try?*

When my son was an infant, he said to Susan and me, "Mom, Dad—I'm giving up on walking, because I'm sure I'm gonna fall. Mom and Dad, there are sixty-year-old men who trip and fall. Who has never fallen? So in my deep humility I'll just acknowledge my failure and stay in bed the rest of my life."

Actually, he didn't say that. He was a child. Children just keep trying. (Surely God doesn't want us to become like a child, does He?)

Philip Yancey tells how a solo violinist came to the great composer Igor Stravinsky and said, "I can't play this piece. I've given it my best and found it too difficult, even unplayable." Stravinsky replied, "I understand that. What I am after is the sound of someone trying to play it."[1]

Is that what God wants? Jesus didn't say, "He who hears these words and *tries* is like a wise man who built his house on the rock." Jesus says, "He who hears these words and *does* them." *Yikes!*

Well then, has anyone ever built his house on the rock? Heard these words and *done* them? Certainly the crowd would have thought of the scribes and Pharisees. They were absolutely stringent about the Law. They confessed, "Lord, Lord" and did "many mighty works" and great deeds in His name.

But remember, Jesus just told them:

MATTHEW 7:21–23: *Not every one who says to me, "Lord, Lord," shall enter the kingdom of heaven, but he who does the will of my Father who is in heaven. On that day many will say to me, "Lord, Lord, did we not prophesy in your name, and cast out demons in your name, and do many mighty works in your name?" And then will I declare to them, "I never knew you; depart from me, you evildoers."*

The scribes and the Pharisees said, "Lord, Lord" and did "great works," yet they didn't do the Father's will, and Jesus doesn't know them.

Building on the rock is like *hearing* and *doing* the words, which is somehow knowing *the* Word—the One who speaks.

> *What is the rock?*
> *Has anyone ever built their house on it?*

The next time Jesus talks about the rock is in Matthew 16:13–18. He's hanging out with His disciples and asks, "Who do men say that [I] am?" Petros (that is, Peter), answers, "You are the Christ, the Son of the living God." Jesus says, "Blessed are you, Simon Bar-Jona! For flesh and blood has not revealed this to you, but my Father who is in heaven. And I tell you, you are Peter [Petros] and on this rock [*petra*] I will build my church."

Well, somehow Peter *is* the rock. Roman Catholics argue that Peter *is* the rock and that here Jesus inaugurates the papacy. Protestants argue that the rock was the confession of Christ *in* Peter. Both would agree that ultimately the rock is Jesus.

In fact, it's all through the Old Testament: "the Lord is our rock," "a rock of refuge," "a sure foundation," "a rock to make men stumble," yet also "the rock of our salvation."

Paul writes that on the wilderness journey the Israelites "all ate the same supernatural food and all drank the same supernatural drink . . . from the supernatural Rock which followed them, and the Rock was Christ" (1 Corinthians 10:3–4).

Paul may mean a particular rock actually followed them, or he may mean that Christ was like every rock where Moses spoke in faith . . . like the narrow gate that's everywhere, like a pearl in every oyster, like a treasure in every field.

Whatever the case, in 1 Corinthians 3:11 Paul writes, "No other foundation can any one lay than that which is laid, which is Jesus Christ."

So not only are Christ's words like a foundation, He—the Word— *is* the foundation—the rock. Yet He says, "On Petros—Peter—this rock—I will build my church."

Peter did *try* to do Jesus' words. He was like Captain Liquefaction, Jell-O Man, but He did *try.* And Peter did *know* Jesus. In fact, after the Sermon on the Mount, Peter went on a journey with Jesus—just as Israel, after the Law on Mount Sinai, went on a journey with the Lord. You really get to know somebody on a journey, especially a journey through a storm. By the end of Matthew, Peter doesn't only know *about* Jesus; he *knows* Jesus.

The Pharisees refused to go on the journey with Jesus. They knew the good in their heads but would not know Him in their hearts. They would not walk with Him. They used knowledge *about* good to guard their hearts from knowing *the* Good—Jesus.

In the movie *Good Will Hunting,* Will Hunting is a genius. He knows about everything with his head, but he uses that knowledge to hide from pain in his heart. He meets a counselor (played by Robin Williams) and guards his heart from the counselor by dissecting the counselor *with* his knowledge and crucifying the counselor's passions for art and his bride, *on* his own knowledge. The counselor confronts him in a garden:

If I asked you about war, you'd probably throw Shakespeare at me, right? "Once more into the breach, dear friends." But you've never been near one. You've never held your best friend's head in your lap and watched him draw his last breath, looking to you for help.

And if I asked you about love, you'd probably quote me a sonnet, but you've never looked at a woman and been totally vulnerable . . . known someone who could level you with her eyes . . . feeling like God put an angel on earth just for you, who could rescue you from the depths of hell.

And you wouldn't know what it's like to be *her* angel, to have that love for her and be there forever, through anything, through cancer. You wouldn't know about sleeping sitting up in a hospital room for two months holding her hand, because the doctors could see in your eyes that the term "visiting hours" didn't apply to you. You don't know about real loss, because that only occurs when you love something more than you love yourself. I doubt you've ever dared to love anybody that much.[2]

Will Hunting knew *about* beauty, truth, love, and life. But he was too frightened to *know* beauty, truth, love, and life, and live. Because he wouldn't know, he wasn't known. He was an act hiding a wounded heart.

> *"Behold, I never knew you," said Jesus.*
> *Does He know you . . . or only the act?*

By the end of Matthew, Simon Peter knows beauty, truth, and love. He knows life, because he's walked with Him. He journeyed with Him all the way to the cross. He knows and is known.

Jesus *is* beauty, truth, love, and life, and I believe He is waiting for you in every painting and every person, in every war, and in the pit of every disease, waiting to *know* you if you'll only "hear and do" . . .

> *That is, have faith;*
> *that is, trust Him enough to try to obey;*
> *that is, give up your control and surrender to His*
> *control—let Him lead you in His dance.*

We're afraid to try, because we're afraid we'll fail and He'll fail, so we'll drown and die, because God really isn't good and He can't be trusted. That is, He's not a rock, or the storm is more powerful than the rock. So we dare not follow His counsel.

In Matthew 14, the disciples are perishing in a storm. Jesus comes walking on the water. Peter calls out, "If it is you, bid me come to you on the water." Jesus says, "Come," and Peter did. He got out of the boat and walked into the storm. Peter tried doing the word of His Lord, and, if only for a moment, Peter walked on water (see Matthew 14:22–33).

Peter tried, but I doubt he was even conscious of trying. I mean, his right hand didn't know what his left was doing. He wasn't conscious of himself; his eyes were fixed on the Rock, the Rock in the midst of the storm—Jesus. When Peter came to himself and saw the storm, he sank. He stopped dancing. Peter failed.

The other disciples *didn't* fail . . . or did they? They didn't sink, but they never *tried*, so they didn't *know* their failure. Because they didn't know their failure, they didn't know what Peter knew next. He called out to Jesus in the storm. He called to the Rock, and the Rock moved. The Rock came to him and saved him.

> So Peter knew Jesus: the beauty, truth, love, and life.
> And Peter knew Jesus: the rock of his salvation.

Perhaps you can't really know your own failure
until you've tried to walk in the storm.

Perhaps you can't really know the Savior
until you truly know that you've failed.

When your heart admits that you've failed, that you're drowning and have no control, then you've become "poor in spirit." Your heart "mourns," you are "meek," you "hunger and thirst for righteousness"—the Rock. Then blessed are you. The Rock moves for you and saves you. You meet the rock of your salvation—Jesus. He moves for you, under you, and in you. You are His house. He is your foundation.

The scribes and Pharisees thought the temple was their house that they built. They thought they built on the Law, Mount Sinai, and Mount Zion. In reality they built on sand. They never really attempted the Law. They moved the Law around like sand in order to conform it to themselves and maintain control.

In Matthew 21:21 Jesus said, "If you have faith and never doubt . . . if you say to this mountain, 'Be taken up and cast into the sea,' it will be done." When Jesus said that, He was standing by Mount Zion.

In Scripture the sea is a metaphor for chaos and the home of the nations. When Christ was crucified, Mount Zion—the sacrifice, the atonement, and the covenant—was cast to the nations. The Rock moved to save the world. The foundation moved to save its house. When Jesus was crucified, the sacrifice, atonement, and covenant moved from Mount Zion to Mount Calvary and to the ends of the earth to save His temple. His temple is His people. They are His house.

Matthew records that when Jesus was crucified, the earth moved. The mountain moved. Whatever that means, whatever Matthew 21:21 means, we do know this: the Rock moved to save His people.

We come to know a Savior when He saves us, but some people don't want to be saved. It's too much of a threat to "their house." They build on sand even in an earthquake.

Overcome with fear, Peter failed to hang on to the Rock when Jesus was crucified. He took his eyes off the Rock and denied the Rock three times. Yet he called to the Rock to save him, and the Rock moved to save him. And then Peter *knew* Him: the Savior. He was anchored to the Savior, dependent on the Savior.

We come to know a Savior when He saves us. He is the "Rock of our salvation." Be built on Him.

The scribes and Pharisees—the religious folks—despised the Savior and so hated the Rock. They refused to be built upon the Rock. They crucified Jesus to maintain control of their house. They tried to push the Rock around with their house. And to quote Jesus, "Great was the fall of it."

In AD 70 the Romans obliterated it. They literally plowed the old temple into the ground, and it hasn't been built since. Yet by AD 312, the Roman emperor himself confessed to living in Christ's house . . . His temple, His people, His church, built on Peter the rock.

Has anyone ever built on the rock? Christ has. He said, "You are Peter, and on this rock I will build my church, and the gates of hell shall not prevail against it." Jesus is the Rock, and Jesus was in Peter, for Peter surrendered control to Jesus. And so on that Rock (Jesus in Peter) Jesus built His church . . . and still builds His church.

Pharisees see that and try to build houses that look the same. But they're the exact opposite at the foundation. They're built on the glorification of self rather than the surrender of self. They're built by the flesh rather than the Spirit.

The religious spirit is a spirit of control. It uses God to *maintain* control rather than *surrendering* control to be used by God.

What are you standing on? Some formula, some system, some philosophy, some idea with which you hope to control God and move the Rock?

What are you building with? Your wisdom, deeds, knowledge, goodness? Spiritual nuggets, chunks of Jesus, as if He's your building material?

If that's the case, you're still building *your* house, aren't you?

He's the Rock, and He builds His church. You don't build *your* house with *Him* so much as He builds *His* house with *you.*

Peter writes, "Come to him, to that living stone, rejected by men but in God's sight chosen and precious; and like living stones be yourselves built into a spiritual house" (1 Peter 2:4–5). He builds His house with you, on Himself, and the gates of hell—storms of hell—cannot prevail against it.

His house, His New Jerusalem, withstands every storm. But more than that, His house is on the move, for He is on the move. He is storming the gates of hell.

Several years ago I was with my associate pastor, Aram Haroutunian, and we were praying with a friend who at the time struggled with demonic spirits assigned to her from her past of satanic ritual abuse. At 2:00 a.m., Aram and I were at her place, and obviously we were not in control. It was a crazy storm, and we were in way over our heads. Yet clearly Jesus was calling from the storm.

I've been saddened that we religious people won't walk into storms like that. We'll say, "That violates my boundaries," or "You need an expert for that, someone who knows what he's doing." Experts can be helpful, but control in a storm is an illusion. We need something more stable than that: the Rock.

- The Rock moves, for He is a living presence.
- The Rock moves, but nothing in all creation is more stable or dependable.
- The Rock moves, or perhaps everything else moves relative to Him.

We were praying against a demonic spirit that took the name "Control" and had convinced our friend to hide from her heart and maintain a good, religious act. At one point it manifested in her body and choked her. Aram and I watched as she stopped breathing and fell over lifeless on the floor. I put my face by hers, and there was no breath.

I thought of everything I knew. I began reciting every religious formula I could think of . . . "I take authority in Jesus' name! I command in Jesus' name! I rebuke in Jesus' name!" . . . tongues, gifts, whatever. Aram prayed and I yelled, and still she wasn't breathing. All of our religion had gone bad.

I looked at Aram, he looked at me, and we realized we were going down! The church was going down. It was 2:00 A.M., and we were in a single woman's house—a *dead* single woman's house. Sure, the cops would understand . . . "It was a demon, officer!"

Well, almost unconsciously I forgot what I knew and thought of the one I know. I stopped trying to dance and surrendered to the dance. Like a child, from somewhere deep in my heart, I mumbled, "Jesus, help us." At that, she suddenly gasped for air. We continued the fight, and the gates of hell could not prevail against us: the church on the Rock in the wild sea.

We were drowning in the sea, and the Rock rose beneath us and stormed the gates of hell.

I hope I'll never forget that. I think the Lord was reminding me, "Peter, with all this religion, all your knowledge, formulas, systems, and theology, never forget I'm the Rock. I will build My church and I will take you into the storm so you can know the Rock of your salvation, and I can build My house out of people who trust Me."

Jesus is the Rock. Put it another way: if I want to dance, it's not about learning a million steps or formulas or theories; it's hanging on to Him.

We're at the end of the Sermon on the Mount. I suspect that we all thought Jesus was preaching about *us* and what *we* must do.

I think that's bad religion.

I think Jesus was preaching about *Himself* and what *He* would do.

I think that's grace.

For by grace you have been saved through faith; and this is not your own doing, it is the gift of God—not because of works, lest any man should boast. For we are his workmanship, created in Christ Jesus for good works, which God prepared beforehand, that we should walk in them. (Ephesians 2:8–10)

I think Jesus was preaching about Himself and what He would do *in* us.

Now, that's amazing grace.

From Mount Sinai to Mount Calvary to Mount Zion—the Sermon on the Mount.

CONCLUSION:
THE EASY YOKE AND THE
LIGHT BURDEN

MATTHEW 11:16–30

MATTHEW 11:11, 15–17: *Truly, I say to you, among those born of women there has risen no one greater than John the Baptist; yet he who is least in the kingdom of heaven is greater than he. . . . He who has ears to hear, let him hear. But to what shall I compare this generation? It is like children sitting in the market places and calling to their playmates, "We piped to you, and you did not dance; we wailed, and you did not mourn."*

God has issued the great invitation: His heart nailed to the tree.

Remember what we've said. God is like a dance: three persons, one dance:

and that dance is *love*

and love is *life*

and life is *self-giving*.

And all that join this self-giving dance are the kingdom of heaven. "What is outside the dance is strictly and solely hell."[1] We dance to the music of the kingdom of heaven. Music seems illogical, but it's ultralogical. Music is more logical than the human mind can comprehend; yet we can recognize it and surrender to it. We cannot comprehend music, but music can comprehend us. It can find a place in us—bypass our conscious mind and will, cause us to lose ourselves and dance entirely free and unrestrained yet entirely ordered by the rhythm of the dance.

Jesus is the *Logos*—the Logic—the Word—the Rhythm of the Dance. "The Word became flesh and dwelt among us" (John 1:14).

Dance makes music visible

Like song makes rhythm audible.

> Jesus is the Word of God incarnate;
>
> Jesus is the Love of God manifest.
>
> > He is Love descended into our hell,
> >
> > Dancing alone but calling us to come join Him.

On the cross, the rhythm of the dance is revealed at great pain. The cross is the judgment of the world.

For all that are offended at Jesus and hate the music, they doubt Him away. They explain Him away. They may have a million facts, but none have meaning. They are alone in hell.

But for all who hear the music and come to the cross, for all who weep for their sins and dance to the tune of God's grace, they pass through the cross (die and live) and join the great dance.

At the cross, the piper piped, and He's still piping. It's not proofs and reasons that lead to the piper. It's the piper that leads to reason (like Led Zeppelin sang). He may use science, philosophy, and Bible studies, but the piper always leads us to reason. He *is* the reason . . . for everything. In other words, "Faith cometh by hearing, and hearing by the word of God" (Romans 10:17 KJV) or "word of Christ" (NIV).

The Word of God is the rhythm of the dance.

And then walking by faith is not making yourself or forcing yourself to believe, so much as surrendering to a music, a logic that's all around you, the Word that upholds all things. We exist in it, like the fish in the bottom of the ocean, like the baby in his mother's womb. When music plays, it vibrates everything—everything moves, but only the living can hear it and dance to it. The music is love. God is love. "In him we live and move and have our being" (Acts 17:28). But will we dance? That's the question.

Every day you do your thing and order your world, but there's music playing. Perhaps once in a while you forget yourself and weep with someone weeping, or rejoice with someone rejoicing. You actually love without trying. You move in rhythm to the music greater than yourself. You move in rhythm; you move in Jesus—His body—making the music visible. You begin to dance His dance. And to the extent you dance, you walk in faith. The faith isn't forced, like a great dance isn't forced. It's not you; it's the music that's found a place in you. If it's a choice, it's not a choice you can take credit for. It's not your choice; it's God's choice in you. It's Jesus in you. It's faith.

St. Augustine writes, "If there is faith in us, Christ is in us. For what else says the apostle: 'Therefore, [my] faith in Christ is Christ in [my] heart. That Christ may dwell in our hearts by faith' [Ephesians. 3:17]."

The Greeks had a legend that Amphion built Thebes with the music of his lute, which was so melodious that the stones danced into walls and houses voluntarily.

I believe that's the way Jesus builds the New Jerusalem. We're like stones: so dead we can't even hear the music, and we don't want to dance. Yet He calls us and chooses us to choose Him in freedom. So He enters us with His music and dances His dance. We become His body—His dwelling—the living stones—the New Jerusalem. The question is not "Is God real?" but "Am I real?"

Dancing with Jesus makes us real forever.

Jesus said that the least in the kingdom is greater than John, and the kingdom is constructed of the childlike (Matthew 11:11; 19:14). What can children do better than John the Baptist? Weep . . . and then *dance*. Children forget themselves very easily because there's not much of them to remember. Their hearts are easily captured; they easily forget themselves and surrender to the piper.

Robin Gunn writes:

> She stood a short distance from her guardian at the park this afternoon, her distinctive features revealing that although her body blossomed into young adulthood, her mind would always remain a child's. My children ran and jumped and sifted sand through perfect, coordinated fingers. Caught up in fighting over a shovel, they didn't notice when the wind changed. But she did. A wild autumn wind spinning leaves into amber flurries.
>
> I called to my boisterous son and jostled my daughter. Time to go, Mom still has lots to do today. My rosy-cheeked boy stood tall, watching with wide-eyed fascination the gyrating dance of the Down's syndrome girl as she scooped up leaves and showered herself with a twirling rain of autumn jubilation.
>
> With each twist and hop she sang deep, earthy grunts—a canticle of praise meant only for the One whose breath causes the leaves to tremble from the trees.[2]

Maybe that's what God wants: not that we'd "figure it out" or finally "do it right"; not that we'd be "smart enough" or "good enough." Maybe all creation, even the Fall and redemption, the law and the prophets, is all a part of God's asking a very different sort of question: not "Are you smart enough or good enough," but "Do you want to dance?"

Robin Gunn continues:

Hurry up. Let's go. Seat belts on? I start the car. In the rearview mirror I study her one more time through misty eyes. And then the tears come. Not tears of pity for her. The tears are for me. For I am far too sophisticated to publicly shout praises to my Creator.

I am whole and intelligent and normal, and so I weep because I will never know the severe mercy that frees such a child and bids her come dance in the autumn leaves.[3]

She may never know that particular severe mercy. But God is an expert at severe mercy . . . isn't a cross a rather severe mercy?

One Sunday I came to church with a cross on my back.

- Matthew 10:38: "He who does not take his cross and follow me is not worthy of me."
- Matthew 16:24: "If any man would come after me, let him deny himself and take up his cross and follow me."

I said, "This is what that looks like: they would flog you, then put one of these on your back, march you through town, nail you to a pole, and then watch you die . . . alone."

Then we read:

MATTHEW 11:17–19: *"We piped to you, and you did not dance; we wailed, and you did not mourn." For John came neither eating nor drinking, and they say, "He has a demon"; the Son of man came eating and drinking, and they say, "Behold, a glutton and a drunkard, a friend of tax collectors and sinners!" Yet wisdom is justified by her deeds.*

So we're supposed to weep and dance. Well, the weeping makes sense. Next verse:

MATTHEW 11:20–24: *Then he began to upbraid the cities where most of his mighty works had been done, because they did not repent. "Woe to you, Chora'zin! woe to you, Beth-sa'ida! for if the mighty works done in you had been done in Tyre and Sidon, they would have repented long ago in sackcloth and ashes. But I tell you, it shall be more tolerable on the day of judgment for Tyre and Sidon than for you. And you, Caper'na-um, will you be exalted to heaven? You shall be brought down to Hades. For if the mighty works done in you had been done in Sodom, it would have remained until this day. But I tell you that it shall be more tolerable on the day of judgment for the land of Sodom than for you."*

Imagine what it must have been like to be Jesus. Imagine the burden of having to speak God's Word and be God's Word. What weary labor! Imagine the pain of being rejected by those you love. You can feel the cross already. What a yoke He bore!

I learned two things from carrying that big cross: (1) carrying a cross is not easy, and (2) a cross is a heavy burden.

MATTHEW 11:25–30: *At that time Jesus declared, "I thank thee, Father, Lord of heaven and earth, that thou hast hidden these things from the wise and understanding and revealed them to babes; yea, Father, for such was thy gracious will. All things have been delivered to me by my Father; and no one knows the Son except the Father, and no one knows the Father except the Son and any one to whom the Son chooses to reveal him. Come to me, all who labor and are heavy laden, and I will give you rest. Take my yoke upon you, and learn from me; for I am gentle and lowly in heart, and you will find rest for your souls. For my yoke is easy, and my burden is light."*

"My yoke is easy, and my burden is light." I can think of only one burden we're commanded to bear, only one yoke we're commanded to wear. The easy yoke and the light burden must be a cross. Isn't that His yoke and His burden?

Yokes were for oxen. They were custom-fit for each ox and attached to a plow. If a yoke was for farming, what is Jesus growing? In Matthew 9:37, looking over the crowds of burdened people, Jesus said, "The harvest is plentiful." And now He says that He has a "yoke." The only thing resembling a yoke that we see on Jesus is a cross.

He says His yoke is "easy"—it fits.

- Yokes are for work, yet His gives rest.
- Yokes are a bondage, yet He talks like His sets you free.

Jesus says, "Take up a cross and follow." "My yoke is easy, and my burden is light." How can His cross be easy and light?

Maybe His yoke and burden is like a *dance*. C. S. Lewis referred to the self-giving at the cross as the central movement at the Great Dance, like the rhythm of the Dance.[4] So Calvary is our initiation into the great dance . . . like a "severe mercy" that frees us and bids us "come dance in the autumn leaves."

A dance is bondage, but then again, it's not. It's bondage in that you're bound and ordered by the music, yet it feels like freedom. If your self makes your self do the dance steps, it feels like bondage. But if you lose your self in the rhythm of the dance, it feels like freedom.

And a dance is toil, but it feels like rest. Aerobics is toil because your *self* makes your *self* dance to lose weight. But if you just lose yourself and dance because you love the music, it doesn't feel like toil. You burn just as many calories, and it feels like rest. Perhaps the cross is like a dance, and since we can't hear the music, the cross only appears heavy and hard.

The dance also is *love.* So the cross is the revelation of love in a world that doesn't dance and can't hear the music. Therefore, in this world, love only *appears* heavy and hard. Yet once you *do* love, it make burdens light and yokes easy. Once you hear the music and like it, calisthenics become dance, and aerobics become light and easy.

I work really hard for my money, and then I just give it to this woman, and these five people spend it. When I think about it, I realize they are an incredible burden. Yet they are an incredibly light burden— my wife, Susan, and my four children. Love makes burdens light.

I'm yoked to my wife, and we've plowed the field and produced fruit: Jonathan, Elizabeth, Becky, and Coleman. And it was pretty easy. Now, Susan had great labor, but her love made the labor easy. I had great labor (paying the bills for her labor), but love made the labor easy. But in this world, most labor lacks love—real love. So the burden appears heavy and the yoke exceedingly hard.

It can be extremely hard to dance in this world. But, you know, it's easy to dance on the moon. I have an old picture of an astronaut grabbing a satellite with his hands. The satellite must weigh several tons— an *incredible burden* in this world. But not in space.

Henry Drummond, in *Pax Vobiscum,* writes, "The weight of your burdens depends upon the attraction of the earth."[5] Jesus said, "My burden is light."

Dancing, love, and *other worlds* may be clues as to how our burden can be light. But I need to confess: I don't feel qualified to speak on this, because I often feel so burdened. That is, I (myself, me) feel heavy and uneasy and restless, which confuses me, because I thought Jesus gave me the burdens. But He says His burden is "light." Jesus preached, and I believe He called me to preach, but I need to tell you: it often feels like an *immense burden.*

For one, I don't know what to say. The more I know, the less it seems I understand. For instance, in Matthew 11:20–24, Jesus speaks judgment on Chorazin, Bethsaida, and Capernaum because they did not weep and dance. But then He thanks His Father because He has . . . hidden the music from them. They deserve judgment for not dancing, but it seems they had no choice. Chosen to not choose . . . I guess.

I can't get my brain around that, but it must be true, and I'm called to preach it, but I feel like an idiot. Then I think, *Or maybe I am an idiot. Maybe that's God's will . . . or is it all my fault, or both?* So I don't know what to say, and then when I feel I've said something great, it's as if people can't hear the music. They reject me and don't see Jesus. Then I feel futile and fruitless.

But many times I'll preach, people will hear, and they'll write a great note. And I'll think, *Oh no . . . they're going be so disappointed next week.* What a burden!

You all know that burden in different forms: preaching, mothering, laboring . . . the fear that "I can't be what I'm called to be."

I can't make myself,

I can't create myself,

I can't save myself,

I can't be good,

I can't obey God's law.

His law is summed up in one word: *love.*

I've failed at loving God and loving my neighbor.

I've drunk too much, eaten too much, said too much or too little.

I've glared at women and pictures of women with lust.

I've treated my bride as an object of consumption.

I've used the bride of Christ as a means for my own advancement.

The failures of my past are a great burden now. Then I look to the future, and that becomes an unbearable yoke. How can I preach, pastor, father, and provide? I'm not only worried about myself; I'm worried about *you,* because I'm worried I can't or won't help you. And if I don't help you, I'm worried no one else will. If I don't save you, who else will? We're talking about God, judgment, and eternal destinies, and I'm a *pastor.* That yoke does not feel easy to me. I think I'm a failure and I'm going to be a failure. Then Jesus says, "Take my yoke . . . ." Ugh!

It's as if I'm laboring under a curse—called to be fruitful yet cursed with futility.

Long ago in a garden, when Adam and Eve were not yet fully made (on the sixth day of creation), they tried to make themselves in God's image. They stole fruit from the "tree of the knowledge of good and evil"—the law. And God spoke the curse.

The woman was to bear children before the curse; it was a great gift. But after the curse, the fruit of her womb would be a great labor. The man was to work before the curse; it was a great gift. But after the curse, tilling the garden would be toil in unfruitful fields. God subjected creation to futility, and He drove them from that world into this world. He had told them, "The day you eat the fruit of the tree, you will die."

Do you understand my burden? My burden is *me.* It's taken me awhile to see it, but my burden is *me.* Do you ever want to get rid of your burden? lay it down? The problem is, you can't kill your self with your *self.* You can kill your body, but you can't give rest to your soul. You simply add murder to your burdens.

Bill Maher said, "Suicide is saying to God, 'You can't fire me. I quit.'" He's right. It's just you seizing control of you, which is more *you.* You are your own restless, weary, painful yoke, and you are your own unbearable burden.

Now listen to Jesus:

The Easy Yoke and the Light Burden

MATTHEW 11:28–30: *Come to me, all who labor and are heavy laden, and I will give you rest. Take my yoke upon you, and learn from me; for I am gentle and lowly in heart, and you will find rest for your souls. For my yoke is easy, and my burden is light.*

In that day, yokes were built for two. His yoke is a cross. Crosses kill people. He's offering to help you die to your *self.*

Your *self* keeps you from loving—

loving is losing your self in another.

Your *self* keeps you from dancing—

dancing is losing your self in the music.

Your *self* is the heavy burden and uneasy yoke.

Your *self* can't help you with that burden;

you need Jesus.

How can His cross be easy and light? It *kills* us. It kills the prideful, insecure, arrogant, shameful, fearful, self-conscious, old zombie that is *me.* It brings me to the end of myself. I see the truth. I'm dead. I can't save me. I need Him to live His life in me.

Brennan Manning writes:

Probably the moment in my own life when I was closest to the Truth who is Jesus Christ was the experience of being a hopeless derelict in the gutter in Fort Lauderdale, Florida. . . . Walker Percy says: "Only once in my life was the grip of everydayness broken: when I lay bleeding in the ditch." Paradoxically, such an experience of powerlessness does not make one sad. It is a great relief because it makes us rely not on our own strength but on the limitless power of God. The realization that God is the main agent makes the yoke easy, the burden light, and the heart still.[6]

Well, hopefully you don't have to drink yourself into a ditch to come to Jesus. However, you do need to admit you're hopeless without Him and enslaved to your lousy self. The priest Anthony DeMello said:

I'm going to write a book someday and the title will be *I'm an Ass, You're an Ass.* [He must be referring to donkeys.] That's the most liberating, wonderful thing in the world, when you openly admit you're an ass. It's wonderful. When people tell you, "You're wrong." I say, "What can you expect of an ass?"[7]

The pressure's off. You know, the cross isn't just for the end of your life or the beginning of your Christian life. It's for every day. If I really carried Jesus' cross every day, I suspect I'd still preach, pastor, father my kids, and provide for my wife. But I'd do it without the burden of *me* . . . always conscious of my *self* and conscious of my *steps.* My life might still hurt, and I'd burn as many calories, but it would be an easy yoke and a light burden, for my life would be like a dance. I'd constantly be losing myself in the dance and finding myself *dancing.* Jesus would be my dance partner. He leads, and I follow . . . to the rhythm of His love.

I can really only dance *now,* in the present moment, with Him. I can't be thinking about the steps I've missed in the past; I can't be thinking about possible dance steps required in the future. My only burden is an infinitely small moment we call *now.*

I think that's how Jesus lived and danced in space and time. I mean, He surrendered Himself to His Father each moment. He bore a cross every day. But only on one day did He cry, "My God, My God, why have You forsaken Me?" Even though He knew that day was coming, He didn't let it stop the dance the rest of the time. He lived each moment by His Father's lead, and their dance is love.

When the people rejected Him, He knew His Father was leading the dance still. He prayed, "Thank you." To constantly give thanks is to remember that your Lord is leading the dance—sovereign over all things. The dance is love.

In Matthew 11:27, He prays, "All things have been delivered to me by my Father [or "are delivered unto me" (kjv)]; and no one knows the Son except the Father, and no one knows the Father except the Son and any one to whom the Son chooses to reveal him." Then He says, "Come"—dance. "Come to me, all who labor and are heavy laden."

So why don't more come? Why don't we come all the time? Maybe because we're not "weary and heavy laden" enough. Maybe because we're not "poor in spirit, meek and mourning." Maybe because we're not "hungering and thirsting for righteousness," because we think we have it. The law tells us we don't *have* righteousness, but that we *need* it.

- Adam and Eve ate the "fruit of the tree of the knowledge of good and evil" (the law), and it told them they were incomplete.
- On Mount Sinai, Moses gave more law.
- In the Sermon on the Mount, Jesus gave even more law.
- His cross reveals the meaning of the law—Himself.

Paul writes, "Law came in, to increase the trespass" (Romans 5:20): that is, to help us know we deserve death and are dead.

The Pharisees profess to be experts in the law. Jesus says, "They bind heavy burdens, hard to bear, and don't bear them themselves" (Matthew 23:4). They haven't digested the fruit of the tree—the law—for themselves. If they had, they'd be "weary, heavy laden, and hungering for righteousness." A Pharisee still thinks he can make himself, save himself. So a Pharisee hates Christ's cross, for it's *too heavy* and *too light* all at once.

- The cross is too heavy, because it's the fulfillment and revelation of the law. The cross reveals what's truly good. Jesus is the Good, and He reveals we are evil and need to die. So Pharisees don't look.
- The cross is too heavy, yet it feels too light. The cross reveals we're dead (that's heavy), and it reveals we're forgiven (that's light). Pharisees want to pay, but we can't pay.

Suicide is trying to pay, but you can't pay. If you've ever really received forgiveness, you know that the burden is that you want to pay and you can't pay. The burden is its very lightness. *It's free!*

How can His cross be easy and light? After it kills me . . . *it sets me free!* I don't pay for the free me.

Jesus prays, "You've hidden these things from the wise and revealed them to babes" (see Matthew 11:25). Jesus wants us all to enter as children. Children have a very easy time *not paying* and a very easy time *dancing*.

> *The burden is light: the burden is, in fact, grace.*

After watching a great dancer, you never say, "How beautiful! That was very responsible dancing." You say, "Wow! That was so *graceful!*" The burden we lay down is sin, and sin is self. "I'm gonna lay down my burden, down by the riverside." "Do you not know that all of us who have been baptized into Christ Jesus were baptized into his death?" (Romans 6:3).

> *The burden we lay down is self;*
> *the burden we pick up is grace.*

"Come to me, all who labor and are heavy laden, and I will give you rest. Take my yoke upon you." A yoke is for tilling and farming. Yet His yoke is easy and His burden is light. The work is like rest, and the order is like freedom. Jesus sounds like Adam before the Fall. Better yet, Jesus sounds like Adam if he had trusted God until the seventh day when God rested and he was to be perfected. Jesus sounds like Adam from the other side of the curse.

Paul writes that Jesus *is* the Adam—the ultimate Adam. He also tells us that we are Christ's bride. Jesus is the true Adam come for His bride, but Eve is dead under the curse. We're all Eve. He tells us, "Come to me, all who are weary and heavy laden" . . . "Eve, take my yoke upon you."

Outside of Scripture, most of what I've learned of the easy yoke and light burden has been through my friend who was raised in a coven, abused, and afflicted with the most horrible burdens. One night around two or three o'clock in the morning, having prayed through some awful memories, my friend not only remembered things done to her in the past but also things that *she* had done in the past. She cried and sobbed to Susan and me, "I hate myself. I want to die." We'd already gotten rid of an evil spirit named "Suicide," and so now I knew it was *she* who wanted to die.

I finally said, "Tell Jesus." She did . . . and then Jesus gave her wish to her. She had a vision. She saw that old self she hated (the heathen) nailed to a cross. Then she saw the self that hated the old self (the Pharisee) also nailed to the cross. Then she watched Jesus nail Himself to the same cross. She watched herself die . . . with Him.

The yoke is easy; it fits us; it's made for us, made for two, and we need to die. The burden is light, for we even *want* to die.

Yet Jesus said, "*My* yoke is easy, and *my* burden is light." Jesus didn't need to die. He wasn't under the curse. But Scripture tells us that on the cross He became a curse for us, like He bit the fruit for the love of Eve, for He would not leave her nor forsake her. On the cross, He bears our curse (every pain and burden) and then dances in hell. He's faithful to His Father unto death on a cross outside Jerusalem.

How can that be easy, and how can that be light? He must be making, growing, harvesting something or someone He loves very much.

Jesus is the Ultimate Adam come for His bride, but Eve is dead under the curse. On the cross, He bears her curse and gives her His life. Eve—His bride—His church, is made with His own body and blood. Eve is created and re-created at Adam's bleeding side. That sounds familiar . . . almost as if God knew what He was doing all the while!

As I was saying, when my friend had her vision and watched herself die on this cross with Jesus, no sooner had she died than all at once she saw herself standing alive and dressed before the cross in a beautiful, white wedding gown, white as snow.

His yoke is easy, and *His* burden is light for the love of you—His bride. "To have ever suffered the Passion for you," said Jesus to Julian of Norwich, "is for me a great joy, a bliss, an endless delight; and if I could suffer more I would do so."[8]

I can only guess in wonder, but perhaps:

- What looks like a yoke of bondage in this world looks like the greatest freedom in another world.
- What looks like the greatest burden of shame in this world looks like the greatest glory somewhere else.
- What looks like a beaten, naked man hanging on a cross here looks like a great Lion and Lamb standing on His throne in absolute splendor someplace else.

Maybe this world is upside down, and the cross is right side up. Maybe in the other world everyone dances, and it looks like heaven (because it is). In this world, only One danced, and it looked like a cross.

In Isaiah, the Lord says, "I have trodden the wine press alone" (63:3). In that day, treading the winepress was to be a communal celebration. But the Lord says, "I have trodden the wine press alone." In Isaiah He tramples Israel's enemies in wrath. By the New Testament, we find that Israel's enemy is herself.

In the Revelation, the Word that is Christ "will tread the wine press of the fury of the wrath of God" (Revelation 19:15). Blood flows from the winepress and fills Israel to the depth of a horse's bridle. It's blood that is wine, and wine that is blood. That winepress is outside the walls of Jerusalem. I believe that winepress is the cross, our Lord's yoke. He tells us, "The harvest is plentiful." He takes our burdens—"the fruit that befits repentance"—our confessed sins, and He crushes them. They turn into wine—His gospel of grace.

> Grace to those who are being saved;
> wrath to those who hate the gospel.
> Grace to those who want to dance;
> wrath to those who hate the dance.
> Wine for His bride;
> fire for the ancient dragon.

Blood that is wine, and wine that is blood: the judgment of this world. "Now is the judgment of this world," Jesus cries in John 12, "and I, when I am lifted up from the earth [on the cross], will draw all men to myself." At the cross, Jesus died alone, but He won't remain alone. There He romances us to Himself. The winepress looks like a tremendous burden in this world. But maybe in another world, it's more like a dance.

As I studied these verses in Matthew, I couldn't get a picture out of my mind. It's a scene from the movie *A Walk in the Clouds*. At the turning point of the film, a group of women tread a winepress in a beautiful California vineyard. It's a great deal of work, a yoke and a burden, to work that harvest. They trample the grapes, but they do it to the sound of music. They dance. As they dance, they pull a young man into the winepress. He turns out to be the groom who rescues the bride from tragedy. They all trample the grapes together. They dance, and the dance grows as they chant, "Crush the grapes, crush the grapes," to the rhythm of the music. In that place, in that way, at that time, the groom leans over and gives his future bride her first kiss.[9]

The cross is a winepress. Jesus meets His bride in the winepress and no longer dances alone. We are joined with Him in a death like His and will surely be united with Him in a resurrection like His (Romans 6:5). And all our weeping turns to dancing *forever*. It's deliverance from bad religion and an introduction to Jesus. We meet our Lord at the winepress (the cross) like Ruth met Boaz (her kinsman-redeemer) on the threshing floor. A threshing floor is where you sift grain for bread. A winepress is where you make juice for wine. Sometimes they were the same place.

On the night He was betrayed, the day that He was crucified:[10]

MATTHEW 26:26–29: *Jesus took bread, and blessed, and broke it, and gave it to the disciples and said, "Take, eat; this is my body." And he took a cup, and when he had given thanks he gave it to them, saying, "Drink of it, all of you; for this is my blood of the covenant, which is poured out for many for the forgiveness of sins. I tell you I shall not drink again of this fruit of the vine until that day when I drink it new with you in my Father's kingdom."*

That must be how He makes old zombies dance. Believe the gospel.

Are you weary and heavy laden? Take a moment to close your eyes and picture the cross. Perhaps you can even picture Him—Jesus—standing next to the cross. Whatever the case, speak to Him.

Confess, saying, "God, I believe . . . help my unbelief."

Surrender, saying, "Jesus, I surrender my burden. I surrender me to You."

Invite, saying, "Spirit of Jesus, come dance in me."

Now, if you did that, you're dead. There's no point in hiding that fact like some sort of religious zombie. And there's no use in killing yourself. You've been crucified with Christ—that is, you are forgiven. You must consider yourself "dead to sin."

And if you did that, *you're alive*, but what's truly living in you is Christ, as Paul said: "It is no longer I who live, but Christ who lives in me" (Galations 2:20). You still battle your old nature, but you battle it with the cross, believing His love and so loving in return. You battle by partaking in His life, not by exerting your old life. The life is in His blood, and you become His body. You are the body of Christ. "You also must consider yourselves dead to sin and alive to God in Christ Jesus" (Romans 6:11). You're not a zombie. You are the body of the Dancing God—the Lord of the Dance—just now rising from the dead.

ENDNOTES

Introduction: The Wild Man

1. Freud, Sigmund. *Civilization and Its Discontents.* Trans. James Strachey. New York: W. W. Norton and Co., Inc., 1961.

2. Sayers, Dorothy. *Creed or Chaos.* New York: Harcourt, Brace and Co., 1949, 5.

3. Lewis, C. S. *The Lion, the Witch and the Wardrobe.* New York: MacMillan, 1950, 76.

4. Manning, Brennan. *The Signature of Jesus.* Sisters, OR: Multnomah, 1992, 194.

Chapter 1: When Jesus Gets Famous

1. Kierkegaard, Søren. *Provocations.* Farmington, PA: Plough Publishing, 1999, 23.

2. By the way, if you have HIV and surrender it and yourself to Him, God will take it away in eternity. And He might even take it away here. Whatever the case, God says, "My grace is sufficient for you, for my power is made perfect in weakness" (2 Corinthians 12:9).

3. Calver, Clive of Advancing Churches in Missions Commitment (ACMC). Joint plenary session, General Assembly of the Evangelical Presbyterian Church. Greenwood Community Church, Engelwood, CO. 23 June 2001.

Chapter 2: Salt and Light

1. Campolo, Tony. *Let Me Tell You a Story.* Nashville: W Publishing, 2000, 101.

2. Draper, Edythe. *Draper's Book of Quotations for the Christian World.* Wheaton, IL: Tyndale, 1992, 5891.

3. Budde, Michael, and Robert Brimlow. *Christianity Incorporated.* Grand Rapids: Brazos, 2002, 65.

4. Patterson, James and Peter Kim. *The Day America Told the Truth: What People Really Believe About Everything That Really Matters.* New York: Prentice Hall, 1991, 143.

5. Willimon, Will. "Thy Kingdom Come." Chapel address. Duke University, Durham, NC. 25 July 1993.

ENDNOTES

Chapter 3: Trouble with Zombies

1. Chalmers, David. "Zombies on the Web," http://jamaica.u.arizona.edu/~chalmers/zombies.html (16 November 2004).

2. Barclay, William. *The Gospel of Matthew,* vol. 1, rev. ed. Philadelphia: Westminster, 1975, 128.

3. Brown, Steve. "Key Life." *Christianity Today.* March-April 1994.

Chapter 4: Church Chat (and Hell)

1. Craddock, Fred. *Preaching Today* [audio], as recounted in a sermon by Tony Campolo. Bel Air Presbyterian Church, Los Angeles, CA. January 1988.

Chapter 5: Adultery (in the Worst Places)

1. Center for Spiritual Exchange. *Anthony De Mello: Writings Selected with an Introduction by William Dych, S. J.* Maryknoll, NY: Orbis, 1999, 96.

2. McQuilkin, Robertson. "She's My Precious." In *More Stories for the Heart: Over 100 Stories to Warm Your Heart,* ed. Alice Gray. Sisters, OR: Multnomah, 1997, 123-25.

Chapter 6: The Oath (Is "Jesus" a Swear Word?)

1. Ortburg, John. *The Life You've Always Wanted.* Grand Rapids: Zondervan, 1997, 17.

2. Bromily, Geoffery W., ed. "Covenant." *International Standard Bible Encyclopedia,* vol 1. Grand Rapids: Wm B. Eerdmans, 1988, 791.

3. Mote, Edward. *My Hope Is Built (The Solid Rock).* 1834.

Chapter 7: Stupid Philanthropists

1. Nouwen, Henri. Quoted in Brennan Manning, *The Signature of Jesus.* Sisters, OR: Multnomah, 2004, 126–27.

2. Bonhoeffer, Deitrich. *The Cost of Discipleship.* New York: MacMillan, 1949, 8. Deitrich Bonhoeffer, *Life Together: The Classic Exploration of Faith in Community.* New York: Harper & Row, 1954, 13, from introduction. Quoted by Brennan Manning. Retreat address. Lookout Mountain Community Church, Golden, CO.

3. Brewer, Mark. "The Life of Paul." Sermon. Lookout Mountain Community Church, Golden, CO. 11 June 2000.

4. The word "workmanship" is also translated "masterpiece."

5. MacDonald, George. *Unspoken Sermons: Series I, II, III.* Johannesen, 1997, 11–12.

6. Lewis, C. S. *The Problem of Pain.* New York: Simon & Schuster, 1996, 137-38.

Endnotes

Chapter 8: Discipline to Dance

1. Lewis, C. S. *Perelandra*. New York: The MacMillan Company, 1944, 136.
2. *The Jerk*. Directed by Carl Reiner. Hollywood, CA: Universal Studios, 1979.
3. Wurmbrand, Richard. *In God's Underground*. Glendale, CA: Diane Books, 1968, 50.
4. Nietzsche, Friedrich. Quoted in Anne Lamott, *Traveling Mercies*. New York: Anchor, 1999, 86.
5. Lewis, C. S. *Mere Christianity*. New York: MacMillan, 1960, 151–53.
6. Willimon, Will. Quoted in Michael Yaconelli, *The Adventure of Childlike Faith*. Colorado Springs, CO: NavPress, 1998, 91.
7. Incidentally, this is the Lord's apologetic. That is, according to Jesus, this is the way the world is to be convinced of the truth. "By this all men will know that you are my disciples, if you have love for one another" (John 13:35). They will know, when we all dance to the same tune, and the tune is love.

Have you ever watched a musical with the sound off? People are walking around doing their own thing, when all at once they begin to be coordinated in their motions. Their motions don't have to be the same—in fact, it's best when they are not—just harmonized. At that point, you realize those people are listening to a music you can't hear. When Christians dance to the rhythm of God's love, they are animated by His Spirit. They move in harmony to a reality greater than any one individual, and the world begins to wonder, *Maybe there is something greater than the self, and maybe the something greater is good.* When they surrender to it, it looks like a dance.

When you truly love, you bear testimony to the dance, for your actions can't be explained by anything in this world.

8. Lewis, C. S. *The Problem of Pain*. New York: MacMillan, 1962, 145.

Chapter 9: How to Pray

1. *Monty Python's The Meaning of Life*. Directed by Terry Jones and Terry Gilliam. Hollywood: CA: Universal Studios, 1983.
2. Luther, Martin. Quoted in Frederick Dale Bruner, *The Christbook: A Historical/Theological Commentary*. Waco, TX: Word, 1987, 237.
3. Augustine. Quoted in Frederick Dale Bruner, *The Christbook: A Historical/Theological Commentary*. Waco, TX: Word, 1987, 236.
4. Kierkegaard, Søren. *Provocations*. Farmington, PA: Plough Publishing, 1999, 345.
5. L'Engle, Madeleine. *Walking on Water: Reflections on Faith and Art*. Wheaton, IL: Harold Shaw, 1980, 24.
6. Luther, Martin. *A Mighty Fortress Is Our God*. 1529.
7. Hewett, James S., ed. *Illustrations Unlimited*. Wheaton, IL: Tyndale, 1988, 250–51.

8. Foster, Richard J. *Prayer: Finding the Heart's True Home.* San Francisco: HarperSanFrancisco, 1992, 99.

9. Forsyth, P. T. Quoted in Richard J. Pryor, *Finding the Heart's True Home.* San Francisco: Harper San Francisco, 1992, 99.

10. Stone, Samuel J. *The Church's One Foundation.* 1866.

Chapter 10: Treasure Hunting

1. Cloud, Henry. "Biblical Leadership That Meets the Demands of Reality" seminar. National Pastors Convention. San Diego, CA. 26 February 2003.

2. Jones Gunn, Robin. "Real Treasure." In *More Stories for the Heart: Over 100 Stories to Warm Your Heart,* ed. Alice Gray. Sisters, OR: Multnomah, 1997, 268.

3. Weekly Illustration. www.preachingtoday.com (September 2000).

Chapter 11: Psyched Out

1. U2. *Stuck in a Moment You Can't Get Out of.* Polygram Int'l, 2001.

2. Hewett, James S., ed. *Illustrations Unlimited.* Wheaton, IL: Tyndale, 1988, 258–59.

Chapter 12: Judgment and Pearl Casting

1. Harvey, Paul. Radio broadcast, 1994.

2. Kierkegaard, Søren. *Provocations.* Farmington, PA: Plough Publishing, 1999, 3–4.

3. Lawhead, Stephen R. *Merlin.* New York: HarperCollins, 1988, 220.

4. Lewis, C. S. *Voyage of the Dawn Treader.* New York: MacMillan, 1952, 90.

5. Yancey, Philip. *Church: Why Bother?* Grand Rapids: Zondervan, 2001, 52.

6. Bonhoeffer, Deitrich. Quoted in Johann Cristoph Arnold, *Why Forgive?* Farmington, PA: Plough Publishing, 2000, 131.

Chapter 13: The Gate

1. Chesterton, G. K. *Orthodoxy: The Romance of Faith.* New York: Bantam, 1990, 49.

2. L'Engle, Madeleine. *Walking on Water: Reflections on Faith and Art.* Wheaton, IL: Harold Shaw, 1980, 61.

3. Tolkien, J. R. R. Quoted in Philip Yancey, *The Jesus I Never Knew.* Grand Rapids: Zondervan, 1995, 218.

4. Chesterton, G. K. *Orthodoxy: The Romance of Faith.* New York: Bantam, 1990, 94.

5. Buber, Martin. Quoted in Anne Lamott, *Traveling Mercies.* New York: Anchor, 1999, 115.

6. Lewis, C. S. *The Magician's Nephew.* New York: Macmillan Publishing Co., Inc., 1955, 173–75.

7. Barth, Karl. Quoted in David L. Mueller, *Karl Barth.* Waco, TX: Word,

1972, 103. "I would not seek you, if I had not found you already in the depth of my heart" (St. Augustine). "In this function this man is the object of the eternal divine decision and foreordination. Jesus Christ, then, is not merely one of the elect, but *the* elect of God. . . . His election is the original and all-inclusive election; the election which is absolutely unique, but which in this very uniqueness is universally meaningful and efficacious, because it is the election of Him who Himself elects Of none other of the elect can it be said that his election carries in it and with it the election of the rest."

8.   The barrier has made Himself the gate. And by the way, we're cut by the flaming sword—the Word that is living and active and sharper than any two-edged sword. He pierces to the division of soul and spirit (Hebrews 4:12). He rides a white horse (Revelation 19), and out of His mouth issues a sharp sword with which He smites the peoples. We die with Him and are resurrected with Him. He is the gate.

Chapter 14: Tree Story

1.   Schroeder, Gerald L. *The Science of God.* New York: Broadway, 1998, 60.

2.   Wiesel, Elie. Quoted in Lewis B. Smedes, *Forgive and Forget: Healing the Hurts We Don't Deserve,* rev. ed. San Francisco: HarperSanFrancisco, 1996, 116–17.

3.   *Toy Story 2.* Directed by Lee Unkrich and John Lasseter. Hollywood, CA: Disney Studios, 1999.

Chapter 15: Wolves in Sheep's Clothing

1.   Church isn't a place to "hide the poop." It's a place to surrender it at the foot of the tree, to confess it to the light. "When anything is exposed by the light it becomes visible, for anything that becomes visible is light (Ephesians 5:13).

2.   *Dogma.* Directed by Kevin Smith. Hollywood, CA: Columbia/Tristar Studios, 1999.

3.   Colson, Charles. "Making the World Safe for Religion." *Christianity Today.* November 1993, 33.

Chapter 16: Rock On

1.   Yancey, Philip. *Church: Why Bother?* Grand Rapids: Zondervan, 2001, 99.

2.   *Good Will Hunting.* Directed by Gus Van Sant. Hollywood CA: Miramax Home Entertainment, 1997.

Conclusion: The Easy Yoke and the Light Burden

1.   Bruner, Frederick Dale. *The Christbook: A Historical/Theological Commentary.* Waco, TX: Word, 1987, 345.

2.   Jones Gunn, Robin. Quoted in *More Stories for the Heart: Over 100 Stories to Warm Your Heart,* ed. Alice Gray. Sisters, OR: Multnomah, 1997.

3.   Jones Gunn, Robin. Quoted in *More Stories for the Heart: Over 100 Stories to Warm Your Heart,* ed. Alice Gray. Sisters, OR: Multnomah, 1997.

4.   Lewis, *C. S. Mere Christianity.* New York: MacMillan, 1960, 153. C. S. Lewis, *The Problem of Pain.* New York: Simon & Schuster, 1996, 152–53.

5.   Drummond, Henry. *Pax vobiscum*, rev. ed. J. Pott, 1891.

6.   Manning, Brennan. *The Signature of Jesus.* Sisters, OR: Multnomah, 1992, 115–16.

7.   Center for Spiritual Exchange. *Anthony De Mello: Writings Selected with an Introduction by William Dych, S. J.* Maryknoll, NY: Orbis, 1999, 110.

8.   Nelson, John, ed. *Julian of Norwich: Journeys into Joy.* Hyde Park, NY: New City Press, 2001, 72.

9.   *A Walk in the Clouds.* Directed by Alfonso Arau. Hollywood, CA: Twentieth Century Fox, 1995.

10.   In the Hebrew calendar, the day begins at sunset.